D0829307

Wandering with Sadhus

This book belongs to:
HOLMBERG - MARCH

CONTEMPORARY INDIAN STUDIES

Published in association with the American Institute of Indian Studies

Susan S. Wadley, Chair, Publications Committee/general editor

AIIS Publications Committee/series advisory board:
John Echeverri-Gent
Akhil Gupta
Brian Hatcher
David Lelyveld
Martha Selby

Books in this series are recipients of the
Edward Cameron Dimock, Jr. Prize in the Indian Humanities
and the
Joseph W. Elder Prize in the Indian Social Sciences
awarded by the American Institute of Indian Studies and are published with the Institute's generous support.

A list of titles in this series appears at the back of the book.

Wandering with Sadhus

ASCETICS IN THE HINDU HIMALAYAS

Sondra L. Hausner

INDIANA UNIVERSITY PRESS
BLOOMINGTON & INDIANAPOLIS

This book is a publication of

Indiana University Press
601 North Morton Street
Bloomington, IN 47404-3797 USA

http://iupress.indiana.edu

Telephone orders 800-842-6796
Fax orders 812-855-7931
Orders by e-mail iuporder@indiana.edu

© 2007 by Sondra L. Hausner
All rights reserved

No part of this book may be reproduced or utilized in any form or by any means, electronic or mechanical, including photocopying and recording, or by any information storage and retrieval system, without permission in writing from the publisher. The Association of American University Presses' Resolution on Permissions constitutes the only exception to this prohibition.

The paper used in this publication meets the minimum requirements of American National Standard for Information Sciences—Permanence of Paper for Printed Library Materials, ANSI Z39.48-1984.

Manufactured in the United States of America

Library of Congress Cataloging-in-Publication Data

Hausner, Sondra L.
Wandering with sadhus : ascetics in the Hindu Himalayas / Sondra L. Hausner.
p. cm. — (Contemporary Indian studies)
Includes bibliographical references and index.
ISBN 978-0-253-34983-5 (cloth : alk. paper) — ISBN 978-0-253-21949-7 (pbk. : alk. paper) 1. Sadhus—India—Social conditions. 2. Sadhus—Nepal—Social conditions. 3. Sadhus—Social networks—India. 4. Sadhus—Social networks—Nepal. 5. Asceticism—Hinduism. I. Title.
BL1241.53.H385 2007
294.5'6570954—dc22
2007022645

1 2 3 4 5 12 11 10 09 08 07

for my parents, the *yoginī*-householder and the wise old man

The ordinary person takes reality to be . . . everything which has come into their consciousness as pertaining to themselves—body, etc. This they have to unlearn.

ŚRĪ RAMAṆA MAHĀṚṢI

Contents

ACKNOWLEDGMENTS

Ten years have passed since I began the research for this book, and my debts have mightily accumulated. First, my thanks to my three primary informants, Pāgal Bābā, Rādhā Giri, and Mukta Giri, who has since passed away. Their support for and patience with this project in both India and Nepal made it possible. I also offer my thanks to Pāgalānanda, the first *yogī* I knew, and his respected *guru*-brother, Dr. Tyāgī Nāth Bābā, at Paśupatināth, and also Nānī Mā, in Sainj, Uttaranchal, for teaching me so much.

My gratitude to the President's Council of Cornell Women and the Cornell University Mario Einaudi Center for International Studies for early support, and to Cornell's Department of Anthropology for being my home base while researching the book and writing the dissertation that preceded it. All four of my dissertation committee members, David Hines Holmberg, Ann Grodzins Gold, Natalie Melas, and Christopher Minkowski, guided my work with exacting gentleness, in four disciplinary languages. Professor A. Thomas Kirsch started my training as an anthropologist of religion, and his memory has shaped the contours of this book.

Deep thanks go to the American Institute of Indian Studies, first for funding much of the research, and then for awarding the manuscript the Elder Prize. Frederick Asher, Pradeep Mehendiratta, Purnima Mehta, Ralph Nicholas, and Susan Wadley provided constant and genuine support throughout the process of the book's research and publication. Thank you to the Awards Publication Committee and to two anonymous reviewers for their faith, and also Ernestine McHugh for her warm response and helpful suggestions. At Indiana University Press, I thank Rebecca Tolen for the work of a masterful editor, and Laura MacLeod and Neil Ragsdale for their help. Kevin Bubriski and Bernard Hausner graciously provided photographs, and the School of Anthropology at Oxford offered generous support at the last moment, for Laurie Winship's professional index.

For thoughts, experiences, hospitality, and introductions that made this research possible, thank you to masters of the scene: the late, great Jasper Newsome aka Rām Giri and his *guru*-brothers in Ānanda Akhāṛā, Maṇgalānand Giri, the late Ali Bābā, the mad Macchendra Giri, Paul Giraud, Rampuri, Shiv, Cynthia Gould, Dudh Bābā, William Forbes, Caitanya from Lubljiana, Caitanya from California, Beppe, Ishtar, Chandeen, Denis and Alain, the late and loved Bhaskar Bhattacarya, and Dolf Hartsuiker. For help with yogic interpretation and instruction, my gratitude to Mrs. Menaka Desikachar, Kausthub Desikachar, and Shaheeda at the Krishnamacharya Yoga Mandiram in Adyar, and to the late Harish Johari in Hardwar.

Many, many loved ones have supported the research, writing, and completion of this book. Thank you to my late teacher, Kunzang Dechen Lingpa, and my parents and sister, Bernard, Nancy, and Ellen Hausner. For inspiring me early and explaining things often, my respectful thanks to Gen. Monty Palit and Meryl Dowman. Greta Austin, Sonam Bennett, Suzie Burns, Jeff Cranmer, Gregory Dicum, Mitchell Duneier, Laraba Friedman, Lindsay Friedman, Elyse Genuth, Julie Hemment, Ariel Kaminer, Martin Kaminer, Meena Khandelwal, Carole McGranahan, Peter Moran, Anne Rademacher, Andrew Rosenberg, Melanie Ross, Pam Ross, Jennifer Senior, Punam and the Vajracharya family, and Andy Young have put up with my comings and goings with alacrity.

A tale of wandering is bound to be the product of many places. In San Francisco, Mary Boardman provided a haven to write and Richard Olsen continued to provoke new thoughts. In Winchester, I thank Princess Jyoti and Pragya Shah-Singha for their refuge and Rosemary Ross-Skinner for her kindness. The sacred valley of Kathmandu sustained this work from beginning to end. And in New York City, a sacred center in its own right, thank you to Susan Falk for letting me return to my longest extant home, a loft-bed on Bank Street, to Ricki Fier and Dr. Henry Kaminer, and to the 4B Academic Library for its beloved desk and comfy gray couch, both of which invited me right on in.

NOTE ON TRANSLITERATION

Words transcribed from Hindi, Nepali, and Sanskrit are transliterated using standard diacritical convention, although I have used English suffixes (*sādhus, tantric*). Words that have become standard in English (yoga, ashram) have been neither italicized nor diacriticized, except when part of a larger name or when their use in the original language may differ slightly from their use in English (*yogī*). Words that may be familiar to readers without diacritics are spelled out in Roman (*chillum* instead of *cilam, chai-wallah* instead of *cāyvāla*), for maximum comprehension.

Personal names (Pāgal Bābā, Nānī Mā, Śankarācārya) and their referents (Mātājī) are transliterated with diacritics, as are deity names (Śiva, Viṣṇu, Satī, Paśupati). Accordingly, the names of temples honoring these deities are transliterated (Paśupatināth) as well. Contemporary place names, however, (Kathmandu, Himalayas, Hardwar [following its Śaiva spelling]) are written in standard English convention, and accordingly, ancient place names (Mayapur, Prayag) are, too.

Wandering with Sadhus

Introduction

WANDERING WITH RENOUNCERS

For close to three thousand years, ascetics have wandered the Indian subcontinent. On their way to sacred places in the mountains or at the confluences of rivers, they have traveled through cities and through forests, sleeping under trees or by riverbanks as they sojourn. They might be headed to a religious festival determined by the astral calendar, or to a cave in the Himalayas for a period of solitary retreat. Laypeople with whom these renouncers of society came into contact would probably cringe at their otherworldliness—they might be naked, or clothed in only a loin-cloth, or covered in ash from funeral pyres. Their matted dreadlocks would hang long, covering their bodies, or be wrapped tightly onto their heads, into turbans of human hair. They might speak only praises to God, or remain mute out of a vow of silence.

To convince laypeople that they were worthy of public respect and support—that they were real or accomplished religious practitioners—they might display the fruits of religious labor in a show of physical strength or austerity. They might keep one arm perpetually raised, for example, letting their fingernails pierce their own atrophying flesh, or lift heavy stones with their penises to display the ability of their bodies to manipulate the material world at will. Depending on the inclinations of village housewives, who would most likely regard them tentatively—with a combination of fear and respect—they might be offered a meal, or a few *paisā* with which to buy rice. After a night or two in any given village, they would continue on their way.

« *Jūnā Akhāṛā*

In the fifth century BCE, the Buddha followed the practices of Indian wandering ascetics, in an effort to renounce the suffering he perceived in the cycle of birth and death. Alexander the Great sought the advice of the "gymnosophists" in the third century BCE, wondering how they held their reign as powerful but naked men of wisdom (Mishra 2004). A thousand years later, the eighth-century Indian philosopher Śaṅkarācārya systematized their sectarian structures, naming them *sannyāsīs,* or "renouncers," so that their previously dispersed or isolated religious efforts would contribute to the project of supporting Hinduism during a period of religious embattlement.

By the twelfth century, religious renouncer orders had become military regiments, some of which men and women of any caste could join. In the middle of the nineteenth century, the British colonial government in Bengal went to war with renouncers: the *yogī* regiments that patrolled the region were claiming their own share of land tax, which was not acceptable to the colonial officials (Chandra 1977). In 1930s pre-independence India, Mahatma Gandhi affected the loin-cloth-clad guise of a *sādhu* to spread his anti-caste message. Now, just after the turn of the twenty-first century, renouncer festivals are touted by the world media as the largest gatherings on earth, and Himalayan *yogīs* are invoked by advertisements for fancy teas, boasting the wisdom of mountain solitude and high-altitude daily regimens. *Sannyāsīs, yogīs*—renouncers, as they are called by scholars of Hindu society, or *bābās,* as they are called in Hindi—are a perennial presence in South Asia.

This book is written in the spirit of an old-fashioned ethnography, in that it describes the study of a group, however its contours are defined. The chapters that follow explore the cultural meanings of the material world for the Hindu renouncer community of South Asia. In turn, they describe how space, time, and matter, especially the material body, are constructed, experienced, and understood by *sādhus* in contemporary Nepal and India. Through this ethnographic exploration, the book shows how these three facets of the material world are used to create and reproduce meaning among members of the Hindu ascetic community.

To link the words "ascetic" and "community" may sound paradoxical, but this book is indeed about an alternative social community. Members of the Hindu renouncer community are known simply as *sādhus* throughout Nepal and India; they are visibly distinct from householder families and communities through their clothes and possessions, their actions and practices, and the places in which they choose to live. In this book, I am interested in how ascetics form a community, despite an ideology that values solitary or isolated religious practice. The crux of this question is how renouncers themselves differentiate their communal life from normative Hindu householder social worlds.

The term "householder," a literal translation of the Sanskrit word *gṛhasthī*, refers to people in that phase of life most directly concerned with marrying, bearing children, and raising a family. The household—the nest, the hearth, the home—is a metaphor for the stability of productivity and procreation by members of lay society. It is this social mainstream that *sādhus* explicitly renounce: their reputation as wanderers sets them apart from those who are, by contrast, metaphorically settled or fixed in location. Scholars of South Asia use the term "renouncers," those who leave, in opposition to the term "householders," those who constitute normative, procreative Hindu society. Renouncers have left those domains behind, usually rejecting them outright in favor of an alternative community devoted to God.

Lay practitioners of Hinduism tend to discuss renunciation in an idealistic or even theoretical way, through a consideration of what revered Hindu texts say a *sannyāsī* should or should not do.[1] Similarly, many university scholars tend to think about renunciation through textual description. Even real *sādhus* quote famous Hindu texts—the *Bhagavad Gītā*, the four volumes of the *Veda*, the *Upaniṣads*—when explaining the lifestyles and daily practices of renouncers, or when describing the ways they should view or use their bodies in religious endeavor. Textual sources that dictate the ideals of renouncer life—the *Sannyāsa Upaniṣads* (Olivelle 1992), for example, collected texts on renouncer conduct, and *The Laws of Manu* (Doniger and Smith 1981), a sourcebook on Hindu social life and conduct written around the beginning of the common era—precisely lay out how a renouncer should conduct himself ritually, and in relation to lay society. The definitions of society are described in detail in these texts, as is the distinction between a householder, who upholds these laws of social order, and a renouncer, who departs from them.

This book discusses renunciation from an ethnographic perspective, not a textual one, which implies that the researcher spent some months or years following the patterns and practices of a particular community. Textual traditions lay out the ideals of renunciation, which real-life renouncers sometimes try to attain but sometimes self-consciously defy. Part of the point of ethnography is to convey a sense of the empirical practices of people—in this case, to show how renouncers actually live, think, and practice—rather than to reproduce textual ideals, or theories from any tradition, which will never be fully realized.

Instead of focusing on the textual dictates of renunciation, then, I use real-life stories, quotations, conversations, and observations from the period I spent working with contemporary *sādhus* to convey the dimensions of Hindu ascetic communal life at the turn of the twenty-first century. In the sense that I use it, ethnography is the study of communal experience, a description of community in a particular place—or series of places—and time. Renouncers' own analyses of space, time, and matter, and the ways my informants described their experiences to me, constitute the base of my arguments. Through the expressions of renouncers in contemporary India and Nepal, this book shows how the structures of this self-identified group—an anti-social society—are rehearsed, memorized, and performed, internalized as well as externalized. My hope is that through thinking about a dispersed community as unified through cultural meanings that are not rooted in place, we will arrive at new ways of understanding space as a factor of collective life, and new ways of imagining how embodied experience both shapes and is shaped by the experience of place.

An Ethnography of Wandering

If ethnography is the description of culture, it is also the product of a researcher being immersed in a specific cultural context. When I set out for my first research trip to Kathmandu in 1997, I knew I wanted to understand the way South Asian *yogīs* interpreted embodiment, but I did not know how I would go about finding out. The famous interpretive anthropologist Clifford Geertz recommends "deep hanging-out," but how exactly does an anthropologist-in-training arrive on the scene and start doing it? With whom should she hang out, exactly, and where, and for how long? Planning something as nebulous as hanging out seemed logistically counterintuitive to me, especially because my study population lived in so many places. How was I supposed to assess a system of cultural values and meaning when the community with whom I wanted to work was located in sites of Hindu practice that spanned the entire Indian subcontinent?

I knew more about specific locations where I might be able to find *sādhus* than whom, in particular, I might meet. As a child, I had lived in Kathmandu, Nepal,[2] the location of one of Hinduism's most sacred temples, Paśupatināth. In 1975, my father was posted to Kathmandu as a United Nations official, and my mother, recently trained as a yoga teacher in suburban New York, resolved to study her new trade with authentic practitioners in their home terrain. She would wait for my sister and me to come home from Kathmandu's American International School and then drive us to Paśupatināth, where she had started to study with Pāgalānanda, an ash-clad *yogī* who could manipulate his body into the most astonishing positions. Sometimes she would send the car to bring Pāgalānanda back to our compound on the other side of town, where he would give us yoga lessons on the lawn.

Pāgalānanda's name, "Crazy Bliss," reflects the reputation for divine madness that *yogīs* sometimes acquire, but his physical capacity was beyond question. Now, more than twenty years later, I reasoned that if I wanted to find *yogīs* who actively considered how their bodies could be used as part of a spiritual pursuit to understand the world, Paśupatināth would be a good place to start. I remembered that in the '70s and '80s, we had sat with Pāgalānanda in a small room, which had belonged to his teacher, set back from the holy Bagmati River, the local manifestation of India's Ganges.[3] The river flowed through the center of the temple grounds, the site of both earthly and otherworldly concerns: on one bank, people washed their clothes; on the other, they burned their dead. Pāgalānanda's teacher and the lineage over which he presided were based in a room located directly behind the temple's public cremation *ghāṭ,* a landing on the riverbank. From either a scholarly perspective or a yogic one, this seemed an appropriate location from which to consider the nature of the material world. In any cultural context, watching human bodies burn leads to a reflection on how ephemeral our time on earth is, and how fragile our material bodies are.

My memories of Paśupatināth suggested that the temple complex was an important destination on renouncer routes. In particular, I recalled that

Hindu renouncers from all over the subcontinent traveled to Nepal for Śiva Rātrī, the annual spring festival in honor of the deity Śiva. The temple compound was a sufficiently prominent site that I knew I would meet renouncers there both during the festival and during their pilgrimages at others times of the year: I remembered that *sādhus* of all sects visited the temple grounds often, wandering through the large wooded area in which it was located, drinking tea, and bathing in the river. I suspected that even in the twenty-first century, Paśupatināth would remain a highly respected center of Hindu practice, a symbolic pivot of Hindu—and Nepali—sacred geography, and might be a sensible starting point for meeting diverse members of the *sādhu* community.

Ethnography as Anthropological Research

On the day before I left New York for my first research trip to Kathmandu, I went to my advisor, Professor A. Thomas Kirsch, a scholar of Thai Buddhism and a much beloved anthropologist. He was known for his equanimity and his gentle humor, such that he was thought of in our department as very Buddha-like himself. I was leaving for the summer after a heady year of being introduced to continental philosophy, theoretical anthropology, and academic politics. I went to say goodbye, but also, now that I was actually getting on a plane, I wanted to ask him what it was, exactly, that I was supposed to do when I got to the field. I had been gifted books on writing ethnographic field notes, and advised to bring novels, but I was still uncertain as to what the practice of ethnography entailed. How was a researcher supposed to perform deep hanging out with *sādhus* when equipped only with the name of an urban temple?

Professor Kirsch had had throat cancer, and spoke through a voice box to teach and advise. The device gave him the appearance of an older gentleman smoking a pipe, but also gave his words unusual weight and solemnity because the sound it produced had a monotone gravity. When I posed my question—what was I actually supposed to do to accomplish this ethnography?—he nodded sagely, implying that I should listen carefully to his response. "Aha," he said. "I asked the same question as I headed to northern Thailand five decades ago. I will now tell you what my advisor, the famous Cora DuBois, told me." Aware that I was being anointed into an esteemed lineage of ethnographers, I nodded respectfully.

"Take a lot of pencils. And be careful of the dogs."

I have since learned the South Asian lore that insists that every teacher teaches in his own way and suggests the humble student should not press. But at the time I submitted to the American cultural imperative that encourages young people to be dynamic individuals who speak their mind as evidence of the individual power and bravery to which we so ardently aspire.

"That's it?" I whined, the outspoken graduate student. "Aren't there some details I should know? What do I *do* when I get there?"

Pressed, he did give a little more.

"Try to find out how people live their daily lives, their rhythms. See if you can establish the way time is used. The best is if you can live by it."

My advisor's initial reluctance to give me anything concrete as send-off advice and his simultaneous insistence that he was passing down received wisdom that would serve me well speaks to the conundrum of ethnography. Ethnography is a responsive method, a commitment to attuning oneself to circumstances that present themselves, and to regarding the dynamics of real life as both present at face value and as hidden at many levels beneath the surface, in the context of every encounter. There is so much information in any one place, in the observation of any one interaction, that if the data gleaned from casual conversation, attuned observation, or the experience of participation can be verified, it becomes meaningful. All circumstances, like all experiences, are endlessly interpretable. But if you hear the same thing from more than one person, over and over again, or from many different kinds of sources, something has been corroborated; some aspect of the narrative conveys collective cultural meaning. Whether what you hear—collective narrative—is consonant with what you see—collective cultural practice—is another aspect of ethnography: what people say and what people do may not always be the same. The assessment of how narrative is reconciled with practice, and how individual voices are reconciled with communal systems, is the product of ethnography as used by anthropology.

This ethnography is my interpretation of the years I spent with members of the Hindu renouncer community in South Asia, rooted as much as possible in the disciplines of social science. The research I conducted for the book took place between 1997 and 2001, with Śaiva, or Śiva-worshipping, *sādhus* in Nepal and India. Śaiva *sādhus,* or *bābās,* are a subset of Hindu renouncers, affiliated more strongly with the worship of Śiva than with Viṣṇu, the other deity of the Hindu pantheon primarily associated with *sādhu* orders. Śaivites are known as the wildest *sādhus,* farthest away from the structures of normative society, in most blatant disregard of social strictures. Lord Śiva, after all, is the patron deity of ascetics, himself a naked *yogī* living high in the mountains at a river's source, covered only with a leopard skin. Generous with his intake of hashish, he is totally unconcerned with his social image. The ultimate *yogī,* he knows on a visceral level that all he perceives—his own body, the world around him, and all thoughts that he or anyone else cognizes—are simply states of illusion, false dualistic divisions of a sacred oneness that unifies all existence.

Studying Space, Time, and the Body

The experience of embodiment for South Asian Hindu renouncers is one of the primary topics that follows, and, at first, it was the underlying question of my fieldwork. Interested in phenomenological and feminist writings on the experience of embodiment, I was curious about how renouncers used and thought about their bodies, these "vessels" through which we all perceive and experience reality. Both Euro-American scholars of embodiment and South Asian religious practitioners explicitly grapple with the ways in which the human body contains, informs, produces, and negotiates experience. This book brings theorists of the body and materiality into hypothetical conversation with religious practitioners whose primary project is to comprehend the nature of the material world.

Over the course of my travels, between fieldwork in one hemisphere and my U.S. academic institution in the other, I defined, refined, and redefined the question I was asking of *sādhus,* as well as my understanding of their responses. On a few cherished occasions, I worked with scholarly renouncers who offered their own personal interpretations of the texts and commentaries they studied. In these instances, we actively engaged in a collaborative philosophical project about materiality and the material body. But most members of the renouncer community with whom I worked were largely uneducated, and this posed a very different kind of fieldwork.

I had imagined that *sādhus* would be actively concerned with questions about the nature of their bodies, given renouncers' reputations in South Asia, Europe, and the U.S. as practiced *yogīs* who aspire to attain extreme control over matter and bodily form. And yet most of the renouncers with whom I worked closely did not seem to place any particular emphasis on bodily experience, either in my conversations with them or in their daily practices. Conversations on embodiment were often quite strained, in fact, and usually resulted in a distilled oration on the illusion of form, or the outer-sheath-like quality of the material body, as presented in the *Bhagavad Gītā,* for example (Zaehner 1973).[4] Active discussions on the nature of the material body occupied very little public space in renouncer life, and, to the extent that I was invited into personal realms of experience, seemed to occupy very little private thought as well.

Rather than a topic of philosophical concern, the body presented itself as a chore in the lives of renouncers, something to be fed and kept healthy and presentable. More often than not, the physical body was regarded as the regrettable obstruction between mundane daily life and true religious experience. The body was basically a hassle, worth maintaining because it provided the only way to experience material reality. This implicit tension around the concept of embodiment—how the chore of the body as it is articulated in place sits in uneasy connection with the valorization of the body as the only viable means of experience—makes up the primary paradox of this book, and is, in my view, one of the core nexuses of experience in renouncer life, rippling outward to constitute both the physical plane and the social world.

The topic that did seem very natural in conversations with and among renouncers was not embodiment, but space. The community of South Asian renouncers is a social web that spans a large territory, and almost all conversations I heard and participated in began with those questions that travelers or wanderers, or, in this case, members of a dispersed community, ask of one another: Where do you live? Where are you traveling from? What route did you use to get here? And do you know my friend in the last place you have been? Renouncers are known as wanderers precisely because they do not belong to settled or sedentary societies. Travel routes, gathering places, and pilgrimage circuits clearly comprise the concrete spatial bonds of their dispersed community. Despite not sharing lives in a particular locality, the Hindu renouncer community produces and reproduces itself through shared meanings of space and place.

All the places renouncers talked about traveling from and heading to, I noticed, were pilgrimage sites: an unstated logic clearly determined that Hindu renouncers belong in a place of Hindu practice, if nowhere else. Many pilgrimage sites were famous because they marked a unique geographical phenomenon: the source of a river, for example, at Gangotri, or the exact point where plains turned into mountainous foothills, for example, in Hardwar, invariably became the location of a shrine to which both lay pilgrims and *sādhus* traveled for blessings. These spots were sacred ground, I learned, because they drew a pilgrim's attention to the wonders of landscape, the vastness of nature, and the way individual places are connected to one another through the flow of water or the undulating surface of the earth.

In addition to their geographic qualities—or perhaps because of them—pilgrimage locations were usually described to me as the sites of particular mythic events or activities in the lives of deities. Often they were linked to a specific body part of Lord Śiva or his wife in one of her many incarnations as the goddess Satī, Pārvatī, Umā, or Kālī. Renouncers talked with pride as they recounted their visits to Amarnāth, an ice *liṅgam*, or phallus, in Kashmir, Kedārnāth; a mountain shrine in Garhwal that represents part of a buffalo that Śiva briefly became; Mount Kailāśa, the Tibetan mountain home of the celestial couple; or Paśupatināth, the temple I remembered visiting as a little girl in Kathmandu, named for Śiva in his manifestation as a gentle deer. These are stories I heard again and again as I asked both renouncers and lay pilgrims why a particular pilgrimage site was significant. I began to wonder whether this collective preoccupation with mythical space might ground a methodology that looked at the links between disparate places and asked how those links created community.

The multiple locations of Hindu worship were the closest renouncers came to having a communal home: unlike householders, who might affect an ascetic's religious demeanor for a brief pilgrimage journey, renouncers are intended to be full-time religious practitioners who can only rightfully reside in a place of practice. As do members of any community anywhere, renouncers, it appeared, defined themselves through place. But instead of being based in one particular place, the community of renouncers inhabits a circuit of sites, a series of pilgrimage places linked through myth and geography. Renouncers do not ask each other, "Where are you from?" but rather, "Which place have you come from now?" *Sādhus* form community not despite their seeming transience, but because of it: they move on a circumscribed route—any famous place of Hindu practice may legitimately be a *sādhu*'s homeland—where they are sure to find each other again. Although the terrain through which renouncers relate to one another is much larger than a village, or even an urban center, the community holds its coherence through shared experiences of—and relations to—physical space.

If pilgrimage circuits constitute communal conceptions of space for *sādhus*, festival cycles constitute communal conceptions of time. First in Hardwar in 1998, and then in Allahabad in 2001, I attended two Mahā Kumbh Melās, the enormous religious festivals which serve as the gathering point for an otherwise far-flung community. This cyclical gathering was clearly the temporal calendar by which the community collectively regenerated its public role, and its private coherence. For months before and months after both festivals, renouncers asked each other and the pilgrims who came to visit them whether they would go or had been to the Melā. Time mattered to renouncers when they planned to be in particular places, with other members of their community, on particular solar or lunar dates: astral temporal planning was required to participate in communal events.

Landscape circuits and astral cycles were the natural sites of articulation for a community dispersed across space, regenerating itself over time. And if circuits and cycles of nature are the mechanisms through which the renouncer community explicitly connects, the bodies of renouncers are the locations of individual knowledge. Renouncers' bodies are the vehicles of experience, they told me when explicitly asked, through which concepts of space, time, and community are materialized. As David Harvey writes in a different context, "the manner of production of spacetime is inextricably connected with the production of the body" (2000:100). A recreation of the body is the first ritual act of renouncer life—a ritual of death to former family, caste, and name, and a ritual birth into a new body, name, and lineage—and is the ground for each subsequent ritual of initiation, act of devotion, and practice of daily life.

I posed the possibility of linking or making parallel the three themes of space, time, and embodiment to two scholarly renouncers who had created a contemplative ashram a few hours north of Uttarkasi, in what is now the new Himalayan state of Uttaranchal. They told me that space, time, and embodiment formed a natural triad, and were thought of in Śaṅkarācārya's commentaries, for example, as the three fundamental building blocks of material existence. Arguably, space, time, and embodiment can be understood anthropologically as three basic elements that communities or cultures produce, and in turn use to produce themselves. This book lays out the particular manifestations of space, time, and body in the context of Hindu renunciation, as both a "thick description" of renouncer life, to use Geertz's concept of what anthropology is good for (1973), and as a contribution, I hope, to the larger discussions of the ways these fundamental human experiences are constituted and connected.

The Mechanics of Method: Places, People, Practices

One of the premises of this book is that, despite the geographical dispersion of renouncers in contemporary South Asia (and the mythic representations of isolated renouncers who wander alone in unpopulated landscapes), Indian and Nepali *sādhus* actively reproduce and participate in communal structures.[5] *Sādhu* lineages, families, and administrative institutions create communal life even across space—they are the social structures that convey the shared practices and the shared concepts that form the common ground of renouncer identity. South Asian Hindu renouncers may live across the Indian subcontinent, but they know how to recognize each other, greet each other, and categorize each other. The historical traditions of South Asian renouncers show us that far from being an exclusively contemporary phenomenon, communities have forged common identities across space for well over two thousand years.[6]

Most multi-sited ethnographies are designed to work with fairly sizable communities in each of multiple places.[7] My methodology required something different, however: the Hindu renouncer community is spread out over an extremely large region, and usually only very small groups or individuals live in each location. Moreover, *sādhus* are renowned as wanderers who live in no fixed location at all. I quickly found that most renouncers do actually base themselves in a particular place, usually a pilgrimage destination in its own right, and this, at least, would make it easier to ground my research in a few specific locations. But even if I began at Paśupatināth and then worked my way to other pilgrimage places, how would they connect to one another, and what would the contours of my field site be?

The "Subcontinent"

India is of course the "traditional" home of Hindu renunciation, but I did not want to confine my research to Indian territory. I knew the Hindu religious view of space encompassed the holy terrain of the Kathmandu Valley, in particular the prominent Hindu temple Paśupatināth, the symbol of the (erstwhile) Kingdom of Nepal. Indeed, many Hindu practitioners I spoke with—both lay householders and long-time *sādhus*—argued for an incontrovertible religious connection between Nepal and India, evidenced through the mythical links between each country's most revered Hindu shrines. Just as Kathmandu's Bagmati River is symbolically connected to the Indian Ganges River, Paśupatināth is connected to a circuit of prominent Śiva temples in India that spans the entire subcontinent, from the high mountains to the Deccan Plateau. The Himalayas are home to Lord Śiva, and temples in his honor—the representation of his *liṅgam*—are sprinkled throughout the countryside, across the border, ranging from tiny stone mounds in remote forests to large, gilded sanctums in busy urban centers. Nepal, as home to the world's highest mountains, is an important stop on pilgrimage routes even for Indian ascetics precisely because the Himalayas are so integral to the worship and lore of Śiva.

I chose my region of focus by latitude, in a sense: I would work with renouncers across the lower Himalayan belt of North India and Nepal. For both Indians and Nepalis, the border is an open one: no visa is required and public busses ply the land routes between Delhi, Varanasi, and Kathmandu, trundling through the southern plains of Nepal. I was told repeatedly that the international border is a political line, not a religious one; more than one renouncer suggested to me that man-made frontiers falsely carved up the unity of sacred terrain, although some also identified their nationality with pride.

On both sides of the border, Nepal is generally considered the little cousin of vast, sprawling Mother India. Broadly speaking, Nepal's enormous diversity, water reserves, sacred history, and recent Maoist insurgency all mean that India likes to keep Nepal under some degree of political and economic control. As a result, Nepal—both the quickly changing government and also most Nepali citizens—tend to regard the Indian state with equal measures of deference and defiance. In both India and Nepal, Hindu nationalists have been eager to maintain Nepal's status as a Hindu kingdom, although Nepal is more likely well on its way to becoming a republic. The neighboring relation between the countries throws into relief the social hierarchies at work, within and across the national border, in relation to caste, nationality, and religious affiliation: many so-called low-caste Nepali wage laborers, for example, are content to migrate across the Indian border where they are classified simply as "Nepali"—who are considered rather provincial in India—rather than by their caste status.

The decision to work in both India and Nepal was also consistent with the routes of the renouncers I worked with and spoke to, almost all of whom had at some point traveled through the national border to dispersed sites of Hindu practice. Speaking Nepali helped with research in the mountainous regions of North India that border Nepal to the west, since the local Hindi dialect spoken there, Pahari, or "Hill-language," is closer to Nepali than is the Hindi of the plains. Some of my North Indian informants also came from Nepali families, although they were born in Himalayan India, and felt as comfortable communicating in Nepali as in Hindi. Most interviews in the Indian mountains were conducted in some combination of Nepali, Hindi, and Pahari, which seemed to suit everybody.

The Method of Wandering

The research for this book was ultimately focused in the Nepali capital, Kathmandu, and in the Indian states of Uttar Pradesh and, after November 2000, Uttaranchal, in particular the Himalayan region of Garhwal. But for four years, back and forth between graduate school in the U.S. and field sites in South Asia, in the effort to meet and speak with renouncers as often as possible, understand the principles and practices of Śaivism, and participate in *sādhu* life as much as I could, I myself was largely a wanderer between sacred Indian and Nepali pilgrimage towns. This was only correct: to write about the experience of wandering, one must fairly wander.

Multi-sited research translated into not only a good deal of travel between the various locations of fieldwork, but also a reflection that different ethnographic themes might be elicited in different places. First, to research space in mountainous terrain, I used as a base the sacred city of Hardwar, prominent in symbolic representations of Hindu geography because the town marks the place where the Ganges River emerges from the Himalayan mountains and flows into the plains. In mythical renderings, the flowing Gaṅgā emerges from Śiva's matted hair, and the river serves as a geographical pivot for many renouncers' wanderings—some walk from her source in the mountains of Uttaranchal to her outlet in the Bay of Bengal on one bank, and back up again on the other.

I too traveled—first by car and then by foot—the popular pilgrimage route to the source of the sacred Ganges and back down again, meeting and living with renouncers along the way. During this journey, it became clear to me that the terrain of ascetic wandering is determined not by national borders but by the geography of rivers and mountains. The rich quality of Hindu legends that take place in Himalayan territory—combined with the importance of Garhwali pilgrimage routes in renouncer travels—meant that my own sojourns were a way to meet and interview renouncers who either lived in pilgrimage places or were themselves traveling to sacred shrines.[8] To understand how spatial networks that connected a dispersed social web derived from mythic stories laid onto natural landscape, journeys through the region became part of my fieldwork method.

Not coincidentally, Hardwar is also the source of a mythic circuit which links the multiple parts of the goddess Satī's body. A woman of noble birth who hailed from Hardwar, Satī married Śiva over her father's protests that he was a lowly ascetic who lived in the forest, poorly dressed and penniless. For the duration of their marriage, Satī suffered her husband's ignoble rejection by the rigid world of social convention that he had himself rejected. When her father refused to invite his son-in-law to a feast of noblemen—Śiva was simply too rugged to be a proper guest at a distinguished dinner table—Satī could stand no more. Mortally insulted, in righteous fury over her father's treatment of her husband, she spontaneously immolated herself, in a location honored by a modest, open-air temple in Hardwar.

Grieving and enraged at the loss of his wife, Śiva circled the world with Satī's decomposing body. Eighty-four sacred sites mark the terrestrial locations where the pieces of her body fell to earth (Sircar 1973). Today, the Himalayas are scattered with shrines to the discrete parts of Satī's body—in Uttaranchal, her eye and her ear, in Himachal Pradesh, her neck and her tongue, in Kathmandu, her "secret part." These locations mark Satī's bodily testament to the impossibility of resolving the relations between renouncers and householders.

If Hardwar is point zero in the circuit of places that honor Satī's body, Kathmandu is home to one of the most revered sites of the goddess. To understand how renouncers viewed the body, I used as a base the Hindu temple complex that encompasses both Paśupatināth and his consort, Guhyeśwarī, where Satī's "secret" body part fell.[9] The manifestation of Śiva as he is worshipped at Paśupatināth is as Lord of the Animals, or progenitor of creatures: his icon throughout the temple is an erect stone phallus, and indeed women pray to this fertile power so that they might conceive. The temple complex as a whole honors the fertile and gendered bodies of procreative deities, but also testifies to the mortal aspects of embodiment, both through its reverence for a goddess's bodily death and through the constantly burning cremation grounds that line the river. Indeed, Śiva in his incarnation as Lord of the *Yogīs* sits in a charnel ground, surrounded by burning bodies.

At Paśupatināth, I worked primarily with an elderly woman *sādhu,* technically called a *sādhvī,* who lived in a small room in a domestic courtyard, tucked in between the temples which honored Śiva's phallus. The images of the divine organs of creation that so dominate the mythic landscape of the temple combined with the real physical ailments she confronted made this location an appropriate place from which to ask questions about the nature and experience of embodiment. At Paśupatināth, as in Hardwar, myths about bodily, sentient activity—and the commemorative structures humans build to recall them—appeared to pepper the geography of the earth, creating a link between body and place.

Finally, as part of the way I researched time, I participated in two consecutive Mahā Kumbh Melās, which I translate as "Great Festivals of the Nectar Jug." Attending these massive festivals was critical to understanding how a community dispersed across space reproduces itself over time. At both the 1998 festival in Hardwar and the 2001 festival in Allahabad, where India's two most sacred rivers, the Ganges and the Jamuna (popularly described as the Gaṅgā and the Yamuna, the river of Śiva and the river of Viṣṇu), converge, I saw how these festival events acted as the gathering points for the entire renouncer community. As calendrical moments when new members are initiated and old members are promoted and honored, the Melās mark a cycle of regeneration. The renouncers I spoke with used the festival as a fixed point of time from which they counted their years as renouncers, and around which they planned their pilgrimages. The myth of the Nectar Jug—whereby four drops of the nectar of immortality fell from the Kumbh, or jug, that is the festival's namesake—poses a cosmic view of transcendent time that symbolically represents the religious project of the renouncer community.

Three different kinds of mythic locations—a region, a festival, and an urban temple— therefore became a tripartite fieldwork approach to living with and learning about the South Asian renouncer community. The links I have drawn between these three places and the themes they elicited—traveling through a region as a way of learning about space, attending consecutive festivals as a way of learning about time, and using temple symbolism as a way of learning about the body—were not planned but organically developed from the research methods I used and the research questions I asked. When I mapped my travels, I found that the themes I had worked on formed a kind of dialectic with the locations I had worked in.[10] Each place of research informed an ethnographic theme, and each theme of research demanded a particular method. Gradually, I hoped, I would develop personal connections in each of these contexts, so that I could trace the social dimensions of renouncers' lives alongside their philosophical orientations and their places of practice.

Informants and Connections

Very early on, I realized that the most appropriate method for my fieldwork would be to get to know a small number of individual renouncers well, if I could, and also interview members of the renouncer community more broadly.[11] This approach would mean a comfortable and sustained interaction with a few people, and also determine my particular locations: I could stay where my key informants chose to live and travel. More importantly, focusing on the stories and perspectives of a few individuals (who turned out to come from very different backgrounds and levels of education) would also allow me to explore the range of renouncers' life histories and religious perspectives at the same time that I was trying to draw conclusions about the practices and approaches of the community as a whole.

Over a total of nineteen months of active fieldwork between 1997 and 2001, I worked closely and consistently with three renouncers with whom I built steady relationships over time and place. Over the years that I traveled back and forth between the various places of my particular field, however, I met hundreds of renouncers and had informal conversations with scores of *sādhus,* some over the course of a few days, some in the context of a one-time meeting. I met and re-met renouncers at different pilgrimage points and, sometimes, at consecutive festival events. Hearing that I had been traveling in Garhwal or from Kathmandu, renouncers would ask me if I had come across a friend or a fellow member of their lineage, and we would compare notes on who had been where when, and catch up on the latest whereabouts, health, or even scandal that surrounded our mutual social connections.

However brief, all these encounters influenced my thinking about the nature of living as a Hindu renouncer, especially because the variable kinds and durations of interactions I had with members of the *sādhu* community seemed to me typical of the come-and-go, sometimes-brief and sometimes-sustained meetings in which renouncers themselves participate in contemporary South Asia. Even conversations that were one-time encounters appear in this book—isolated interactions are as much a part of *sādhu* life as large communal festivals are.

The pages that follow detail the structures, views, and practices of the *sādhu* community as a whole, but the range of *sādhu* experience is much broader than I encountered or can convey. I discuss the "renouncer community" as a singular entity despite this individual variation because the overarching argument of this book is that the experience of renunciation—first a ritual of initiation and then a self-conscious separation from householder society—links *sādhus* together despite varied backgrounds, divergent practices, and dispersed locations.

The plan to work closely with a small number of individual renouncers solved the problem of where I should physically base myself in the Himalayan region, but produced a series of other intellectual conundrums. How was I to select the individuals with whom I would be able to build close relationships? How would I choose three people to work with, or know a real renouncer when I met one? A series of initial attempts failed dismally when one informant with whom I had worked closely over a summer was kicked out of town for impregnating too many women (despite his stated *tantric* ability to withhold semen), and a second made clear after an initial period that our conversations would come to fruition only if I met him late at night at the temple and brought him a watch from America.

After these fruitless attempts, I became despondent at the thought that I would never be able to build a relationship of trust and open communication with a dedicated renouncer, and that the community I had chosen to work with fulfilled its reputation as an ordered set of charlatans, outcasts, criminals, mentally ill individuals, and men who wanted only to smoke hashish in a fraternity-like setting.[12] Certainly I learned from these groups that the social and therapeutic roles of renouncer institutions needed to be taken seriously: *sādhu* society clearly offered alternative community structures for people who were not welcome in householder society or who could fit nowhere else. But in these large, single-sex groups, male renouncers in particular seemed indeed a bunch of louts, and I was dismayed to think of writing an ethnography about a community that used religion exclusively as an excuse to forge an unproductive brotherhood.

This methodological stalemate was broken when I began to seek out women *sādhu* informants, not because women were purer renouncers, but because I did not have to break down what seemed an impermeable gender barrier. I had been reluctant to write a dissertation based exclusively on women's experiences because I was committed to writing an ethnography about the entire renouncer community. Of an estimated two million renouncers in South Asia, probably only 200,000 (or 10 percent) are women.[13] Writing exclusively on women, I felt, would limit the kinds of questions I could ask and the scope of understanding I would have of the community as a whole: I wanted to understand renouncers' views not of the gendered human body, for example, but of the material human body, of which gender is only a part.[14]

Beginning my research by working with women broke down certain barriers for me as a fieldworker, however, which eventually opened up the larger field. I felt more comfortable with women renouncers than I did with men, and they were more open with and accepting of me. In part, this was because many *sādhvīs* were Nepali or of Nepali origin.[15] Most importantly, working with women immediately defused some of the tensions around gender and sexuality that were part of my research agenda, but that were inevitably heightened when a lone young woman arrived at the sacred fire-pit of an exclusively male lineage, as I did many times over the course of fieldwork. Having gained a certain degree of fieldwork confidence by working with women, I began to have more relaxed and natural conversations with informants—both women and men—sometimes about gender, but more often about renouncer life as a whole.

Although my research with women was in many ways smoother than my research with men, this book remains an ethnographic study about the larger renouncer community, roughly 90 percent of whom are men. But I warn my readers that my key informants are not a representative sample: of the three key informants with whom I eventually worked closely, two are women. The third, a man in his sixties, was perhaps my closest informant, however. My work with him showed me that doing research across gender lines was in fact possible and could, in the right circumstances, be extremely productive.

Searching for One Who Has Found

Those early despondent fieldwork moments pointed to some unspoken exigencies of field research (cf. Gold 1988; Lamb 2000), but also to an important aspect about the myths and realities of renouncer life. Looking for a "real" renouncer seemed to resonate with a larger Hindu devotional project. Many lay Hindus I met told me they had no tolerance for the vast majority of renouncers, but that there *were* a select few (some people specified 5 percent, or 1 percent, or even less than that, a tiny number symbolized by flicking the thumb) who were on a genuine religious path and who could convey religious knowledge. Meeting them, of course, depended entirely on one's *karma*. I witnessed a number of heated arguments between householder Hindus about what constituted a "real" renouncer and what kinds of *sādhus* could be counted as legitimate. Almost everybody—even highly suspicious householders—eventually agreed that a committed devotee might be able to find a real renouncer, who would be a realized or spiritually advanced person who spent his or her days in meditative contemplation, and whose steadfast efforts produced religious power.

The institutions of Indian monasticism fulfill the needs of people requiring social welfare, to be sure, but they also provide a structure for people on genuine mystical quests. These two populations sometimes merge, and social and religious motivations for renunciation sometimes coincide. People with social disadvantages and economic needs may find solace in religious faith and material sustenance in alms offered by pilgrims. Conversely, people who come from wealthy backgrounds may leave all their possessions behind in order to find God. Indeed, legends abound about accomplished religious beings of noble birth who take on the guise of a mendicant to free themselves from all attachments or to test public perceptions.

People become renouncers for many reasons, including an inability or an unwillingness to fit into normative society, on one hand, and a profound desire to understand the meaning of existence, on the other. The larger *sādhu* fraternity with whom I had such trouble working and toward whom lay Hindu householders are so suspicious shows that the social and economic aspects of community are as important to contemporary renouncers as questions of religious ideology. Most often, I found that members of the renouncer community—like members of any community—were people who experienced moments of genuine religious reflection, and also moments of worldly or materialistic concern. Many of us shift back and forth between these two poles of thought.

The possibility that a few renouncers are unilaterally focused in their religious efforts and have attained a clearer understanding of the nature of material reality inspires a degree of collective householder faith in the Hindu renouncer community. As I researched this book, I too was interested in finding "real" renouncers, or people whose conduct and beliefs were in some way more deeply informed by religious experience and knowledge than by their membership in an alternative brotherhood. I was at first more interested in Hindu religious philosophy than in pure sociology, and I sought to speak with renouncers who would teach me the core principles of religious thought and practice. In a sense, my project to find renouncers approximated the search for a *guru*, or religious teacher. Central to the tradition of Hindu renunciation are the concepts that first, religious knowledge can only be conveyed through experience, and second, that experience must be directed and guided by a qualified *guru*. Every renouncer I spoke with insisted on this point: the importance of and reliance on a *guru* is a critical part of practice.

To be a true "participant" in renouncer life, or to acquire insight into religious or ritual experience that went beyond simple observation, then, I would have to have been initiated by a *guru* into a renouncer order.[16] I was open to the possibility of initiation during fieldwork—if the dynamics with a particular renouncer inspired such a ritual or if the circumstances seemed appropriate—but my connections with *sādhus* did not come to fruition as such. Perceiving that I intended to understand renouncer philosophies in as much depth as possible, one informant did call me her *celī*, or disciple, but she used the term in a general or colloquial sense. She graciously introduced me as her disciple to other members of her lineage, which provided a comfortable structure for me to do my research, but I did not undergo any formal ritual, which is core to the identity of a renouncer.[17]

As primarily a researcher, I remained outside formal *sādhu* social structures, inhabiting instead the "observer" status of an honorary deep-hanger-on. Not being a formally initiated disciple meant that I paid my service and obligations to renouncers in other ways, more befitting the respectful actions of a lay pilgrim: I made repeated small offerings of money, and I tried to provide whatever material objects or small services my informants might ask for or need. Being an outsider rather than an insider had certain research benefits: I was free to come and go as my own research required, to ask naïve or straightforward questions about many aspects of *sādhu* life, and to work with more than one renouncer, which would have been very difficult had I been initiated by a particular *sādhu*.

This arrangement meant that I developed personal relationships with many renouncers, who usually found their own ways of classifying me. For example, when I first started my research at the Hardwar Kumbh Melā, I went to the camp of a "Western" *bābā* I knew. His sweet, formidable Indian *yogī*-brother, Ali Bābā, was in charge of the compound, and

I approached him to request permission to stay, explaining that I was a doctoral student planning to work with renouncers of different orders at the festival. Rotund, with a turban of matted hair and very dark skin, Ali Bābā was impressed with my stammering attempt to speak Hindi, nonplussed by my obsession with my notebook, and fully supportive of my research efforts. He assured me that I was welcome, and promptly nicknamed me "Babydoctor," a name which reflected my nascent status both as a doctoral student and as an educated but uninitiated member of the camp. Babydoctor—sometimes shortened to "Baby"—was as good as an official designation, and Ali Bābā used it frequently when he summoned me to the main tent, where he sometimes asked me questions in public to show me off as a member of his camp. When we met three years later, at the Allahabad Kumbh, I was known as Babydoctor once again: the name—and the intimate-outsider status it conveyed—had stuck.

Every informant I spoke with over the course of three years insisted, however, that no one would ever be able to understand the principles of Hindu religious life through academic categories. Along with the importance of a *guru,* the impossibility of a purely intellectual grasp of religious endeavor was a universally agreed upon premise. Experience is not an intellectual exercise, my informants argued: mental and bodily disciplines are required to establish enough spiritual depth to translate or interpret religious teachings. In place of becoming an insider, then, which would have meant initiation as a renouncer (and quite likely the abandonment of the ethnography as such), I did engage in my own religious practice, which I was also personally inclined to do. I understood my daily practice (a short period each of meditation and physical yoga exercises) as part of my method, the one part that was implicitly required of me by my informants.[18]

Key Informants

Through a combination of circumstance, perseverance, and luck, I did meet three people who, over time, became close informants with whom I developed a constructive and genuine connection. All three showed compassion and trust and, perhaps most importantly, were willing to take me, a relative stranger, into their confidences and into their lives, while many others refused to have anything to do with me or were interested in my project only because I might provide a link to the material objects or *guru* circuits of the "West."

The three renouncers with whom I worked closely came from very different backgrounds and represented a wide range of experience. Two were from India, one from Nepal; two were women, one a man; two were uneducated, one was highly educated; one had become a renouncer as a child, one as a young woman in her twenties, one as a widow in her sixties. All three were members of the *daśnāmī sampradāya,* or the Śaiva sectarian orders established by the eighth-century philosopher Śaṅkarācārya. The two women belonged to the large and unruly Jūnā Akhāṛā, the only administrative body which initiates women; the single man belonged to the upper-caste and wealthier Nirañjanī Akhāṛā, a much more exclusive order. All three were in their late fifties or sixties when I worked with them, and all three had been initiated into the full rank of *sādhu* maturity.

The closest connection I developed was with Pāgal Bābā, or "Crazy One," a *sādhu* whose formal name was Svāmī Rājeśwarānand Giri. Bābā, as I called him (and as most renouncers are addressed), had spent a little time in Europe through an enduring friendship with a Slovenian man who had traveled to India in the 1960s, and spoke excellent English. He had always lived life as an eccentric, he argued (thus his nickname)—his renouncer organization had funded his Sanskrit education in Varanasi, but he had ripped up his thesis when he got fed up, something he exhorted me not to do. He had been initiated as a renouncer when still a child and so was reared with a firm belief in the value of renunciation, including the steady conviction that normative social life placed real constraints on people.

Because of his natural candor and independence, as well as his experience in Europe and familiarity with Europeans, Pāgal Bābā was as well practiced in explaining his daily actions and the structures of renouncer life as he was patient with my curiosity, naïveté, and sometimes painfully inadequate knowledge. I first met Bābā at the 1998 Kumbh Melā in Hardwar (he had met other members of my family at the 1989 Allahabad Kumbh Melā), and Hardwar remained one of his home bases. When I returned to Hardwar in September 2000, I bumped into him on the street and soon after moved into the small hotel where he had lived on and off for years. There I could visit him daily, take evening walks with him, and wash our dishes if he cooked me lunch, as he often did.

I also met Rādhā Giri at the 1998 Kumbh Melā in Hardwar. A fiercely independent *sādhvī,* she was rumored to have magical powers, and she brooked no disrespect toward or disobedience of the rules she had established around her small quarters on the riverbank.[19] She was fairly reticent about her background, but I did learn that she had been raised and married in the Himalayan area of Kumaon, northern Uttaranchal. She had left her marriage—I wondered if her fiery character had contributed to an unwillingness to play the part of subordinate wife—and followed a *guru* to Hardwar, where she had lived at the same spot on the riverbank for over twenty years. She was clearly motivated by both religious duty and compassion, for she unfailingly paid her daily homage to the river and meticulously maintained the altars around the trees under which she lived, although her tent was rather scruffy.

Rādhā Giri had also taken on the role of protector toward a number of needy creatures and people (including me, on occasion), most notably a baby girl whom she had agreed to raise despite her own ill health and relatively advanced years. Her tent was a haven for many of the homeless neighborhood dogs, and she frequently shared her meals with a mentally ill woman from the area. She was a well-respected figure among members of the Hardwar renouncer community (including the men), and a steady flow of local and traveling renouncers visited her tent. Mai, or Mātājī, as women renouncers are known, was neither particularly interested in my interview questions nor particularly verbal, but she was welcoming, and I visited her often when I returned to Hardwar in 2000. Spending time at Rādhā Giri's home place meant that I could watch for myself how she lived her daily life, and speak with the revolving cast of renouncers who came to visit her tent on their way up to or down from the mountain pilgrimage routes.

The third key informant I worked with was an elderly Nepali *sādhvī* named Mukta Giri. I met Mukta Giri in Kathmandu, at the Paśupatināth Temple, in the early spring of 2000. She had traveled to Nepal to attend the annual Śiva Rātrī festival, and had fallen ill and stayed on. She was very frail and very poor; she lived in a tiny, dark, spare room in a residential courtyard of the large temple complex. Until she felt well enough to travel back to Hardwar, where she lived in an ashram, I spent two or three afternoons a week with her; we sat and talked in the open spaces of the forest area that surrounded Paśupatināth, about the ways she interpreted Hindu precepts and the kinds of social connections she had developed through living in a householder courtyard. Social conditions had clearly contributed to her choice to become a renouncer. She had been a widow for twelve years and faced dire social circumstances (see Lamb 2000). Becoming a renouncer was a freeing, validating act, and she took great solace from the faith that a full-time religious life and a ready-made religious community offered her.

By the time I met Mukta Giri, I had encountered many renouncers, but she was one of the first with whom I was able to establish a steady rhythm of conversation and a genuine level of discussion that broke through the automatic recitation of religious aphorisms. She was clearly happy to be back in Nepal (as was I), but she felt relatively separate from the householders she lived with; I provided company, afternoon conversation, and a little money and medicine. In May 2000, when she felt well enough (or at least sufficiently restored from spending some months in her native Kathmandu), she returned to the Nepali Ashram in Hardwar. When I moved to Hardwar in September, four months later, I tried to find her, but the members of her ashram said she had returned once again to Kathmandu. We reconnected at Paśupatināth in March 2001 and continued our afternoon meetings for a few months, until I left, this time, at the end of my fieldwork period. She had clearly gotten fed up with wandering back and forth across the Indian border; now that she had established the viability of living in Kathmandu as a renouncer, she wanted to remain in Nepal.

A number of Western renouncers were very helpful during my fieldwork: European and American *sādhus* had made for themselves decades earlier the cultural transitions and translations that I was newly working on. I debated whether to work with any in the steady way that I was eventually able to work with Pāgal Bābā, Rādhā Giri, and Mukta Giri, but opted to keep the primary theme of my research the meanings of culture for renouncers of South Asian origin. Although I do not focus on the particular experiences of Western *sādhus* in this book, they did provide me with a great deal of information and on occasion they do appear as informants in the pages that follow.[20]

The Practice of Ethnography

The conversations I had with my informants were by and large very informal. On a few occasions, I scheduled interview times with *sādhus,* but more often I visited renouncers in their home places, hoping to find them in, and in the mood to talk. Fieldwork basically meant sitting with renouncers in a relaxed way, watching their actions and discussing life with them and their visitors. I was usually treated as a guest despite my efforts to learn how to be of service to a *sādhu,* that is, to be a *sevak,* someone who provides service,[21] which I had thought might be a good role for me. But it generally took more effort than it was worth for a renouncer to teach me the proper ways to prepare food on a sacred open fire-pit or to wash dishes with ash. Apart from a few valiant attempts to help serve renouncers and their other guests, I usually just tried to stay out of the way and accepted the tea or food I was offered. I was often reminded that food or drink from the hands of a renouncer was *prasād,* an offering from a holy person or deity, and eventually I learned how to offer a little bit of tea to the fire, or pour a circle of water around my food before I consumed it.

I did not tape-record the conversations I had with *sādhus,* choosing instead to take notes by hand, which I later wrote out in detail. As in the case of many ethnographers (see Desjarlais 1992), the word quickly spread that someone liked to talk to *sādhus* and write down everything they said. I was on occasion asked by *sādhus* or their visitors to read what I had written, a request with which I always complied and which I found to be a very useful fact-checking exercise. I enjoyed seeing how my representation fit with what informants thought they had been saying, and also following the conversations that resulted from a public reading, such as how I had understood or misunderstood important points about *sādhu* life, or how far I still had to go in understanding the nuances of religious philosophy.

The process of distilling my informants' multiple narratives into a coherent analysis has evolved over time: I have tried to keep the conversations and experiences I had with renouncers at the core of both ethnographic and theoretical discussion. I have kept in mind the words of one *sādhvī* who read the detailed notes I had written about an afternoon we had spent together. She complimented my memory on the course of our conversation—I had transcribed the words and the order of our dialogue in accurate detail. But she added that I had understood her words on a very superficial level. I was stricken, but she assured me that my understanding of her words would deepen with time.

This *sādhvī*'s suggestion that successive interpretations of narrative could gradually approach a speaker's meaning became a kind of method for me. I used the conversations recorded in my notebooks as a stable point of reference, and my writing and rewriting as a way to focus and refocus my lens of analysis, whereby my informants' own words could come more clearly into view. As I gradually understood the greater context in which informants articulated their perspectives or experiences, I tried to reinterpret their narratives in a way that was more closely aligned to the meaning intended by the speaker—acknowledging that there would always be a dimension invisible to me—and also that reflected more nuanced layers of the cultural context in which they were uttered. While I did not discount meanings that were observable to me, but not necessarily discerned or discernable by the speaker or subject, I tried to consider what my informants said at face value. Respect for my informants as teachers of a tradition that was not my own was, to the best of my ability, an unarticulated but non-negotiable contract. My hope is that this book—using the language of both Hindu religion and Euro-American social theory—better represents what my informants tried to convey about renouncers' lives and practices than I could understand at the time.

I did not carry a camera during most of my fieldwork—South Asian *sādhus* are a favorite photo opportunity among foreigners, and I wanted to resist being perceived as a tourist photographer if I possibly could. I watched how having a camera seemed to alter every interaction between renouncers and foreigners: *sādhus* were either very hostile toward cameras or very insistent on being photographed, and I did not want to participate in either kind of dynamic. The striking minimalist aesthetic of renouncers means that they are usually represented as glorified "Others," and I wanted to avoid this problem too.[22] Eventually, a close American friend gave me a camera on a brief trip to the U.S., insisting that my experiences should be visually as well as verbally recorded. I dutifully snapped three rolls of film, taking pictures of the renouncers I was close to, before I gave the camera to Pāgal Bābā, who hinted that he needed one, perhaps encouraged by my visible ambivalence about using it.

Religion, Society, and Experience

The book as a whole hinges on three points of tension. These three frames inform a project grounded in symbolic anthropology, whereby shared meanings about the nature of the world create a coherent, if dynamic, religious community. First, focusing on questions of community speaks to the paradox of the renouncer ideology of isolation and the explicit value of stripping away social influence, when renouncers actually live in what is very clearly a fully developed social context. Every renouncer I met articulated the importance of solitude in religious practice, since the explicit goal of renunciation is to remove the habits and rhythms of social life. And yet renouncers clearly relied on each other, and on their lineages and renouncer families, as the enduring units of a community that takes great pains to pass down religious values and instruction. The tension between isolated religious practice and shared communal life is reflected in traditional texts on renouncer conduct and also in contemporary renouncer narratives.

Second, despite an emphasis on the illusory nature of space, time, and embodiment in textual exegesis, renouncers I spoke and lived with struggled with their own perceptions of material reality and, most specifically, with the question of how to worship or engage in religious practices that rely on form and experience. The dilemma between text and lived experience is a scholarly issue for anthropologists and historians of religion, but a very practical issue for renouncers. How does one worship at all if the body is illusory? Hindu practice is based in large part on the detailed calculations of sacred spaces, times, and actions. The renouncers I spoke with explicitly believed these differentiations were constructed human props, or Brāhmanical ways of organizing human thought.

As religious practitioners, renouncers acknowledged they needed those props, and by and large they used the modes of worship affiliated with concepts of form. They participated in rituals that differentiated space, time, and bodies into categories of sacred, profane, pure, and impure. Studying texts that argue that material experience is illusory led renouncers' religious thoughts in one direction, they told me, but their desire to fulfill the tenets of religious practice required another. The renouncers I worked with were aware of this ideological contradiction, but they would rhetorically ask, What other choice do we have, as embodied people? They had to participate in ritual differentiation, *sādhus* told me, until they became realized beings whose bodies were no longer ensnared by illusion.

Renouncers moved back and forth between concepts of the body as a burdensome trap of illusion, on one hand, and concepts of the body as a divine tool of experience, on the other. This final paradox in renouncer narratives—between viewing the body as an obstruction and using the body as a ground of knowledge—reflects a tension similar to contemporary European and American theories of the body (which have self-consciously moved away from what they call the dualist Cartesian model of the body that, these theories argue, has dominated Western thought for centuries). In this book, I show how Hindu renouncers argue for an experiential understanding of the world in some cases, but also rely heavily on a dualistic model to explain the body. They claim the materiality of the body is illusory, they denigrate its functions, and they fear its power. Experience, renouncers argue, is not always a reliable source of knowledge: it can occlude as often as it can reveal. The body may be a reliable source of knowledge in Hindu religious thought, but it is also the unrelenting source of suffering and entrapment.

Rather than try to resolve any of these contradictions, I present ethnographic material that shows how my informants lived with and accommodated these tensions in their daily lives. Isolated religious practice occurs within dispersed but communal structures; illusory states of space, time, and body still form the ground for worship; and the body is certainly our only option as a vehicle of life experience, despite its burdensome demands and illusory allure. Renouncers themselves are sometimes conscious of these tensions, and I recount directly the perspectives of my informants when they discuss them as such. More often, this book sets forward my own interpretations of what renouncers told me, and presents my own explanation of how renouncers understand and reconcile these core paradoxes of human life.

The Structure of the Book

The body of the book is divided into five chapters. Chapters 1 and 2 lay out the theoretical and sociological groundwork for the detailed ethnography that follows. Chapter 1, "The Body and *Sādhu* Society," acts as the theoretical pivot of the book. Contrary to the popular Western or Euro-American view that Indian approaches toward the body defy dualism, I argue that renouncers' narratives about breaking away from householder society are reflected in the metaphor of splitting the soul apart from the physical trap of the body. The social and material spheres of renouncer life are seen as equivalent, understood by renouncers through the same religious model.

Chapter 2, "The Social Structures of *Sādhu* Life," tries to dispel the notion that *sādhus* are isolated ascetics and shows how different kinds of social organizations create and sustain a community of renouncers. I argue that the social structures of *sādhu* life are divided into two distinct but overlapping arenas, renouncer families and administrative orders. These systems serve contemporary functions within the renouncer community, but are significantly shaped by their particular histories. I show how concepts like "family" and "social structure," which are ostensibly renounced by *sādhus*, are recreated with new twists and new meanings in renouncer society. The chapter presents a sociological overview of *sādhu* life, describing the institutions of Hindu monasticism and showing how renouncers participate in collective structures.

Chapters 3, 4, and 5 constitute the core of the ethnography by demonstrating how the conceptual themes—space, time, and the body—around which I organize the book play out in the daily lives, practices, and perspectives of renouncers. This central part of the text is empirical rather than theoretical or sociological, based directly on the stories and narratives of renouncers, and my conversations and experiences with them. By taking up space, embodiment, and time in turn, each chapter demonstrates the meanings of the material world that renouncers create and reproduce for themselves. For each theme, I suggest that the natural or material world mediates between a mythic or transcendent plane of existence on one hand, and the exigencies of communal spatial and temporal life on the other.

Chapter 3, "The Ground of Space," set in Hardwar, shows how a shared mythic view of natural landscape conceptually and practically links renouncers together, despite the geographical dispersion of the community. Rather than wander perpetually (as legends about renouncers imply), most renouncers actually do have a base for their travels, or a "seat." The words for "home" in Hindi and Nepali are entirely shunned by renouncers, but I suggest that specific places, such as caves, jungles, ashrams, and fire-pits, serve as seats for sedentary renouncers. I argue that a network of *sādhu* seats in holy places creates a subcontinental web that comprises renouncers' collective view of space. The natural elements of Himalayan geography, such as mountains, rivers, and valleys, combined with mythic and political readings of the Indian and Nepali landscape, mean that certain places are equipped to support renouncers with social networks, economic sustenance, and religious revitalization. The circuits of local and regional pilgrimage places serve as the primary ways renouncers understand their community in space.

Chapter 4, set in Allahabad in 2001 (although my research on the Kumbh Melā started in Hardwar in 1998), "The Community in Time," describes the great communal festival of Hindu renouncers, known as the Mahā Kumbh Melā. The festival shows us how natural time, or the time measured by the movements of the planets and stars, articulates a collective space-time for the renouncer community. The gathering itself is the forum for initiations, promotions, and the regeneration of communal life, as well as a re-enactment of the military history that developed and expanded the ranks of warrior renouncers. Through a ritual regeneration of community, the festival mediates between the historical reality of renouncer life and the collective experience of temporal transcendence.

Chapter 5, "The Body in Place," set in Kathmandu, shows how renouncer disciplines of the material body mediate between the laudatory and the denigrating passages about embodiment in Hindu philosophical texts. I argue that renouncers view their religious project as one of maintaining the body with as little indulgence as possible, while also giving it its care and its due. This tenuous balance between conflicting ideologies of embodiment is the meaning of *tapas*, or a renouncer's austerity or discipline, and it requires a vigilant attention to the physical world and the physical body. Renouncers' bodily disciplines keep the body in its place, as it were—sustained, groomed, and sociable, but also restrained from entirely eclipsing transcendental consciousness, which is the real goal of renouncers' religious practice.

Apart from brief sections in the first and last chapters, theoretical discussions have been kept to a minimum. A more detailed discussion of major theoretical approaches and literatures has been added as an appendix, however, which can be used by students learning the materials or by scholars who wish for a brief overview of the theoretical literature behind my analyses. Authors whose work has been referenced in the text are cited in standard scholarly fashion: non-academic readers need just know that the name in brackets at the end of a sentence can be looked up in the bibliography at the end of the book.

Certain elements of *sādhu* life are fairly constant over time, while others have been defined by particular political and economic moments in history. The book as a whole is written in the hope that a reader can gain a sense of what it is like to live and think as a Hindu *sādhu* in South Asia around the turn of the twenty-first century. But also, more broadly, by decoding how one community constitutes its own reality at a particular moment in time, perhaps we might understand a little more clearly what it means to be embodied in the world, in culture and across culture.

1 ❁ *The Body and Sādhu Society*

The Hinduism that underscores renouncers' lives broadly overlaps with the Hinduism that householders live, practice, and reproduce. But the point of renunciation is to separate from normative Hindu society. A community that self-consciously splits apart from dominant social structures will inevitably modify and reconstruct core elements of a worldview. As long as we recall that 'Hindu' is itself a culturally constructed category (Dirks 2001), renouncers' views of the material world can expand our grasp of Hindu practices at large, and lead us to a deeper comprehension of the experience of renunciation in South Asian life.

Householders probably only have time for a devotional ritual in the morning, as they begin their day, or in the evening, when their work is done. Renouncers, on the other hand, are supposed to be full-time religious practitioners. Because *sādhus* are meant to be engaged in religious activity all the time—performing rituals of daily ablution, spending hours in private meditation or study, or even devoting one's whole life to continued service or charity, called *sevā* (Khandelwal 2006)—they are presumed to be authoritative teachers of Hindu texts and traditions. The image we have of an ascetic with a begging bowl arriving unannounced in a village is probably not far from the truth. What we might less frequently recall is that, in implicit exchange for a place to sleep and some food to eat, a *sādhu* will offer blessings, conduct a village ritual or rite, or give a lecture on the core tenets of Hindu theology. Every renouncer should be able to recite the *Bhagavad Gītā*, for example, or at least summarize its lessons

« *Three sādhus*

about the importance of religious duty. Even in cities, some renouncers deliver public sermon-like *prachans* to lay audiences, who want to hear renowned renouncers' interpretations of sacred texts (Menon 2006).

The *Gītā* teaches that we need to accept whatever comes in life, be it joy or sorrow, as the inevitability of one's own *karma.* According to the *Gītā,* our bodies—the vessels through which our *karma* in this life is borne out—merely encase our inner, unchanging core. The intention of Hindu practice is to overcome or transcend that outer plane, characterized by dualistic thought and perception, and merge with an undifferentiated, unified plane of being. For both Hindu householders and Hindu renouncers, being reabsorbed into cosmic consciousness leads to *mokṣa,* or liberation from cyclical material existence. Every embodied individual contains a personal spark of divinity, an *ātman,* which strives to reunite with the vast divine force, the *brahman,* from which it came.

Yoga, the mental and physical disciplines that most renouncers practice in some form in order to achieve this state of deep concentration, derives from the Sanskrit root *yuj-* ("to join" or "to unite").[1] Fusion, the real goal of renouncers' practice, is the successful outcome of disciplined religious conduct as articulated in philosophical texts, myth, popular culture, and the narratives of my informants. Ironically, fusion with the divine is only possible through fission, or by breaking apart from the trap of material reality, with its seeming social and physical laws of differentiation. *Mokṣa* literally means "release," final separation from the cyclical world of illusion, the moment when our falsely perceived bodily experiences melt away.

The physical and social worlds are most frequently symbolized in renouncer life by metaphors of breaking apart: separation, fragmentation, incompleteness, and casting away the body are the images used by the community of renouncers to describe both their social roles and their religious practices. The body pieces of the self-immolated goddess Satī show that she does not need to be whole to be worshipped—indeed, she is more accessible to human beings split into fragments. The metaphor of fission—"splitting . . . apart," as Isabelle Nabokov puts it—is an intentional practice designed to transcend a dualistic world (2000:15).

These two fundamental splits—the practical split of the renouncer from householder society and the metaphorical split of the soul from the body—mirror each other. In what follows, I show how the social split enacted by renouncers is paralleled by the religious goal of stripping the body away from the soul, and vice versa. In this way I deconstruct the oft-cited link between Indian minds and bodies and show that the renouncer project may be precisely to split the body, as the symbol of both the social and material plane, from the spirit. This religious project is evidence of the equivalence between materiality and sociality in renouncer thought.

Paradoxically, renouncers' practices suggest that fission facilitates fusion: by splitting apart from society, the body releases the soul. Both separations reflect the renouncer's project of union, or liberation from the dualistic trappings of social convention and material confinement. This chapter analyzes the relationship between householder society and *sādhu* society by asking what social roles renunciation serves. I show how renouncers intentionally treat the body as a metaphor for social life through the language of Hindu philosophy. And I suggest that renouncers regard their bodies as the symbol of both physical and social life: the rejection of the body is analogous to the rejection of society. Renouncers' shared religious beliefs ground both the way they create an alternative community and the way they think about their bodies in religious practice.

This chapter includes the only explicitly theoretical sections of the book—discussing in turn the work of Durkheim, Dumont, and Descartes—which should not put readers off. The first and second sections use a lens from the sociology of religion to look at how renouncers create themselves as a society separate from householders. The third section, at the very end of the chapter, continues this discussion by reflecting on the body as a religious project in India. Based on my interpretations of what Indian scholars or *yogīs* told me, I ask whether we might reconsider the ways anthropology and Indology approach the soul-body split in South Asian thought and experience. (These academic discussions are considered in further detail in the appendix.) The chapter as a whole considers the parallels between these two conversations—one on society and one on the body—suggesting that renouncers' efforts to split from conventional society reflects the Hindu religious goal to achieve transcendence from materiality, to strip the layers away, into being.

The Difference Between Householders and Renouncers

What, exactly, a renouncer opposes in householder life takes many forms. The lives of contemporary renouncers (and of contemporary householders) are so varied that there is no single, unidimensional way to draw a theoretical line between *sannyāsīs,* renouncers, and *gṛhasthīs,* householders, to use the Sanskrit but still active terms for these divergent life paths. Experiences of caste and family undoubtedly shift in the world of renunciation, but the meanings attributed to these categories of identity are so broad that a universal definition seems almost impossible. Personal motivations to renounce householder society vary widely, and the ways an individual renouncer articulates his or her opposition to householder society may change over time, in a social dynamic that is fluid and shifting.[2]

Like members of any community, renouncers are accountable to and connected with one another through the formal lineages and institutional structures that I describe in the next chapter. The split that gives meaning to Hindu religious society is not, therefore, "social" versus "anti-social" or "communal" versus "isolated." Scholars who have tried to find any one, precise, pan–South Asian social category with which to distinguish householders from renouncers have failed, because each possible theoretical distinction breaks down when faced with the range of actual, lived experiences among *sādhus.* Anthropologist Richard Burghart writes, "no simple dichotomy can describe the relation between Brahman householder and renouncer" (1983a:636); Kirin Narayan adds, the "opposition between renunciation and caste . . . like all simplistic divisions . . . obscures the messy variations in everyday life" (1989:75).

The householder social structures from which renouncers are ostensibly free—and from which many willfully flee—do not disappear in renouncer society. Caste and family affiliations, though much mitigated, leave their traces among renouncers, visible in the way renouncers do or do not share food, touch each other, and care for disciples, students, and children. Some ascetics are married, and some do raise children. Many renouncer orders think of themselves as families. And although traditionally renouncers are supposed to wander so as to distance themselves from socialized settings, many *sādhus* are sedentary, and live among householder communities.

Caste

There is no doubt that renouncer society largely opposes caste society, and the symbol of the *sannyāsī* has been held up as a radical critique of caste in Indian political movements by figures as lofty as Gandhi.[3] But the community in its place is not entirely without caste consciousness. My closest informant, Pāgal Bābā, spoke publicly and easily of his own *kṣatriya* caste background. At the Kumbh Melā I was told that the difference in the nature of distinct *sādhu* orders could be attributed to the fact that some sects—like the large and unruly Jūnā Akhāṛā—initiate members of all castes, while others—the wealthy and subdued Nirañjanī Akhāṛā, for example—initiate members of so-called "twice-born," or upper, castes only. I was also told that *sādhu* orders are mapped onto different parts of the divine body of Śiva (a clear parallel to the popular narrative that correlates the four *varṇas,* or castes, with the primordial body of Puruṣa), and thus represent a clear social hierarchy, with those orders closest to the head ranking highest and being considered purest.

Narayan (1989) emphasizes the danger of accepting the distinction between caste householder and renouncer as too stark for the same reasons: caste does not entirely disappear from the world of the renouncer, and too much attention to caste obscures the multiple other social divisions that many renouncers aim to transcend. Narayan's informant comes into willing contact with people from all backgrounds, which she argues speaks as much against gender, religious, and state social divisions as it does against caste (1989:77). My own informants appeared to hold very closely to certain practices that appeared linked to their own natal caste backgrounds—bathing, for example, was important to renouncers who had been born into high-caste families. Those who had not, on the other hand, might have argued that undue attention to preening the body was a sign of vanity.

Family

Although popular rhetoric insists that renouncers sever ties with their natal kin, in truth many *sādhus* keep up connections with their families (Tripathi 1958). One *sādhvī* I spoke with agreed to speak to her family, after trying to hide for months, when she saw how despairing they were of her disappearance. She agreed to be in nominal contact with them, but still cultivated a personal detachment that she felt would further her religious practice. Other *sādhus* saw their parents once every twelve years, in a cyclical rhythm that they argued was permitted. Still others paid their parents surprise visits, or asked their parents to visit them at public occasions like Kumbh Melās. One of India's most famous and respected saints, Ramaṇa Mahāṛṣi, was eventually joined at his ashram by his mother, who lived with him until she died. In this case, the young sage left his family in pursuit of religious liberation, and the family became reconnected later in his life. Still, the story shows no explicit ban on parent-child connection. Although their relationships with natal families are much changed, many renouncers clearly do not hold to the mythical idea that they leave their families never to see them again.

Similarly, I met a number of *sādhu* couples, some of whom had children. The most striking married couple I met lived in an ashram outside Hardwar. Narmada Puri, a German-born woman, and her husband and *guru,* Santoṣ Puri, had been married for thirty years. Both husband and wife, and their three gracious, college-age children, each named for a Himalayan river, were of the Puri lineage, Narmada Puri explained; she and the children all regarded Santoṣ Puri as their *guru* (and his *guru* as their *dādā-guru,* and so on). She defended her marriage as like those of the *ṛṣis,* or legendary sages, who were married, stating that hers was not a marriage of the senses but a spiritual union, akin to the cosmic coupling of Śiva and Pārvatī. Because Narmada Puri was born a foreigner, the marriage contained yet another dynamic to consider. But I also met a number of Indian-born *sādhu* couples, who talked about their marriages in the same way, as cosmic unions consistent with religious life. A married Aghori ascetic living on the outskirts of Kathmandu defended his decision to marry by saying that his personal behavior had nothing to do with what his disciples might think: his *karma* was for him alone to figure out. He told me that his marriage enhanced rather than detracted from his spiritual progress.

I heard the propriety of *sādhu* marital families hotly debated among householders, but married *sādhus* themselves had no reservations about their status as renouncers. None believed that they had strayed from the commitments of renunciation. Their acceptance by *gurus* and lineages similarly indicated that they were included in ascetic institutions despite their familial connections. While these renouncers outwardly engaged in practices that did not differentiate them from householders, they argued that their experience of family structures was so different from lay experience that they legitimately inhabited an alternative universe.

Theoretical Orientations I: A Community Apart

The break between householders and renouncers may not be easily defined or articulated, but the split in Hindu society is important and real. The distinction between householder life and renouncer life was central to the identity of the *sādhus* I spoke with, each of whom, in his or her own way, demonstrated how his or her lifestyle, religious practice, or philosophical view differed from those of householders. While the opposition between renouncers and householders is difficult to assess unilaterally, the public statement of difference is unequivocal.

For all their diverse locations, lineages, practices, and histories, renouncers share a fundamental social choice: religious action is prioritized over householder life. The great sociologist Emile Durkheim argued that religious language and practice was one way communal social life was formed (1995[1912]). For Durkheim, religion could be interpreted as a social language that linked members of a community together through common beliefs and collective rituals that generated and fortified people's identities. The material in this book should be familiar to scholars, students, and observers of Hindu life, but the heart of this ethnography is how renouncers collectively tweak a mainstream Hindu worldview. Renouncers' common rituals, languages, and codes—which are visibly distinguishable from those of householders—are sufficient to establish that they are, indeed, a community apart.

Although Durkheim's work is a century old, his model may still help us understand South Asian renouncer life. Members of the contemporary Hindu renouncer community are linked through shared status as people outside householder worlds, and this social role is articulated through commonly understood religious doctrine and practice. As Durkheim suggests for all societies, in the case of renouncers religious life is coterminous with social life. The ideology of separateness is ironically the glue that binds *sādhus* together across space and time. This separateness is expressed in religious terminology and demonstrated through religious ritual in which the body is the explicit metaphor of social separation.

Caste, family, sedentariness, and the effort to present the body in a socially sanctioned way are qualities that we assume to be common in householder life—and we conclude that if renouncers leave householder life behind, they must leave these features behind, too. A great deal of myth, scripture, and rhetoric supports this view. In reality, however, it is not so much that specific aspects of householder life are forsaken as that new structures and languages are deliberately constructed and put into place by *sādhus,* in order to display their alterity.

Intermezzo: Leaving Householder Life

At the 1998 Kumbh Melā in Hardwar, I witnessed for the first time—albeit briefly—the initiation of a group of men into *sannyāsa,* or renouncerhood. It was the most sacred night of the four-month festival, and a cohort of initiates, barefoot and naked except for a light white cloth tied around the waste, stood around an enormous bonfire, heads newly shaved. As a group, they repeated the Sanskrit chants bellowed by the presiding *sādhu,* a senior member of the order. The nighttime scene—the raging fire, the men's bodies exposed to the elements, the authority of the group's warden, and the ritual accompaniment of bells and conch shells—was powerful: these initiations were not to be taken lightly, by either participants or viewers. The tradition into which these men, young and old, were entering dates back well over one thousand years, and the initiation, despite its counter-cultural resonance, was a venerable and sober event. Struck by the obvious import of the occasion, passersby spontaneously bowed their heads. Aware of the initiates' physical and ritual vulnerability, resident *sādhus* of the camp patrolled the area. I moved as close as I could to the circle of men around the bonfire; I was permitted to watch and listen up to a point, and then I was summarily dismissed.

Life as a renouncer begins with initiation into an alternative social order; the group initiation like the one I saw will likely be the first of many in a renouncer's life. The ritual to become a renouncer demonstrates an explicit, intentional, and fundamental break from domestic householder life and the social and material laws of Hinduism. A new initiate is stripped bare—for modesty, he or she may be covered with a simple white cloth or blanket—and his or her head is shaved. Like a newborn, the new *sādhu* is presented to his or her new community with no possessions or attributes beyond the stark physical form. The *guru* presiding over the initiation ceremony will give the novice a new name and whisper a personal mantra to be used in recitation. Body, speech, and identity are renewed with these rituals, and the renouncer is reborn.

Householder life—symbolized by old names, old families, and, most significantly, old bodies—is ritually removed from the new being that is the renouncer, and they cannot be reinstated. All accounts confirm that the rites of initiation make renouncers dead to the social world they leave behind. I asked my closest informant, Pāgal Bābā, if a renouncer could go back to householder life. In response, Bābā described a case he knew, whereby a renouncer tried to reintegrate himself into householder society when his parents died in order to claim his inheritance. The case went to court, Bābā told me, and the verdict was that the renouncer was not permitted to claim the estate, disallowed because of his renouncer status. A renouncer is still alive after initiation, but his death to the social world of householderhood is real.

By equating the ritual of initiation with death to a renouncer's former life, the community of Hindu *sādhus* asserts a fundamental separation from householder society, beyond that of a life-stage. And yet these two social realms interact and are intimately related to each other in terms of the Hindu worldview they share, their overlapping spatial practices, and the fact that all renouncers started out as householders, consciously opting to leave householder society.

A Place of Refuge

Because the domain of *sādhu* life is so clearly situated away from householder worlds, renouncer society offers a place of refuge from dominant caste society. This is particularly clear in the biographies of women renouncers, who explicitly use the institution of renunciation to escape from emotionally untenable lives as householder women. Many women renouncers I met had become *sādhvīs* in order to escape from the socially confining life of a widow. This is certainly true in the case of Mukta Giri, the renouncer I worked with at Paśupatināth. But other women I met used renunciation as an escape from actual or proposed marriages. Rādhā Giri had left an unhappy marriage as a young woman and became a renouncer in part because there were so few options for a woman who wanted to leave her husband. A young *sādhvī* I met in Gangotri explicitly told me that she had become a *sādhvī* because she was uninterested in marrying at all; her parents had accepted the decision, she said, because she had five sisters.[4]

Women who do not easily fit into marital structures are not the only people who use the structures of renunciation for asylum. A *sādhu* in his thirties whom I met in Hardwar had joined an ascetic order as an orphaned child. He was respected among his peers because he had been a member of the order since childhood and because he had brought a childlike passion to his renouncer's vocation, "riding elephants like they were horses," I was told. Because of its insistence on confronting the limits of householder life, *sādhu* society also certainly includes former criminals, people with mental illnesses, and runaways—those who are not easily accepted back into householder society, and who need alternative social institutions.[5]

The strictness of structured caste society needs a buffer for those who cannot, will not, or choose not to fit; who have nowhere to turn; who need asylum but do not have access to a shelter; or who lose parents or leave marriages, and thereby their connections to larger social networks. The *sādhu* community includes people with all these stories and is structurally willing and required to turn a blind eye to personal—caste, marital, familial, or sexual—history. Many renouncers felt like misfits when they were members of householder societies; as *sādhus,* they are integrated into a separate but internally connected social structure that remains on the outskirts of conventional society, but does so in a collective context.

Both religious practice and participating in a social community that challenges householder values make renouncers' lives meaningful. Ethnographer Robert Gross suggests that:

> asceticism provides a viable alternate life style for individuals living within the rigid hierarchically stratified system of the caste society . . . . [R]enunciation offers a meaningful religious outlet and a constructive release from oppressive social and psychological conditions. In a society where individual choice is limited by many factors, a life of asceticism is the only realistic alternative for many. . . . [A]sceticism [provides] a convenient and

> socially recognized "escape" from the stigma of indebtedness, poverty, and material failure. (1992:415–416)

Gross argues for understanding renunciation in economic, psychological, and social terms, as well as in religious terms. Without underestimating the religious motivation that impels people to become renouncers, we should remember how social factors contribute to the decision to renounce. Certainly the renouncer community serves as an alternative social world, and provides a real social function.

To householders, meanwhile, the *sādhu* community symbolizes the fearsome power of a world outside structural norms, from which there is no return. I heard a number of lay families, even as they outwardly expressed respect for renouncers, tease their children with the threat of giving them away to a wandering *sādhu* if they misbehaved. *Sādhu* society offers for those who need it an alternative communal structure, and, for those who do not, a fearful reminder of what it might be like to belong nowhere.

The Public Display of Departure

Renouncers make it clear that the split apart from normative society is a critical part of their identity not only in their words and in the public role of their community, but in the ways they carry and clothe their re-created bodies. The way renouncers dress and anoint their bodies is an unspoken but visible demonstration of both their break from lay society and their connectedness with one another. Śaiva renouncers almost all dress in orange or pale saffron robes, which ideally have no seams. Early in my fieldwork, wearing the color orange was described to me as a way to align the body with rising energy, since orange is the color of the rising sun, and also as a way to neutralize or cool bodily passions.

I asked two *sādhvīs* I knew about the cooling effects of orange as we sat together in Gangotri on a fall morning. "Blue and white are cooling colors," they corrected me. "Orange is not!" They told me that orange was rather a symbol for the sacrificial fires of Hindu practice, but then they added that in antiquity (and the logic continues through the present) it was a useful way to identify *sādhus,* who could approach the homes of laypeople without having to speak, and householders would know to give them food. Or if a *sādhu* misbehaved, taking liberties with his or her freedom, people would know. "So it's way to identify each other," I offered. One *yoginī* agreed, but then asked rhetorically, "But who needs to identify anyone anyway?" Taking the body too seriously—as indicative of a real person—is how we become absorbed in dualistic thought.

Regardless of the symbolic content of its color, an orange robe publicly designates the wearer as a renouncer of a *daśnāmī,* or Śaiva, order. Many *daśnāmī* renouncers, men and women alike, let their hair become matted into *jaṭā,* or dreadlocks, from the time they are initiated and their heads shaved. The length and thickness of their *jaṭā* serves to show how long they have lived the renouncer life and how religiously powerful they have become.[6] Renouncers with extremely long or extremely thick *jaṭā* are generally considered to be extremely powerful. Most renouncers keep their *jaṭā* tied into a manageable turban, as if to keep the true power of the hair under wraps. The unruly nature of renouncers' dreadlocked hair symbolizes their explicit rejection of normative life and also serves as a public sign of the power of renunciation (Obeyesekere 1981). One *sādhvī* showed me a picture of her *guru,* his hair tousled: "He used to look like this," she told me. "Hair uncombed. And barefoot. Then he went to Brindavan, and people started worshipping him." Her *guru*'s untidy appearance was perhaps evidence of his heightened holiness, but even if something else gave lay observers that impression, his unkempt looks were not something to reproach.

In addition, almost all *daśnāmī* renouncers wear a *tilak,* or a forehead marking of ash or sandalwood paste, in the shape of three horizontal stripes, representing the trident, or *triśūl,* of Śiva. The practice of marking the face with the icon of a patron deity demonstrates how renunciation is in part a public statement of religious devotion, and how renouncers rely on representation to set themselves apart. The ash, or *vibhūti,* with which sādhus mark themselves comes from the personal sacred fires-pits that they tend, or their *dhūnīs.* These fires suggest funeral pyres, and the ash that they produce connotes the base element of matter. Some *daśnāmī* renouncers choose to cover their bodies entirely with ash rather than wear robes of any kind. (Some *sādhus* say ash has a medicinal quality, and is a handy mosquito repellent.) Nakedness defies social norms very visibly, and insists on the natural state for both viewer and viewed. By wearing ash, *sādhus* remind all who see them of the impermanence and substitutability of all material forms.

Many renouncers are also identifiable by what they carry. Fire tongs serve as protection against animals, and one blanket means a *sādhu* will always be able to sleep on or under something warm and soft if the terrain is rocky or the night is cold. Depending on sectarian affiliation and seniority, some renouncers carry a staff (a *daṇḍa*), which cannot touch the ground; many renouncers carry a trident as a symbol of Śiva. Almost all renouncers carry a *kamaṇḍal,* or a water receptacle, for hydration and for hygiene. And most carry a small, embroidered *jholā,* or bag, famous for its hidden pockets, designed to organize compactly those few possessions required for wandering. (Colorful, functional, and emblematic of *chillum*-smoking renouncers, these bags are extremely popular among Western backpackers as well, both the perfect travel organizer and associated with the spiritual path of *sādhus.*) Most *daśnāmī* renouncers carry, wear, or display photographs of their *gurus,* which they tend with enormous respect. Taken together, these possessions assure that renouncers are self-sufficient and mobile.

Just as unkemptness symbolizes departure from social norms, so can ritual display. While some renouncers care nothing for bodily appearance, the presentation of the body is extremely important for others, to a point that reaches well beyond simple maintenance. Some *sādhus* I met obviously took a good deal of pleasure in adorning their bodies, as well as their surroundings and their few material possessions. Over the course of my fieldwork, I saw *tilaks,* or forehead markings, painstakingly applied, and *mālas,* or necklaces, elaborately constructed; I also saw renouncers meticulously smear ash, chalk, or mud over their entire bodies, sometimes with the help of a mirror to ensure precise aesthetic effect. I saw *mālas* or garlands of *rudrākṣha* beads or flowers carefully wrapped around turbans of *jaṭā,* or tied onto arms, or strung around necks. Renouncers consistently described these actions to me as symbols of complete devotion to Śiva, and also as a way to look good. On the subject of orange, one of the *yoginīs* said simply, "It looks nice!"

The ways renouncers adorn (or ignore) their physical bodies deliberately sets them apart from householders and visibly connects them with one another. Renouncers' bodies are publicly marked as separate: their anointments mark them as insider members of an exclusive community and signify the split renouncers have made from householder life. Added to the visual form of renouncers' clothing and possessions is the bodily way renouncers greet and acknowledge one another—usually with a hand on the heart, an upper-body bow, and a mantra of respect which also designates a *sādhu*'s sectarian affiliation. Unlike members of a small tribe or village living in a circumscribed area, renouncers live and travel in and among householder communities across the subcontinent: they must be identified not by where they live but by what they look like and what they say. They are a community set visually apart, through the practices of their bodies.

The Body in Hindu Thought

A core question in contemporary feminist and anthropological theory—how the body mediates cultural experience—is also posed, in somewhat different terms, in Hindu religious philosophy and practice. Most renouncers described to me a physical body and a material world modeled through the explicitly dualist Sāṃkhya school of Indian philosophy. Sāṃkhya doctrine explains how the manifest world—the material plane—is the product of play between the oppositional, gendered forces of the universe. Puruṣa, the masculine force, represents static, unmarked divinity, while Prakṛti, the feminine force, represents change, form, and nature. The active and creative force of phenomena, Prakṛti, molds form out of Puruṣa, the unchanging, primordial divine being. The gendered pair of Puruṣa and Prakṛti are responsible for bringing forth the world of form: bodies, creation, and dissolution are all aspects of Prakṛti, or nature. All phenomena of the material world, including the human mind, are birthed by Prakṛti; the dualistic world of change is a direct product of her power. Each person is a physical manifestation of the ultimate in this model, materialized in the form of mind, body, and that tiny residual trace of divinity.

Five sense organs plus *manas,* the mind or mental activity complex, *buddhi,* or intellect or understanding, and *ahaṃkāra,* the ego-complex, bring individuated humans into existence out of undifferentiated divinity (Hiriyanna 1993; Eliade 1958[1954]). Inner souls at the core of the physical layers of the human body are fragments of an undifferentiable cosmic union. They are untainted by individual markings or characteristics, and lie entirely outside—although within—the realm of differentiated matter. The myth of Satī's body shows us how the dissolution of material form leaves behind traces of sacredness.

In other textual accounts, the Hindu body is described as a five-sheathed affair, where the source of individuated identity, or the divine spark of *brahman* which radiates in every person, is cloaked in progressively coarser layers. The five sheaths, which represent physical-social composites, move from the subtlest inner layer to the grossest outer layer (see White 1996; Johari 1983).[7] In this model, too, the outer sheaths encase the *ātman,* or soul. To liberate the immaterial, undifferentiated Self, Hindu religious practice aims to reject completely the five-layered, variably pure body.

The split between Puruṣa and Prakṛti—between transcendent truth and material form—is the fundamental dualism which represents the core of Hindu religious practice. The religious goal of the ascetic, as the anthropologist Jonathan Parry puts it, is "to get all the way back to the source and realize his identity with Brahma," or to strip away the phenomenal manifestation of Prakṛti and realize his identity with Puruṣa (1992:508). The point of religious practice is liberation from all the excessive and extraneous matter of the body—the five bodily sheaths and the eight components of personhood—which separates *ātman,* or Self or soul, from its origin, the unchanging divine principle.

Anthropologically speaking, caste is the social system through which bodies have been most frequently interpreted and understood by Indologists. Anthropologist McKim Marriott argued that in the Hindu view all organic matter should be understood as "coded substance," physiological matter that is inseparable from its *dharmic,* or caste-behavior, code. Bodies seem to be composed of a fluid substance—one anthropologist suggests it might be thought of as "some combination of neuroendocrinal fluid and blood" (Alter 1992:116)—that travels easily over the seeming boundary of flesh; members of a particular caste already share substance in common.[8] In this model, a Hindu body is partly made of the same substance as another body of the same caste; among members of a caste or family there will be a higher ratio of like substance. Accepting food cooked by someone else means that the body will literally assimilate the substance that has flowed with the food. A renouncer's anti-caste position would therefore explain his or her hypothetical willingness to accept food from any donor.

Every human body is in a state of constant substance flux in this model, mixing and separating the new substances with which it comes into contact, simultaneously absorbing and releasing. This analysis must be extended to encompass every creature, place, and element with which a human being interacts, from the soil of one's home (Daniel 1984) to the power of sacred *tīrthas,* or the "crossing-places" which mark pilgrimage spots (Eck 1981). Even the isolated *yogī* of legend, alone in a Himalayan cave, exchanges substance with other material forms, such as grass, water, and air.[9] "Atoms!" one renouncer yelled, when I asked why one remote place was different from another.

An analog to this model posits that the Indian body can be refined along a continuum of purity and pollution (Carman and Marglin 1985). If a person's caste affiliation determines the base level of purity of the body, his or her subsequent interactions dictate whether the body will be increasingly purified or increasingly polluted. This is the principle behind disciples or pilgrims touching the feet of their *gurus* or other people thought to be religiously advanced: the pilgrim's body will be purified from contact with even the least refined part of a pure being.[10] Refining a body until it is optimally pure is, indeed, one of the goals of religious and ritual practice. As Parry explains, a renouncer is supposed to "refine himself out of existence" (1992:508).

Body, family, and name—which usually carries a caste designation—are the three elements which change when a person dies in Hindu India, since his or her inner soul is reborn with new ones. Parry wonders whether death can really be considered the end of anything in this context, since the physical body of the dead person is reintegrated with the elements, the specific social "codes" of the body—personal connections and caste alignments, for example—are still alive in the dead person's descendants, and the spirit is released, either to take new form or, in the case of a realized being, to merge with the divine (1992, 1994). What does seem clear is that death marks a distinct shift in both social relationships and the form of a body.[11] In this light, the new names, new families, and symbolic new bodies that are given to renouncers upon their initiation into a new way of life are as much a death as any. The new bodies which *sādhus* ritually inherit are untainted with the social residue of their previous lives, and can propel them into states of potential religious and cosmic realization.

The Parallel Split

The community of renouncers is geographically dispersed, but ideologically grounded in a common project of departure from householder life. Despite vastly differing life circumstances prior to renunciation—and the many ways in which people choose to become renouncers—*sādhus* forge a shared identity by breaking apart from mainstream society. The group ritual of initiation is evidence of both the seriousness of the vow renouncers take, and the collective nature of *sādhu* departure. On some occasions, renouncers use ritual gatherings to regenerate their community as a distinct social order. But on a daily basis, in many stated and unstated ways, *sādhus* use religious ideology, symbolic language, and rituals of the body to demonstrate their connectedness to each other and their collective separateness from householder life.

In truth, the respective social worlds of renouncers and householders are not totally distinct. Renouncers rely on householders for financial support (Gross 1992), and householders rely on renouncers for religious teaching (Narayan 1989). Some renouncers have families, and some householders may be deeply religious, committed to devotional practice, and reliant on their *gurus*. The two communities cross over and interact heavily in political and economic contexts as well. Bouillier analyzes the historically interdependent relationship between the Nāth sectarian institutions of renunciation and the structures of state and monarchy in Nepal (1991, 1998), and van der Veer shows how the Rāmānandi monastic orders of Ayodhya interact with the Brāhman *pandits,* or priests, who control the economy of the sacred in the popular North Indian pilgrimage destination (1988).[12] Almost all renouncers and institutions of renunciation interact with caste and householder society.

But in these ethnographies, as in my own discussions with renouncers, *sādhus* speak of themselves and their community as different from householders because they have chosen—or have been chosen—to fulfill an alternative path of full-time religious devotion and practice. Customary ways of differentiating renouncers from householders need to be nuanced in the face of ethnographic reality, but they still must reflect how renouncers describe and experience their fundamental alterity. The self-consciousness of division—and the religious language renouncers employ to describe it—is itself what unifies the renouncer community in opposition to normative, caste, householder society.

Theoretical Orientations II: The Split Between Renouncers and Householders

The break that I argue exists between renouncers and householders reflects the work of French Indologist Louis Dumont (1980[1966]), which was roundly critiqued by Indologists in the decades that followed. Dumont suggested that Hinduism as a social system could best be understood precisely by looking at the dynamic between the householder enmeshed in caste society and the renouncer who lived outside of it. He argued that caste society demonstrated "the meaning of wholes or systems" in a pure, unmitigated form (1980[1966]:41), and that caste in particular derived its meaning from its complement or opposite in the larger structural system of Hinduism, namely the institution of renunciation. The drive to leave the social world—the structured units of caste society—was, Dumont argued, embodied by renouncers. Renunciation was a "social state apart from society proper," Dumont wrote, and one which every Hindu could understand, if not participate in. "The ultramundane tendency," he continued, "does not only hover in the minds of men in the world, it is present, incarnate in the emaciated figure of the renouncer, the *saṃnyāsin,* with his begging bowl, his staff and orange dress" (1980 [1966]:273–274).

To understand contemporary renouncers' lives, I argue, we need to see them as members of a community (which Dumont significantly underplayed) and at the same time, we need to understand how that community is premised upon a collective split from householder social life (which Dumont cogently argued). Dumont's explanation of renouncers' relationship to householder society—an "other-worldly" challenge to a "worldly" web of social life—runs parallel to renouncers' own religious thinking. *Sādhus* described renunciation as both a social and a physical process; in discussing their distance from householder life, renouncers referred both to the social world of attachments and to the material world of the body. Dualism—not in its structuralist sense, but in its argument that social life, language, and other systems of signification are based on relational terms—is a concept internal to Indian religious philosophy, and also to the worldviews of the renouncers with whom I met and lived.

The Split Between Body and Soul

In my discussions with *sādhus,* they always used language that showed that bodies occupy a separate state than do consciousness or souls. Renouncers expressly referred to their inner selves as their souls, or *ātman,* the internal Self that corresponds to divinity. But they referred to their bodies as *sarīr,* the colloquial Hindi and Nepali word for body, and sometimes as *rūpa,* an external form. Renouncers who spoke to me in English often used the phrase "*this body,*" as if to emphasize its character as one of many forms they had had or would have, and one of many differentiated forms that exist in the world. I also heard renouncers refer to their own physical experiences using the phrase "the body," as if it were separate from themselves.

The sheer frustration renouncers felt with their tiresome, worldly bodies was apparent to me on many occasions during fieldwork. A *sādhvī* with whom I worked sighed deeply as she showed me how to let steam out of a pressure cooker. "Oh, this body," she said, regretting having to stop her religious practice—meditation or the study of scripture—to cook or eat: it seemed such a waste of precious time. Like her, other informants would hold out their garments when we started to talk about embodiment, and dismissively tell me, "This body is nothing." The initiation rituals I witnessed in Hardwar, and again at the Allahabad Kumbh Melā, three years later with an entirely new cohort of aspirants, left no doubt that the body of a new renouncer is viewed as frail and vulnerable, having no power to assert itself in the world.

Many ethnographic examples confirm the separation between physical bodies and immaterial souls. The renouncer in Narayan's account tells a young disciple, "Your soul [*ātmā*] must become a *sannyāsī,* you see, not the body" (1989: 65). I heard a public lecture from a well-respected renouncer who announced, "The body is the car, while the soul is the driver." Parry concludes

> I could equally argue that my informants inhabit a markedly dualistic universe. The body is the 'house' of the soul which it leaves behind like 'old clothes'. . . . A degree of dualism is again surely implied by my informants' insistence that each person possesses a unique soul which is entirely particular to him or her alone, while their bodily substance is composed of particles shared with a diffuse set of bilateral kin. (1992:511–512)[13]

One lay resident of Hardwar fervently told me, "The saffron color is a symbol, but the person is not necessarily a *sādhu* inside! Being a *sādhu* must be inside *and* outside." As did many renouncers, this pilgrim emphasized the body's role as an external "casing" which contained the divine and precious *ātman,* invoking precisely the so-called Western split between an interior soul and an exterior body. A Western *sādhvī* explained to me that a true wandering renouncer is "simply waiting for the body to drop." In her construction, the body is extraneous matter, a grave distraction from religious effort and achievement.

The ways renouncers spoke of their bodies were certainly paradoxical at times (as I discuss in detail in chapter 5). In some instances, *sādhus* expressly glorified their bodies as tools or vehicles of religious practice. But the split between spirit—which stands in for wholeness and divinity—and body—which symbolizes the fragmented, material world—is a critical part of Hindu renunciation. The practice of asceticism relies on detachment from material conditions. The explicit project of renunciation is to split the body apart from the spirit, in order to release the transcendent self or soul—*ātman* in Hindu terminology—from the constraints of the material universe. "Who is watching your actions when you are awake?" a *sādhvī* with whom I worked asked me. "The seer [*dṛṣṭa,* or "the one who sees"] is also watching the self in dreams. . . . But all those dreams—and the waking hours too—are like a play, or a river flowing by. You can get involved with the characters, happy or sad. Or you can sit back and watch. It's all happening, but the *ātman* is immortal—so watch the play, joyfully." The way my informant talked about true consciousness as entirely separable from the daily experiences of the body reflects classical Hindu religious goals to separate transcendent consciousness from material sensation. This project resembles religious endeavors all over the world by placing more weight on divine spirit than on individual physical form—and strongly refutes Orientalist ideas that the mind-body split is somehow mitigated in Indian or "Eastern" religious or medical bodily traditions.

Theoretical Orientations III: Embodied Dualisms

If Louis Dumont's dualism marks the predominant social split in models of South Asian religion, Rene Descartes' dualism marks the predominant physical split in models of Western thinking about the body. The so-called Cartesian dualism between mind and body refers to the French philosopher's attempt "to reconcile material body and divine soul by locating the soul in the pineal gland whence it directed the body's movements like an invisible rider on a horse," as Nancy Scheper-Hughes and Margaret Lock describe it. "In this way Descartes, a devout Catholic, was able to preserve the soul as the domain of theology, and to legitimate the body as the domain of science" (1987:9). In the contemporary West, we are told, the Cartesian split between mind and body still reigns supreme: science is uninterested in mental or psychological dimensions of physical illness, and secular culture prioritizes materiality over non-existent spirit at all costs.

Conversely, in the "East," many theorists write, Descartes has not had his effect, and the energetic influences that connect mind or spirit with body are equally tended to by doctors, psychics, performers, and religious practitioners. South Asian approaches to the body have been lauded as a theoretical counter to the Cartesian split still prominent in Western medicine and science, and this is a source of relief and pride to Indologists and ethnographers, asserted with remarkable consistency and surety: "The Hindu conception of the self does not posit a quasi-Cartesian division of body and soul, as is found in contemporary Western thought," van der Veer argues (1989:458). Alter similarly states, "In Hindu philosophy the mind and the body are intrinsically linked to one another . . . There is no sense of simple duality" (1992:92).[14]

These arguments are muddled on both sides. First, Descartes himself argued not for a split between body and mind but for a split between body and soul: "What Descartes accomplished was not really the separation of mind from body," Elizabeth Grosz writes, "but the soul from nature" (1994:6).[15] Second, in the Hindu context, the Sāṃkhya school very explicitly posits a dualism, again not between mind and body, but between body-mind and soul, or materiality and transcendence. Minds and mental functioning are certainly part of a physical or material dimension in Hindu thought, but the mind-body complex remains fundamentally opposed to the soul, or the Self. Descartes and Sāṃkhya philosophers may disagree about the particular roles and capacities of bodies and souls, but both schools argue for a theological division. Materiality—the body and the mind or mental activity—occupies one domain, and transcendence—the soul or the *ātman*—occupies the other. Far from turning Cartesianism on its head, Hindu body-soul dualism looks remarkably similar to Descartes' original formulation.

Indologists have ignored the philosophical base of a body-soul split in Hindu thought for at least two reasons. First, bodily practices in South Asia precisely mediate between serving the needs of the material world and fulfilling the religious goal of transcendence, as chapter 5 will detail. The integrated function of bodies in Hindu practice—consider the explicit way in which the social division of caste is upheld through eating—seems to indicate a philosophical monism. Second, because Hindu conceptions of the body usually include the mind and mental processes such as emotion and thought, they have been held up as a response to what seems an exclusive physicality in Western biomedicine, for example. Critics argue that Western culture pays too little heed to the mind as a contributing factor of illness or wellness, and look to Eastern traditions for more integrated methods of diagnosis and healing.

Jonathan Parry questions whether the collective refusal to think of South Asian embodiment as a dualist enterprise might be Orientalism at work, rather than an accurate view of the relationship between body and spirit.[16] Quoting Ronald Inden (1990), Parry suggests that the emphasis on coherence or fusion as a way Indian religious systems see the body may be rooted in an Orientalist tendency to view "'the essence of Indian civilization [as] just the opposite of the West's'" (Inden in Parry 1989:513).[17] This philosophical orientation means that the persistent denigrations of the body (and mind) in Hindu religious rhetoric have not been systematically analyzed in Indological anthropology.

Dualism—that model of reality eschewed by contemporary anthropologists as too structural and confining—may be an appropriate model for social relations between Hindu householders and Hindu renouncers because it may help us to understand the relationship between the material and the transcendent for renouncers (Dumont 1980[1966]). Although there is no one category that distinguishes renouncers from householders, the intentional separation from householder society is itself a fundamental, shared part of renunciation. The social break enacted by renouncers is consciously reflected in the religious effort not to unify, but to split the body from the spirit. Material reality does not say it all, renouncers argue: there are powerful forces beyond the scope of our bodies, which we cannot access without the help of religious life.

The Metaphor of Fission

The social and physical dualisms of Hindu thought give renouncers a clear way to articulate their religious efforts: normative householder society must be consciously rejected, and the body—and mind—must be carefully monitored, their influences controlled, in the hope that embodiment, too, will cease as a meaningful category. Renouncers know that leaving the social world is not simply a question of spatial departure: the body has to be disengaged as well.

Two metaphors operate in renouncers' narratives to show how their bodies have been disconnected from householder social life. First, the metaphor of death is the clearest way to demonstrate that a body no longer exists in its previous state. The rituals of ascetic initiation mean that a renouncer has proceeded to a new life-stage, past the social householder world. If Hindu householders' bodies explicitly carry and convey social rules and hierarchies, Hindu renouncers' bodies, in their metaphorical death, have split away from both social and physical laws.

Second, the metaphor of splitting the soul away from the body demonstrates the core of the renouncer project. In this metaphor is both a religious goal, liberation, and a demonstration of the breakable nature of the social world. The possibility that the physical body—which in Hindu thought so clearly carries and perpetuates social codes and experiences—is damaging to religious fulfillment reflects the idea that the social world, too, can be constraining and painful. *Sādhus* choose to renounce householder society for many reasons, and do so in different ways, but all use the process of renunciation to step apart from householder social structures. Renouncer society offers some *sādhus* the bodily and social refuge they needed from previous living situations, while it offers others the possibility of reappropriating the power they were denied as householders.

Not unlike phenomenologists or cultural anthropologists, Hindu renouncers argue that the body is the manifestation of social reality. Their project is to depart from both, by transcending what they call physical and social non-reality. The Hindu religious experience that renouncers seek is the fission between material processes and transcendent consciousness. Only upon achieving the rare Hindu religious goal of liberation is dualism possibly transcended, and fusion possibly attained, renouncers told me: at the level of society, culture, and body, we are necessarily immersed in perception, thought, and language. For all but the most realized among us, experience is based on dualism—be it Sāṃkhya philosophy or Cartesian reason. The very process of differentiation creates the social and material worlds.

2 ❁ The Social Structures of Sādhu Life

Despite setting themselves apart from normative householder life, Hindu *sādhus* live in a socialized world. In practice if not in theory, *sādhu* society is communal, constituted through a set of shared meanings that structure the living, dynamic organizations of social life. The symbolic links, connecting mechanisms, hierarchies, and kinship terms used by renouncers certainly differ from those used by householders, but they exist nonetheless as the functional terms of contemporary Hindu *sādhu* society. In the last chapter, I considered how breaking apart from householder life was a central aspect of renouncer experience and identity. In this chapter, I describe the organizing principles of the community created by that split, and review the social structures of the contemporary Hindu *sādhu* community.

By their very name, and in any society, renouncers are supposed to leave behind the trappings of daily socialized existence. In real life, however, renouncer life is supported through the communal activities of powerful institutions. *Sādhu* society demonstrates fully developed social mechanisms—lineages, families, institutions, and rites of maturation—and also the unavoidable social practices of gossip, politics, and rivalry. Being a renouncer in contemporary South Asia means sharing cultural understandings about how space, time, and matter are constituted or stripped away, but it does not generally mean isolation, individuality, or separation from social existence. Despite its explicit purpose—and religious mandate—to strip away society's influence, renouncing the world remains a social act.

« *Three women sādhvīs, Allahabad*

Certainly monastic orders in traditions other than Hinduism rely on alternative communal structures. But many world renouncer traditions are exclusively based in monasteries, while Hindu renouncers' home bases are located thousands of square miles apart from one another, across national borders, in vastly differing physical terrains and social contexts. The Hindu renouncer community is unusual in that its structures and practices cut across geographical distance. Networks of space and place precisely constitute community in this instance, and social structures that do not require physical proximity, such as alternative families and lineages, transcend spatial distance.

The Image of Isolation

Both classical texts in India and modern social science about India have emphasized the anti-social and isolated project of the Indian renouncer, the *sannyāsī.* The *Sannyāsa Upaniṣads,* which were written over many centuries as a textual guide to renouncer life, are very explicit that renouncers must break away from society and exist in anti-social isolation: "Wearing a single garment or none at all, his thoughts fixed on the One, let him always wander without desire and completely alone" (*Nāradaparivrājaka Upaniṣad* 141 in Olivelle 1992:177).[1] The solitary quality of renouncer life is clear in every part of the verse: the renouncer must be alone; the renouncer must clothe himself in such a way that his departure from social norms is apparent; the renouncer must be free from worldly desire (and therefore produce neither children nor attachment to any worldly possession); the renouncer must not allow his mind to stray into the realm of the mundane. In the traditional *āśrama* system that categorizes Indian life stages, *sannyāsa* is the fourth and last stage, when an adult leaves his home and family and, through the model of isolated renunciation, prepares for death.[2]

The usual sourcebook for textual injunctions about the appropriateness of life processes is *The Laws of Manu,* the core treatise of Hindu *dharma* (translated variously as law, principle, religion, or proper conduct), written around the beginning of the common era. The text is very clear on the matter of an ascetic's departure from social life:

> When a man has departed from his house, taking with him the instruments of purification, he should wander as an ascetic hermit, indifferent to the desirable pleasures that may come his way. He should always go all alone, with no companion, to achieve success; realizing that success is for the man who is alone, he neither deserts nor is deserted. (*The Laws of Manu* 6.41–42 in Doniger and Smith 1991:121)

The ascetic is the person who leaves the social system entirely—"all alone, with no companion"—and who stands in opposition to the Brāhmanical householder, the person who stands at the hierarchical peak of the caste system.

The notion that renouncers are socially isolated figures, wandering alone in the Indian landscape, is both part of the Indian textual tradition and a product of Western social science. Louis Dumont's argument that Indian renouncers were the solitary individuals of Indian society perpetuates this idea: "The renouncer leaves the world behind in order to devote himself to his own liberation. He submits himself to his chosen master, or he may even enter a monastic community, but essentially he depends upon no one but himself, he is alone" (1980[1966]:274). In his famous treatment of renouncers as the individuals of Indian society, this is Dumont's only mention of a monastic community. In his construction, renouncers could be seen as the outside to Indian society's inside: the two together made up the bounded whole. For the French ethnologist, Indology could be pushed to its limit by the case of renouncers, who lived outside the normative structures of householder Hinduism.

Ethnographies about real renouncers in contemporary South Asia show that *sādhus* are neither isolated nor alone, however, but instead create a nuanced society of their own (cf. Burghart1983a; van der Veer 1988; Gross 1992). Among anthropologists, Richard Burghart first suggested that the individual isolation theorized by Dumont was mistaken (1983a). Dumont approached renunciation from the vantage point of the householder, Burghart argued, focusing on the relationship between the renouncer and the householder. When renunciation is read rather from the renouncer's own point of view, he suggested, the seeming antisocial quality of renunciation is replaced by a sense of social identity: *sādhus* explicitly define themselves in terms of which orders they belong to and which orders they do not. Burghart describes the importance of properly identifying with home institutions for renouncers by showing how clothing and bodily discipline, for example—classic ways of defining oneself in relation to others, which I described in the last chapter—demonstrate the differences between ascetic orders. They may have left the conventional world, and sometimes dramatically so, but renouncers create new social orders that give life and texture to a community that defiantly sits outside society.

The Reality of Community

By explaining how renouncers define and use lineages, administrations, family networks, and maturity rites—those mechanisms that connect and socialize all communities across space and time—this chapter expands upon Burghart's argument that renouncers think of themselves not as isolated individuals in the world but as members of a society, and I follow his example by examining *sādhu* structures from within. Learning the structures of *sādhu* life was no easy task, however, as I learned over time. Both the cultural codes and the social divisions among *sādhu* sects and lineages proved to be inexhaustible fields of knowledge, with highly intricate subdivisions that refer to numbers of initiations, kinds of practice, and lines of knowledge transmission. Each informant I asked gave me new insights into—and new details about—*sādhu* social structures, and new interpretations about what they meant. More than three years into fieldwork, when I finally felt relatively comfortable with the basic social structures that define *sādhu* society, I was given directions to a *sādhu*'s sacred fire-pit, or *dhūnī*, that used as a point of reference an obscure social category that I had never heard before. Each *sādhu* belongs to multiple orders and suborders, and while some are apparent from a *sādhu*'s given name or the style of his or her dress, others are revealed only when necessary.

After many months, I realized that this knowledge is deliberately complicated: the detail of the system guarantees that it is not too easily available, and that the society of renouncers may keep to itself in some measure, choosing when and to whom social and religious information is passed on. The intricacy of *sādhu* structures shows how important the social networks of renunciation are to the institution's identity and longevity. In part because the community is so dispersed, renouncers need a way to ascertain who is a bona fide *sādhu* from another part of South Asia, and who is just a householder temporarily begging for alms at a local festival. Knowledge about *sādhu* social orders is a legitimate passport for entry into private or exclusive forums or events. Despite the enormous variety in individual *sādhus'* lives and religious practices, renouncers think of themselves as members of an exclusive social community.

Although it took me many years to understand the labyrinthine details of renouncer society, my informants were very clear about the categories of membership available to *sādhus*, and how they fit into them. Some of the structures that I describe (in particular the administrative structures) overlap or affiliate with each other, or subdivide into progressively smaller administrative categories, but in the interest of clarity and broad understanding, I do not detail these complexities. I am more interested in providing a context for social life and the mechanisms of community and connectedness than with cataloguing the minutiae of *sādhu* social ordering. Understanding the primary social categories through which renouncers classify their community—and the religious and historical frames of these structures—is the base of an ethnography of renunciation.

In both historical and contemporary contexts, the social organizations of *sādhus* are formidable, with strict laws of affinity and conduct. The contemporary institutions of renouncer life reflect a series of religious ideologies and political structures that have shifted over time. As historian William Pinch writes, Indian asceticism is not "timeless and static (which is how *sādhus* often represent the religious worlds to which they belong)" (1996:23), and this chapter describes the historical structures of *sādhu* society that remain extant. It first provides a broad social overview of Śaiva, or Śiva-worshipping, renouncers and outlines the religious philosophies on which these orders were theologically based. The second part of the chapter centers on the kinship system that is created from the *guru*-disciple bond and explains the familial structures that constitute renouncers' most intimate social connections. The third section details the military history and reputation of the *sādhu* administrative orders, tracing the institutional structures that are still in place today.

Śaivas, Vaiṣṇavas, and Religious Philosophy

Formal *sādhu* sects, known as *sampradāyas,* are broadly divisible into Śaiva and Vaiṣṇava orders. There are a small number of Sikh-inspired orders, as well, known as Udāsīn *sampradāyas.*[3] Most ethnographic work with *sādhus* has been conducted with Vaiṣṇava (Bairāgi or Rāmānandi) orders, which break down further into Tyāgī, Nāgā, and Rasik sects (see Burghart 1983a, 1983b; van der Veer 1988; Gross 1992). Śaiva orders have been the subject of significantly fewer ethnographic field studies, probably because of their reputation as less approachable and more reckless, with much higher rates of drug use. Also, Śaiva *sādhus* do not conduct group practice, as do Vaiṣṇavas on occasion, and are therefore less apparent as a coherent social sect.

At the most visible level, Śaiva *sādhus* usually wear orange (a few sects wear black) and mark their foreheads with three horizontal lines, the symbol of Śiva's trident. Vaiṣṇava *sādhus* largely wear white and use vertical designs for their *tilaks.* These are not hard and fast rules—variations are plentiful. Explanations to foreigners about sectarian divisions tend to rely on this level of distinction, but in truth the separation between Śaiva and Vaiṣṇava orders derives more from different historical approaches to religious practice than from a significant difference between the sects' respective patron deities. While the orders do differ in attire and in ritual emphasis, the *sādhus* I met did not identify themselves as devoted exclusively to either Śiva or Viṣṇu. For example, members of Śaiva orders greet each other by offering praises to Viṣṇu: "Om Namo Nārāyaṇa," which means "reverence to Nārāyan," another name for Viṣṇu. Conversely, members of Vaiṣṇava orders sometimes clean or adorn themselves with ash, which is symbolic of the funeral pyre where Lord Śiva conducts his meditative practice.

The division between Śaiva and Vaiṣṇava orders reflects rather the religious philosophies of the founders of the respective sects. Śaiva orders are accredited to the philosopher Śaṅkara's organizational efforts in the late eighth century while Vaiṣṇava orders are attributed to those of Rāmānuja about three hundred years later, in the late eleventh century. At the broadest level, the theological positions of these two religious scholars laid the foundation for the social structures and religious practices of the monastic institutions they created.

The Path of Knowledge

In eighth-century India, Buddhist and Jain ascetic religious movements were growing rapidly, partly because they offered an alternative to rigid Hindu caste society. In the face of these radical social changes, the prolific high-caste philosopher Śaṅkara looked to the institution of *sannyāsa*, renunciation, to ensure that Hindu caste society retained its position as the dominant social order of the day. By organizing the fragmented sects of Hindu ascetics into a single institution, Śaṅkara believed that he could both support the practice of Hindu asceticism—and with it the study of Hindu philosophy—and bolster Hindu mainstream society. In addition, Śaṅkara intended to remove from the larger institution of Hindu asceticism the counter-social Pāśupata and Kāpālika sects, *tantric* orders which explicitly rejected all forms of social division, accepted renouncers from all castes, and engaged in explicit practices of the body— perhaps more than they engaged in disciplines of the mind. To protect caste hierarchy, which he saw as integral to a functional and thriving religious society, Śaṅkara designed an all-encompassing institution that would consolidate the previously dispersed efforts of solitary, high-caste renouncers and array them against the combined threats of Buddhism, Jainism, and *tantra* (Thapar 1979; Ghurye 1995[1938]).

Śaṅkarācārya, or "the great teacher Śaṅkara," as he is popularly known, is generally credited with catalyzing the gradual progression from solitary renouncer life into institutionalized renunciation, thereby radically altering Indian monastic history (Thapar 1979). Not only did he establish four regional centers for the administration of religious affairs in India which remain in place today, led by four regional chiefs known as Śaṅkarācāryas in their own right,[4] but—more importantly for the discussion here—he established ten structured lineages for renouncers, which he named the *daśnāmī sampradāyas,* the "Orders of the Ten Names." Contemporary renouncers still refer to "Ādi Śaṅkarācārya"—the first, or archetypical, Śaṅkarācārya—with great reverence, as one of their primary teachers.

Śaṅkarācārya established the *daśnāmī* orders for serious renouncers who would exclusively follow the *jñāna mārga,* or the path of knowledge. As a system of religious practice, the path of knowledge is based on extensive philosophical commentaries that Śaṅkara wrote, establishing a school of thought known as Advaita Vedānta. In his interpretations of the *Upaniṣads* (the last part or the end of the *Vedas,* or "Vedānta"), Śaṅkara argues that although reality seems dualistic (*dvaita*)—by which he means that form, language, and experience falsely appear to have qualities or attributes that we can differentiate—it is in truth non-dual (or *advaita*).[5] The Vedānta scriptures on which Śaṅkara is the best known commentator argue that the world of form is wholly an illusion. The ultimate divine experience is by contrast inarticulable, inexpressible, imperceptible, and inexhaustible; the absolute *brahman,* that sacred principle which my informants described as ultimate consciousness, has no attributes at all. If the world of form is itself entirely an illusion, all elements are equally sacred, or equally profane. "Everything is the Lord's play!" one *sādhu* proclaimed to me, and many others voiced similar sentiments. It is the mind of the practitioner which determines how something is experienced.

Although Śaṅkara wrote his commentaries twelve centuries ago, they remain part of a daily practice of study and meditation for contemporary scholarly renouncers, who may spend many hours each day reading his work (or subsequent commentaries which my informants said were slightly easier to understand) and all their waking hours attempting to live by his philosophy. One *sādhvī* with whom I worked was in the process of reading Śaṅkara's text *Aprokh Anubhūti,* or *Direct Experience,* in which he discusses how the mental and physical steps of a yoga practice can further an accurate perception of non-dual reality. At the end of a long afternoon of study, my friend put down the text, ready to eat something and go to bed. "Time just flies!" she exclaimed. Fully immersed in the text, she had lost all sense of time's passage, perhaps approaching or experiencing the state advocated by Śaṅkara. The path of knowledge advocated by Śaṅkara's texts requires stripping away deluded actions, thoughts, and perceptions so that each being's *ātman* may remerge with its source; the mundane act of preparing food seemed at that moment the antithesis of Śaṅkara's teachings. In a state of true knowledge, form—a body in time—is entirely superfluous, and material reality is directly understood as a multifaceted projection of undifferentiated oneness.

The Path of Devotion

About three hundred years after Śaṅkara, a South Indian religious activist named Rāmānuja popularized the practice of *bhakti,* or devotion, which remains one of the most important cross-sectarian elements of Hindu practice today. Rather than arguing for the illusory quality of the material world, Rāmānuja embraced it, believing that devotional rituals of worship were the most effective path to religious experience. His organizational efforts were instrumental in linking diffused patterns of worship into a singular model of religious practice, which emphasizes devotion to the supreme, universal force in the form of Viṣṇu, or Nārāyaṇa, the highest deity (Ghurye 1995[1953]:55). The Vaiṣṇava *sādhu* orders which Rāmānuja established are still focused on training practitioners in devotion, faith, and a sometimes passionate aspiration to merge with the divine, who takes form and has recognizable attributes.[6]

As the world of form is an active part of religious devotion in the *bhakti* model, religious attainment is possible through precise assessment of which parts of the world are sacred—which places, or which times, or which parts of the body—and should therefore be heightened, and which parts of the world are profane, and should therefore be avoided. On the *bhakti mārga,* or the path of devotion which Rāmānuja advocated, the differentiated nature of the universe is used to further religious experience. The divine takes the form of gods who can be worshipped: the body is a vehicle for ritual, particular days and times are sacred and auspicious, and particular places are more or less holy. Conducting oneself properly, in the right place and time, is the foundation for proper devotion to god, and this in turn facilitates realization.

These two paths of religious practice, the *bhakti mārga,* the path of devotion, and the *jñāna mārga,* the path of knowledge, broadly represent the religious paths followed by contemporary Vaiṣṇava and Śaiva renouncers, respectively. Ideally, renouncers in Vaiṣṇava orders would worship using particular places, particular times, and their bodies as ways to heighten their understanding of the sacred principles of the universe. For renouncers in Śaiva orders, places, times, and actions would be equivalent, and sacredness would equally infuse all objects, people, and occasions. These two ways of talking about divinity—as with or without attributes—are known both in popular language and in religious texts as *saguṇa* (with characteristics) and *nirguṇa* (without characteristics).

The difference between these two perspectives—one advocating worship in a world of form, the other knowledge in a world of illusion—is one of the pivotal, contradictory, unresolvable themes in this ethnography. Śaiva *sādhus,* the subjects of this book, should all ideally should follow the *jñāna mārga,*[7] but if this were the case, I would not need to address why different places or times are holy for *sādhu* communities, because space, time, and matter would all be equally considered an illusion. Attaining a realized view where the material world is properly understood and experienced as illusory was described by my informants as a long and arduous process. Most Śaiva *sādhus* I met demonstrably used elements of worship and devotion in their religious and ritual activities, as evidenced by the altars to various deities placed in every *sādhu*'s home place, the respectful phrases of greeting they offered to one another, the mantras they repeated, the prayers they said before eating their food, and the invocations—"Bom Śiva!" or "Bom Śaṅkar!" (another name for Śiva, not the philosopher, who would not have approved)—before smoking their pipes.[8]

Just as living practices do not always conform to textual exhortations, clear ideological divisions blur over time, and most contemporary renouncers blend elements of both religious paths in their practice and orientation. As one often hears in India, I was told, "There is a path for everyone, in all these different forms and combinations. . . . The images of the different gods are there so that people with different natures can find a deity that suits them." In part, Gross is right when he finds that "*sādhus* have a 'fragmented' knowledge of any particular ascetic philosophical tradition and . . . there is a tendency to mix together several religio-philosophical approaches" (1992:204). But most of my educated informants understood worship and knowledge as two stages of development, rather than as two opposing philosophical schools.[9] A close informant told me, "*Bhakti* and *jñāna* are two wings of the same bird. *Bhakti* is where there is form of the divine—here is duality; *jñāna* is where there is no form, and no duality." Eventually, she continued, "*bhakti* will give way to *sādhanā,*" meaning that acts of worship will, in due course, become the higher practice of knowledge.

I challenged Pāgal Bābā directly on the uses of worship when I returned to Hardwar after traveling in Garhwal. In the mountains famous for adept renouncers, I had indeed met strict *jñāna mārga* renouncers—*sādhus* who told me clearly that the body was based on illusion and that physical practices had no relevance—and I could not understand how yoga and meditation practices remained important parts of *daśnāmī sādhu* traditions. Trying to use the language of his order, I asked Bābā directly, "Aren't we supposed to forget about the body?" "Waalll, yess," he answered in his characteristic drawl, "but that's only at a very high point. Before that stage, you need it. You need to worship." Although he clearly identified himself as a member of the Śaiva Giri order, and as a follower of Śaṅkara's teachings, his statement shows how worship, although it might be thought of as a lesser form of religious practice among Śaiva renouncers, was an appropriate—indeed a required—use of the body. He was one of many renouncers who told me they *need* the world of form—and its differentiation into more or less sacred places, times, and ways of using the human body—in religious practice, until such time when the human need to distinguish slips away.

The Orders of the Daśnāmī, or the Ten Names: Teachers, Lineages, and Families

Contemporary Śaiva *sampradāyas* fall into two basic categories: the Nāth sects (see Briggs 1973[1938])[10] and the *daśnāmī* orders, or the Orders of the Ten Names, with whose members I primarily did my fieldwork. Nāth lineages probably derived from orders that engaged in *tantric* religious practice, while the *daśnāmī* orders were almost certainly developed by Śaṅkara to support the Brāhmanical Vedānta tradition (McEvilley 1981; Olivelle 1992). The term *yogī,* colloquially, *jogī,* meaning someone who trains the body or mind to acquire religious knowledge, generally refers to members of Nāth sects—those orders with a history of anti-social or counter-cultural activities—but I also have heard the term used for naked *sādhus* of any order who are visibly committed to mental or physical disciplines. While a renouncer of any order may be called a "*sādhu,*" a colloquial term, only members of *daśnāmī* sects are technically known as "*sannyāsīs.*"

Among the Śaiva *daśnāmī* renouncers with whom I worked, two overlapping but distinct systems served as the main organizing structures: the lineages of the ten names, and the *akhāṛā* administrations. The *daśnāmī* lineages, discussed here, provide a family structure through which religious knowledge is passed down; the *akhāṛā* institutions, discussed in the next section, maintain the social and economic power of renouncer orders. Together, these two systems create a social system that defines the contemporary Śaiva renouncer community, and allow a dispersed community to be linked across the wide regions through which they wander. Both are classic social structures in that they require formal initiation, produce debated hierarchies, ensure systems of promotion and punishment, and are constituted by webs of personal connection. In the case of South Asian renouncers, these personal links are formal ones, established through the rite of initiation with a *guru.*

Gurus

The most important social connection for every *sādhu* I spoke with was the link with his or her *guru.*[11] Looking for or meeting a *guru* marked the beginning of renouncer life in almost every narrative I heard. A renouncer's teacher is the pivot in his or her social world, but more importantly, a *guru* is the route to spiritual awakening, on any path. Only through the guidance of a realized teacher, I heard again and again, can an aspirant hope to achieve any kind of religious experience.[12] A *guru* performs a novice's initiation into ascetic life, providing a new name, a new religious practice, or *sādhanā* (which usually includes a spoken mantra and a form of daily prayer), and a plan for religious education. There is no prohibition on having a *guru* of the opposite sex: women's *gurus* are often men, and men's *gurus* are sometimes women.

In the course of a *sādhu*'s lifetime, he or she will likely take initiation with a series of *gurus,* reflecting advancing levels of progress along the path of spiritual achievement and institutional hierarchy: a new initiation is required into each level. Sometimes householders choose to renounce after they have already received a mantra from a *guru,* in which case the renouncer's *mantra-dikṣa guru* would not be the same as the renouncer's *sannyās guru,* who would formally initiate a *sādhu* into a renouncer order. Different *gurus* are known for different styles of teaching or instruction: some teach harshly, while others are gentler; some wait for disciples to approach, while others take a protective stance. All questions about religious philosophy and disciplined practice will be directed to the appropriate *guru,* and all religious activities—whether a *sādhu* will conduct a particular kind of austerity or set out on an extended pilgrimage—are either directed or approved by a renouncer's *guru.* Some *sādhus* specifically request instructions from their *gurus,* and in these cases a teacher might be angry if a student does not fulfill a practice. "Don't ask for assignments you won't do!" scolded one practitioner's *guru* when she had been distracted by the beauty of the mountains and gone trekking instead of retreating into a meditative practice.

The importance of the relationship a *sādhu* has with his or her *guru* or *gurus* cannot be overestimated. Even those scholarly Vedānta renouncers whose religious practices explicitly opposed worship were completely and utterly devoted to their teachers. Worshipping deities would perpetuate the illusory world of form, these renouncers told me, but their *gurus* rather symbolized the highest transcendental plane. I pressed one very educated *sādhu* on the seeming contradiction here: if all form is illusory, how could she worship the person of her *sannyās guru*? "*Gurutattvā* is One," she replied. *Gurutattvā* literally means the "element (or the reality) of the *guru*": I understood her to mean that devotion to her *guru* would allow her to transcend the world of form. *Gurus* were described to me as completely realized beings, incapable of human error, and able to convey profound teachings through their simplest actions. Mukta Giri told me the hardest thing about being a renouncer was losing her *guru,* who had died some years earlier. The experience of surrender to a *guru,* I was told, could itself bring about religious knowledge.

A disciple's devotion to a *guru* is reflected in the teacher's protection of and responsibility for the student. "I'm not ready to be a *guru* or have disciples," a *sādhvī* humbly told me. "I'm not realized yet." She was, she said, still "bubbling with the joy of this life"—being a practitioner was her main focus, and she did not feel she could take on the responsibility of tutelage. Being a *guru* is no light task: in addition to setting out a disciple's program of religious instruction and inspiring an experience of faith, a *guru* initiates a new disciple into his or her own lineage. When a renouncer takes initiation with a *guru,* he or she is inducted into a new social order that has a particular identity within the larger *sādhu* community, and the *guru* takes responsibility for the behavior and progress of the student. A *guru*'s own ritual affiliations will determine how and where a new *sādhu* will belong in the larger context of renouncer society, usually for the rest of his or her life.

Upon first meeting, almost all *sādhus* ask one another, "Who is your *guru*?" because the response situates a renouncer as a member of a particular order and the recipient of a particular lineage's traditions and teachings. The *guru*-disciple relationship ensures that a renouncer is never outside of the monastic social structure. Even a *sādhu* who chooses (and is permitted by his or her *guru*) to practice in complete isolation belongs to a social web, and is beholden to *sādhu* society, through his or her connection to his or her *guru*. The relationship between *guru* and disciple precisely *prevents* the social isolation or disconnectedness that might otherwise be expected of renouncers. Through relationships with their *gurus*—often thought of as parent-child relationships— *sādhus* take their place in communal families of religious teaching and ritual practice, even during periods of solitary retreat.

Families

The disciple-*guru* relationship is the core of a lineage, what renouncers explicitly call a "family." Each of the ten names of Śaṅkara's orders is a line of *gurus* and disciples, interpreted by its members as a formal family tree. At the 2001 Kumbh Melā in Allahabad—where *sādhu* orders were eminently visible—I stayed at a camp managed by my informant Pāgal Bābā, a member of the Giri lineage. As part of the ground rules for participating, Bābā told me that I should eat only what was prepared at his camp by a small number of *sādhus* who were members of his immediate cohort, and nowhere else. To make his point, he explained kindly, "We are family." Despite his hospitality, I was confused—didn't renouncers leave behind their families? Was his use of the word "family" a gracious gesture to make me feel welcome, or was he somehow referring to members of his camp? "Family," he repeated, slightly frustrated that I still hadn't fully understood what was, for him, clearly the most important social designation, and one with important ramifications about sharing food: "Giri, Giri." He certainly wished to include me, but he also felt strongly that I should maintain commensal relations—the sharing of food—only with his immediate family group, for my sake and for theirs.

The ten family names of the *daśnāmī* lineages almost all refer to places; *sādhu* lore dictates that the order into which a *sādhu* is initiated will determine where, geographically, a person feels most aligned. The ten *daśnāmī* family names, according to Pāgal Bābā, are as follows: Giri, representing the mountains or hills; Parvata, or high snow mountains; Sāgara, or sea; Puri, or towns; Sarasvatī, institutions and teachers (indeed, most of the strict *jñāna mārga sādhus* I met were in this lineage); Bhāratī, or all-India; Vana, forest; Araṇya, grove; Tīrtha, holy place; and Āśrama, place of refuge (see also Ghurye 1995[1953]:82). The four most represented lines in contemporary South Asia are the Giri, Puri, Bhāratī, and Sarasvatī. When he gave me the list of the ten lineages, Pāgal Bābā added that although many Giris now live in towns—we live in modern times, after all—he himself always feels more at home in the mountains, as befits a man of the "Hill" family.

These family lineages are a source of pride, identity, and social networks. Members of the same *daśnāmī* lineage feel related to and responsible for one another—as might members of a natal family—particularly if they are in the same *akhāṛā,* an institution which I discuss below. A *sādhu*'s name consists of both a given name and the name of the lineage, which serves as a surname. Indeed, renouncers would often introduce themselves to me with an emphasis on their *daśnāmī* family name: "I'm a Giri!" or "I'm so-and-so Puri! Puri!" Like distant second or third cousins who know they are related simply because they share an unusual surname, renouncers in the same family know they are ritually connected, but may not know each other personally. With enormous differences in their personal and educational backgrounds and in their reasons for becoming *sādhus,* all three of my key informants were from the Giri lineage but had never met or heard of each other as individuals.[13]

The lineage system is not just a convenient social structure, but also the source of real kinship intimacy within renouncer relationships. Both symbolically and structurally, a renouncer's *guru* comes to stand in for father, mother, or both, exercising the responsibility for the way a disciple is named, reared, and nurtured through progressive stages of spiritual development.[14] A new *sādhu* is the baby in his or her *guru*'s *daśnāmī* family—consider the ritual of initiation, when a novice is presented as a naked, bald newborn. Many renouncers described to me their "*sādhu* brothers"—their *guru-bhāīs,* or those who were initiated by the same *guru*—not only as spiritual brothers and sisters, but as literal family members. In the context of *sādhu* life, where renouncers have left natal families behind, this brotherhood is deeply meaningful. The relational terms of renouncer orders explicitly reflect a family tree: a fellow disciple of one's *guru* is one's *guru-bhāī, guru*-brother, one's *guru*'s *guru-bhāī* is one's *cācā-guru,* uncle-*guru,* and one's *guru*'s *guru* is one's *dādā-guru,* paternal grandfather, the patriarch of the lineage.

The *guru*—clearly the parent in the renouncer family tree—is the pivotal figure in this family or kinship diagram, the link to other members of the larger society, and the barometer of respect that must be paid to those members. A renouncer (ironically, "ego" in anthropological kinship terminology, or the person whose view we take) is on an equal footing with his *guru-bhāī,* but he must pay proportionately increasing levels of deference and respect to the "relatives" of his *guru,* particularly the *guru* of his *guru.* Kinship links between renouncers are articulated through vertical lines of descent between generations, and horizontal lines of fraternity between members of the same cohort. A vertical relationship demands deference; a horizontal relationship demands fraternal support.

Hindu renouncer families look very similar to Hindu householder families in certain regards: senior members deserve the most respect, members of the same cohort are expected to forge generational bonds, and devotion is due one's progenitor in the lineage. Loyalty to one's *sādhu* family is an unsurpassed value and a serious responsibility. The familial relationship between renouncers is thought to be contained in the body, just as it is for householders. Birth by initiation has as much meaning as a physical or "natural" birth, and renouncer families are as real as householder ones. Renouncer families convey the practices and teachings of a particular lineage, carry the knowledge of a community that extends over space and time, and transmit the ritual substance of a parent-child connection.[15]

The relationship between a *sādhu* and his or her *guru* sustains a social organization that both allows religious teachings to be passed down and ensures that the *daśnāmī* lineages will maintain themselves as whole and vital units, despite the presumed celibacy of the monastic order. Initiation therefore marks a non-procreative form of reproduction. The maintenance and reproduction of renouncer families through initiation pointedly demonstrates the viability of *sādhu* society to the wider world. If in "Brāhmanical conceptions . . . the family is what guarantees human immortality," the renouncer community has created a non-procreative family which similarly assures longevity (Olivelle 1992: 27).[16] The Brāhmanical requirement to produce a son (see Doniger and Smith 1991; Heesterman 1993) is replaced in the context of renunciation by a requirement to sustain a lineage.

Sādhu Akhāṛās: Festival, Ritual, and Order

The ten Śaiva orders are family lineages that guide the training of renouncers, but they are not administrative institutions. The primary organizational structures which administer *sādhu* membership are known as *akhāṛās,* or gymnasia. In contemporary North India, *akhāṛās* are structured social groups whose members come together for a common purpose.[17] In the particular context of the *sādhu* orders, *akhāṛā* means an armed regiment. Gross argues that "it was the rise of militant asceticism . . . that has perhaps more than any other single factor influenced the character of medieval and, ultimately, contemporary asceticism and ascetic organization" (1992:62). The concept of armed ascetics seemed at first highly incongruous to me, but the *sādhu akhāṛās* were in fact historically developed as military regiments. On certain occasions, the *akhāṛās* still assert their identity with outbreaks of aggression and even violence.

There is no one-to-one affiliation between the ten family lineages and the seven Śaiva *akhāṛās.*[18] There are Giri lineages in all Śaiva *akhāṛās,* for example, as there are Puri lineages. Members of the same *akhāṛā* from different family lines will tease each other—"You Puris!"—and members of the same family line in friendly *akhāṛās* feel linked despite being in different *akhāṛās.* However, *akhāṛā* affiliation is by far the stronger identity category at large public events, such as the Kumbh Melā, and while Giris may feel solidarity with each other across *akhāṛā* lines in peacetime, *akhāṛā* rivalry is such that brothers may find themselves hurling stones at one another should a fight break out. Sharing a *daśnāmī* lineage will sometimes soften sentiments about particular individuals, but the history of *akhāṛā* militarism and violent jostling for hierarchy is such that *daśnāmī* lineage cannot mitigate antagonism across *akhāṛā* lines.

Akhāṛās: Historical Militarism

Although their dates of origin are hard to pinpoint, the seven extant Śaiva *akhāṛās* were probably instituted over a period of a thousand years. The first—which aggregated small bands of uninstitutionalized Śaiva ascetics in a maneuver similar to the one Śaṅkara executed on a larger scale a century later—was likely established in the seventh century; the most recent was formalized in the seventeenth century (Farquhar 1925; Ghurye 1995[1953]).[19] The ascetic *akhāṛās* came into political and military prominence around 1200 CE, possibly in response to Muslim invasions in North India (and the presence of Muslim *fakirs* in the Moghul armies), and grew steadily for more than half a millennium.[20] Regiments of armed renouncers became important in campaigns to protect Hindu princely states from each other as well as from Moghul armies.

Gross suggests that the political instability of India during periods of intermittent warfare in the sixteenth and seventeenth centuries resulted in widespread geographical dispersion, making *akhāṛās* institutions that many had reason to join (1992:73). Unemployed, landless, or religiously dispossessed men—it is not clear whether there were any women members—could join the ranks of the *akhāṛā* for safety, wealth, and a sense of purpose. The *akhāṛā* orders represented the possibility of community to dispersed populations: renouncer regiments offered a communal existence—one that did not expressly rely on shared space—to people who might need or want to leave their home settings, places from which they already felt excluded. In their status as roving bands of warriors, *akhāṛās* could both challenge the social requirements of sedentary communities and demand material support from householders in exchange for protection.

As warrior *akhāṛās* became more powerful, they were frequently called upon to protect principalities that needed mercenary services. And as demand for warriors increased, the *akhāṛās* began to recruit lower-caste members in order to build their military numbers, probably toward the end of the sixteenth century (Pinch 1996; Hartsuiker 1993; Ghurye 1995[1953]).[21] Commensal relations were prohibited between these military regiments and other orders of high-caste *daśnāmīs*. The growing ranks of military ascetics serving as mercenary warriors were reputed to use both yogic and militant powers to defend Hindu "tradition," a project that has been recently reactivated by the contemporary Hindu nationalist movement, which frequently uses the symbol of the renouncer (McKean 1996). In different places and times—and to different ends—warrior *akhāṛās* have been held up both as a critique of caste and as a defense of Hindu belief and practice.

By the end of the seventeenth century, military strength had positioned *sādhu akhāṛās* as powerful political and economic forces as well. The regiments owned a great deal of land and had amassed considerable funds through demanding taxes from peasants (Bayly 1983; Cohn 1964; Farquhar 1925). Over the next century, the *akhāṛās* continued to accumulate wealth: not only did the institutions own land and demand taxes, but they also "speculated in real estate and engaged in extensive money-lending activities" (Pinch 1996:24). Alliances with wealthy householder landowners ensured that the lucrative and sometimes violent profit-making ventures of the armed ascetic orders went largely unchecked (Gross 1992). By the late eighteenth century, the *akhāṛās* were available for mercenary hire by British military units as well as by Hindu kings and landlords (Lorenzen 1978). Early colonial support further built up the military and economic domains of the *akhāṛās,* and also established regional protections over pilgrimage routes and monastic land.

In the early days of colonial rule, the English East India Company tried to use the unchallenged dominance of the ascetic regiments for its own benefit. To facilitate economic growth for the Empire, the Company tried to ally itself with the wealthy *akhāṛās,* an endeavor that included, on one occasion, an international trade agreement (Pinch 1996). But the renouncer regiments and the colonial administration were at cross-purposes. The renouncer regiments' growing economic power, their practices of bearing arms, and their direct challenges to British tax collection—including some direct attacks on British tax collectors (Ghosh 1930)—led to a series of back-and-forth confrontations between the armed ascetic regiments and the burgeoning colonial administration during the last decades of the eighteenth century. The "*sannyāsī* rebellion," as it was known, refers to a series of lootings of the East India Company and attacks on its troops in Bengal and Bihar by *sādhu akhāṛās* between 1760 and 1800.[22] During the worst outright battle between the Company and ascetic regiments, in 1773, *sādhus* killed an entire British detachment (Stiller 1989).[23]

As a result of these attacks, British restrictions on the *akhāṛā* structures increased exponentially. Ewing (1994) suggests that all groups of *sādhus* and *fakirs* were assumed criminals because they were wanderers and thus fell outside the dominion of state control (see also Freitag 1985). While colonial rulers may have wished their subjects to remain sedentary so as to be easily controlled, British authorities also wanted to subdue renouncer regiments because the armed bands of ascetics did indeed act as "bandits" in their forcible demands for money and land (Ghosh 1930; Farquhar 1925).

Economic and military rivalries were equally convincing threats to the Company. Pinch argues that the armed, transient, and financially powerful ascetics represented "more than simply a 'law and order' challenge" for the British:

> Armed *sādhus* were the very antithesis of the world the company-state was endeavoring to create in the eighteenth and nineteenth centuries, namely, a settled peasant society that would render forth vast agrarian revenues on a regular basis with as little resistance as possible. The modern state in India could not countenance recalcitrant *sādhus* wandering about the countryside armed, dangerous, often naked, and claiming to represent an alternate locus of authority. (1996:25)

The British administration subsequently banned battles between feuding *akhāṛās* at public religious festivals, such as the Kumbh Melās (Gross 1992:69). British laws also explicitly barred the regiments from carrying arms, and prohibited wandering bands of ascetics in Bengal and Bihar.[24]

The Contemporary Institutions

In contemporary South Asia, *akhāṛās* still possess wealth and valuable land. They remain the institutional centers of Hindu renouncer orders, and they continue to assert political and economic power in a way that transcends regional boundaries, or at least encompasses multiple locations. Each Śaiva *akhāṛā* holds large properties in five or six major pilgrimage cities, usually in a prominent riverfront area (Bedi 1991).[25] Through these large headquarters and many smaller ashrams, *akhāṛās* are the administrative bodies which constitute the bureaucracy of renunciation. While the family connections of the *daśnāmī* lineages ensure the intimate transmission of religious teachings, the administrative centers of the Śaiva *akhāṛās* keep the *sādhu* regiments organized, disciplined, and publicly reputable.

The *akhāṛās* are individually responsible for matters pertaining to internal administration (such as registering *sādhus,* collecting dues, and issuing membership papers), for disciplining members, and for managing each *akhāṛā*'s still considerable funds.[26] Each *akhāṛā* has its own reputed character or personality, its own tutelary deity, its own policies, its own accounts, and its own headquarters. The four Śaṅkarācāryas, the leaders of the four extant monastic centers established by Ādi Śaṅkarācārya, serve as the titular religious and political chiefs of the *akhāṛā* structure. Senior *akhāṛā* officials, elected from the membership of each *akhāṛā,* are posted to headquarter offices, where they work with both the Śaṅkarācāryas and civil government bodies to formulate policies that affect the institutions of renunciation, including government sponsorship or subsides, legal representation, and public religious festivals. Promising young *sādhus* are assigned junior leadership posts that rotate between *akhāṛā* branch offices in Hardwar, Varanasi, and other prominent religious centers. Junior *sādhu* leaders are also posted in *akhāṛā*-sponsored ashrams throughout India.

Unlike seniority in family or lineage structures, which is determined by cohort, *akhāṛā* institutional seniority is a political rank, assigned from above for the lower strata, and elected from below for the upper. The first tier of the *akhāṛā* leadership structure is *mahant,* a title given alongside administrative duties or in recognition of long years of service. At the Allahabad Kumbh Melā, a group of politicized Jūnā Akhāṛā members with whom I was sitting one day were made visibly jubilant at the news that one of their number had been awarded the title. Higher on the political scale is *maṇḍaleśvara,* a group whose duties "include doctrinal inculcation of the inmates into the *akhāṛā*" (Ghurye 1995[1953]:109). At *akhāṛā* gatherings, all junior members publicly pay their respects to *akhāṛā maṇḍaleśvaras* as part of the evening ritual. These homages include an elaborate demonstration of secret *mudrās,* or hand gestures, which mark each *sādhu*'s commitment to the religious teachings of the *akhāṛā.*

At the highest level, each *akhāṛā*'s dozen or so *mahā-maṇḍaleśvaras*—the "great *maṇḍaleśvaras*"—constitute the true administrative power of the institution. This highly respected group is ultimately responsible for internal *akhāṛā* policy; *mahā-maṇḍaleśvaras* are in charge of negotiations with other *akhāṛās* as well as with state and national governments, especially during political conflicts between rival regiments. Interestingly, a number of *mahā-maṇḍaleśvaras* are women—even when the *akhāṛās* they lead are all-male institutions. Two leaders of the exclusive Nirañjanī Akhāṛā—whose membership is entirely high-caste men—are women, one of whom, Yoginī Mātā Mā, is an active lobbyist for creating four leadership posts for women who would serve alongside each regional Śaṅkarācārya, and who would be known as Pārvatyācāryas. She told me at the Hardwar Kumbh Melā in 1998 that her work to establish women in high-level political positions stemmed from her belief that prominent women religious leaders could do the most to improve the lot of religious women. Most *mahā-maṇḍaleśvaras* are respected *svāmis* (or *svāminīs*) in their own right, with busy ashrams in a number of locations of India and, in some cases, the world.

Discipline and Support

If the religious training of an ascetic is largely structured by a renouncer's primary *guru,* who bestows a name on a new disciple, provides a family structure, and guides an initiate through the development of his or her religious practice, disciplining *sādhus* who misbehave is usually an institutional matter. *Akhāṛās* are charged with managing the *sādhu* ranks and maintaining a reputation of order—after all, individual *sādhus* represent not only themselves but their *gurus,* their lineages, and their *akhāṛās.* On more than one occasion, I saw *sādhus* publicly beaten by *akhāṛā* superiors for showing *sādhu* life in a bad light. Once, during the huge annual Śiva festival at Paśupatināth, I witnessed a loud and public thrashing on the riverbank, only to realize that the person being beaten was Pāgalānanda, the *yogī* I knew as a child. The person doing the beating, shouting at the top of his lungs as he slapped and pummeled the cowering *yogī,* was Dr. Tyāgī Nāth Bābā, Pāgalānanda's senior *guru-bhāī,* who had been named the head of their lineage after their *guru* had passed away. Tyāgī Nāth Bābā had come to Kathmandu for the festival, from the Nāth Akhāṛā headquarters in Dang, southern Nepal, expressly to ensure that his lineage was appropriately represented. He had been informed that Pāgalānanda was badly abusing alcohol, and he was absolutely livid at the behavior his dissolute *guru*-brother was allowing the public to see.

While some beatings are deliberately public, others are expressly private—dirty laundry must not always be aired. Even if punishment takes place behind closed doors, however, the mark of shame may remain public, as when a *sādhu*'s hair is suddenly shaved. At the 2001 Kumbh Melā, a *sādhu* I knew appeared one morning with his face scratched up and his head shaved. A member of his *akhāṛā* explained to me that he had gotten into a fight, and that he had been subsequently punished by the *akhāṛā mahants.* The internal rules of social *sādhu* life are strict, and the structures of renunciation do not brook misbehavior even from the wildest and most idiosyncratic individuals. Hierarchies are firmly in place to prevent anyone getting too big for his britches, or using the relative freedom of renouncer life to the wrong ends.

Conversely, *sādhus* who do conform to rules of *akhāṛā* behavior are encouraged to look to the *akhāṛā* for sustenance and support. Just as *gurus* accept the religious training of their students as a serious responsibility, the leaders of an *akhāṛā* offer systematic and caring support for its members. When I worked with Pāgal Bābā in Hardwar in the autumn of 2000, he had chosen to live apart from the *akhāṛā.* Recovering from a stomach illness, he was staying in a small, private hotel room not far from the Nirañjanī Akhāṛā headquarters. The *akhāṛā* administrators thought he was "crazy" not to live at the headquarters, or at least eat with them; they even suggested he bring a "tiffin" from the *akhāṛā* to the hotel if he wished, so that he could take advantage of prepared food and, presumably, shared commensality with the high-caste *akhāṛā.* He had refused because he preferred to cook for himself—he could monitor his own ingredients and adjust them to his individual taste and health requirements—rather than take food which had been prepared for a large group. The *akhāṛā* officials had finally insisted on his taking raw ingredients, which he called his "rations," from the *akhāṛā* kitchen, and these he had gratefully accepted.

Although they usually live far apart in temples and hermitages across the country, the members of each *akhāṛā* do live together for brief periods during the cyclical Kumbh Melā festivals. These festivals mark the occasions when South Asian *sādhu* organizations gather their troops, hold religious meetings, coordinate membership elections, and also reap the fruits of public admiration. Although they are no longer active fighting regiments (apart from the sometimes violent eruption of hostilities at Kumbh Melās), the *akhāṛās* still value their warrior history and reputation. These ritual gatherings remain the most popular forum for the self-conscious display of military culture.

Melās: Public Sādhu Life

The dynamics of contemporary *sādhu* social structures are most apparent during the great festivals organized around the renouncer community, the Kumbh Melās. One of the most visible tasks of the *sādhu akhāṛās* is the organization, in cooperation with state and national governments, of these massive events, which are the largest public religious gatherings in the world. The community of renouncers plays a starring role at these events: all seven major Śaiva *akhāṛās* were represented at the two Kumbhs I attended, each sporting its own symbolic logo in brightly colored light bulbs above the bamboo gates of its main camp. The larger Śaiva *akhāṛās* each have a membership of between ten and fifteen thousand *sādhus.* Probably a total of about a hundred thousand renouncers were in attendance at the 2001 Kumbh Melā in Allahabad.

Renouncers I worked with belonged to one of two primary *akhāṛās.* The Nirañjanī Akhāṛā, the wealthiest *akhāṛā,* accepts as new recruits only members of so-called "twice-born" (that is, not untouchable) castes, and is known as dignified, formal, and proper. The self-conscious presentation of the *akhāṛā* meant that the best and most expensive tents were used for the *akhāṛā* leadership at the Allahabad Kumbh Melā, and that rules about public behavior were strict: members were not allowed to smoke hashish publicly, for example. The camp was constructed in large, roomy rows; the most senior members of the *akhāṛā* lived in the front and central tents along with their renouncer families.

The Jūnā Akhāṛā, Nirañjanī's main rival, is the largest *akhāṛā,* and is reputed to be the oldest as well, although this claim is probably based on the age of a smaller sub-*akhāṛā* which now affiliates with Jūnā (Ghurye 1995[1953]:105). The *akhāṛā* accepts members without regard to natal caste or gender—it is the only *akhāṛā* of *daśnāmī* lineages to accept women—and in accordance with these counter-cultural practices, is known to be wild, unruly, and powerful. At the Allahabad Kumbh Melā, the Jūnā Akhāṛā tents were crammed together for rows upon rows; a large concern among administrators had been how to find room for the overflowing numbers of members. Pilgrims attending the festival spent most of their *sādhu*-viewing hours at the Jūnā Akhāṛā, where *sādhus* engaged in extreme austerities, smoked the most hashish, and generally projected an attitude of fierce revelry. None of this non-conformist or other-worldly behavior was on display in the sedate elegance of the Nirañjanī Akhāṛā.

Rivalry between *akhāṛā* regiments is both a longstanding tradition and a source of much tension for state officials and *akhāṛā* leaders at Kumbh Melās. In the tradition of *sādhu* military history, very violent battles have taken place at Kumbh Melās, despite British colonial attempts to ban them. Many scholars assume that historical references to battles between renouncers refer to violence only between Vaiṣṇava and Śaiva *akhāṛās,* but equally bloody have been the fights between rival Śaiva *akhāṛās,* or between Śaiva and Sikh *akhāṛās.* As early as 1266, Śaiva *sādhus* defeated Vaiṣṇava orders in Hardwar (Gross 1992); in 1760, 1800 *sādhus* were killed in full-fledged warfare between the fighting ranks of two *akhāṛās;*[27] in 1796, five thousand Śaiva ascetics were reportedly killed in battle against Sikh orders, although Sikh orders normally affiliate with Śaiva orders (Ghurye 1995[1953]:111).

Most recently, at the 1998 Hardwar Kumbh, the militant sections of the Nirañjanī and Jūnā *akhāṛās* broke into battle, injuring ascetics from both *akhāṛā* regiments as well as a number of Uttar Pradesh state paratroopers. These were not battles over sectarian philosophy, but over power and precedence. The Melās are a convenient demonstration ground not only because of the unusual proximity of also sectarian orders but because they mark auspicious periods to bathe ritually, and the armed ascetic warriors who bathe first symbolically accrue the greatest benefit from the sacred waters.

Nāgā Bābās: Power, Masculinity, and Adulthood

The armed *sādhus* who comprise the bulk of *akhāṛā* membership are known as *nāgā bābās.* The Hindi word *nāgā* derives from the Sanskrit word *nagna,* which means "naked" (McGregor 1993): the appellation refers specifically to the common (but not required) *sādhu* practice of displaying the naked body as a public statement of having conquered worldly passions. *Nāgā* warrior *sādhus* are known as the powerful, naked renouncers who shun all worldly clothing, posturing, and possessions (except their military decorations and weapons, when in formal procession). A *nāgā* must be initiated by and belong to a military *akhāṛā,* but not all *akhāṛā* members are *nāgā sādhus.*[28]

A newly-initiated *sādhu* begins as a *brahmacārī,* and may eventually be initiated at a Kumbh Melā by his or her *akhāṛā* as a *nāgā*, which marks full maturation as a renouncer.[29] Like any Hindu *saṃskāra,* or rite of passage from one life-stage to the next, each "promotion" requires a new initiation.[30] The renouncer community reproduces itself as a society in part by codifying progressive stages of maturity, which encompass a full range of social development. In a fashion parallel to householder society, renouncers participate in rites of initiation and thereby mark themselves as belonging to a community where growth and development is required, valued, and ritually facilitated. Becoming a *sādhu* requires not just a rebirth, but a full process of social development. The status of militant ascetic is much coveted by many young men who become renouncers. Quite a number of young *sādhus* told me with obvious pride that they were *nāgā bābās,* not just ordinary *sādhus.* Others told me they were waiting until the time they would be initiated as *nāgās,* like young adolescents who couldn't wait to grow up. The status of *nāgā* very clearly represents *sādhu* adulthood.

The process of social maturation corresponds with the symbol of the warrior ascetic through shared connotations of virility, strength, and power. Warrior status recuperates the masculinity that would otherwise be stripped from a non-procreative society, while nakedness proves extreme renunciate behavior, symbolizing complete control over sexuality. The spectacle of ash-covered, naked young men adorned for battle powerfully resonates with cultural images of both celibacy and masculinity, and the potency that each connotes.[31] Restrained sexuality produces otherworldly power and masculine strength much beyond that which can be attained by a householder man (O'Flaherty 1973; Brown 1988). I heard the ideal of *nāgā* strength lauded even by disbelieving laymen: two young men from Hardwar disgustedly told me that all *sādhus* were fakes, and then admitted, "Well, not the *nāgā bābās.* They have real ability."

Nāgā sādhus are the most publicly revered ascetics of the renouncer community. The *akhāṛās* carry social authority in part because they are represented by an (unrestrained, naked) army, members of whom are also religiously armed. The military and masculine power projected by *nāgā bābās* translates into a public statement of religious power.[32] Naked, covered with ash, and carrying weapons, *nāgā sādhus* begin the ritual processions at the Kumbh Melā. Some travel on horseback, with swords drawn, providing an impressive spectacle of might and military prowess. At both Kumbh Melās I attended, the *nāgā sādhus* of each *akhāṛā* processed with the most pomp and circumstance: pilgrims frantically ran to throw and then to reclaim coins and flower petals that made contact with their skin; police, who were on hand in case of violence, brutally fought back crowds. Perceived as untamed and unpredictable by devout pilgrims of all castes, an otherwise suspicious public, and amazed Western photographers, *nāgās* are everybody's favorite *sādhus*.

The religious power, bravery, and brute strength publicly attributed to *sādhus* are validated by violence that continues to break out periodically between rival camps at contemporary festivals, including a serious fight between the Jūnā and the Nirañjanī *akhāṛās* that erupted at the 1998 Melā in Hardwar. The 1998 conflict also demonstrated nascent tensions between renouncer *akhāṛās* and the Uttar Pradesh state government: after the fight, negotiations held to determine whether the state would allow the *akhāṛās* to march lasted through the night before the Royal Procession. The state finally agreed to let the Jūnā Akhāṛā, which was blamed for the outbreak of violence, participate in the *jalūs*, or procession; in defiance, however, *akhāṛā* officials opted to withdraw, leaving their ranks primed for a public ritual and then denied the opportunity to perform. The warrior renouncers, covered in ash and flowers, were visibly crushed by the decision as they made their way to bathe privately in small groups of twos and threes.

Apart from ritual processions, *nāgā sādhus* may or may not live their lives naked, and may or may not carry weapons. Most wear pale saffron robes: the only visible mark of initiation as a *nāgā* is a *tilak*, or forehead marking, of three vertical bright red dots. That their status is latent, allowed to come to the surface only during periods of public display, adds to their reputation as powerful holders of a religious lineage. Women *nāgās*, who are initiated by the Jūnā Akhāṛā on a separate day (under the protection of a blanket and the strict monitoring of senior *sādhus*), rarely process naked or with the accoutrements of battle. While the power of violence and nakedness is exclusively the domain of male *nāgā bābās,* the attribution of advanced religious power is shared between men and women.

The Tenacity of Social Connection

Historically, *daśnāmī* lineages and institutional *akhāṛās* developed for different purposes, and they continue to serve multiple social roles in contemporary renouncer life. If lineages establish renouncer families and *akhāṛās* maintain administrative structures, together they ensure kinship connections, rituals of initiation and maturity, social discipline, and institutional order. Despite periodic flare-ups of violence and internal rivalries, both lineages and regiments unify the renouncer community, across space and across time. As in householder society, kinship structures and institutional orders ensure the transmission of religious values and the reproduction of social practices and communal identities. Through these structures, the renouncer community coheres and is reproduced, even in the absence of biological offspring and even without the shared experience of place. Families, lineages, and administrative orders connect, institutionalize, and reproduce shared meanings that do not need to be locally bred.

There are, of course, *sādhus* who choose to live in solitary settings, and some who consciously resist positions of administrative power in favor of meditation and study. But even those *sādhus* who opt for the more classical practices of extreme isolation remain socially connected within the broader structures of *sādhu* community.[33] This is particularly true by virtue of *sādhus'* relationships with their *gurus* and their lineages. A number of *jñāna mārga sādhus* I met chose not to go to the Kumbh Melā, for example, preferring to stay committed to the regular practice of their *sādhanās,* and choosing to avoid what they saw as a showy, political event. Some of these renouncers deliberately chose to spend the winter months in locations out of reach, such as Gangotri, when the roads were closed and inaccessible. Even if they were not in daily contact, however, these renouncers remained intimately connected to their teachers and to members of their lineages, sometimes traveling great distances before or after their months of isolated practice to receive renewed religious instruction.

Over the course of my fieldwork, a number of *sādhus* told me—often with a sense of regret—that despite their plans for an isolated life, being a *sādhu* meant being a public, social, and active figure. Whether someone chooses to live in a communal setting or an isolated one, the structures of renouncer life ensure social connectedness. In this chapter I have focused on the layered complexity of *sādhu* social structures by describing family lineages and administrative institutions; in the next, I ask how the community of renouncers sustains itself through shared views and experiences of space and place. Breaking apart from householder society is the critical unifying element of *sādhus'* lives, but the formation of an alternative community—through both social structure and cultural landscape—is an equally important aspect of renunciation.

3 ❁ Hardwar

THE GROUND OF SPACE

The city of Hardwar, in the Garhwal region of northern India, is the traditional starting point for pilgrimages to the Char Dham, the four holy abodes located in the new Himalayan state of Uttaranchal.[1] Soon after Uttaranchal's independence was granted on November 9, 2000, Hardwar lost its bid to be the site of the new state's High Court, but the city's fame as a pilgrimage center was untainted. Hardwar marks the point where the Ganges River emerges from the Himalayan Mountains into the Indo-Gangetic Plain. Pilgrims traveling in the reverse direction—from the plains of India into the Himal—follow the Ganges north to its source high in the Himalayan glacier, in the region locally known as Devbhumi, the land of the gods.

One of India's seven sacred cities, Hardwar is the place, I was told, where a pilgrim must abandon all illusions before starting out on pilgrimage (the name of the ancient city was Mayapur, literally "the city of illusion"). Once pilgrims leave their illusions behind, they may travel to Rishikesh, the "city of saints and seers," and on up the Ganges River Valley, the "valley of knowledge," as it was described to me by Nānī Mā, a Western *sādhvī* who had lived by the Ganges for thirty years. Garhwali terrain is dotted with shrines to mountain deities and sacred confluences which fit into the Hindu cosmography that marks India as an organically connected "living landscape," as Eck puts it (1996:142). The topology of Himalayan India and Nepal is cast in Hindu religious geography as a model for materiality: mountains and rivers have physical forms and

« *Sādhu under a tree*

manifestations, just like human bodies. "The whole of India [is] a sacred land," Eck writes, which "adds up to a body-cosmos" (1982:214). This religious imagery has potent meaning for pilgrims from all over India, who come in the thousands to visit Garhwali pilgrimage sites, including family vacationers with children and aging parents, school trips, Boy Scouts outings, and also members of the Hindu nationalist movement, which claims this territory as constitutive of Hindu identity (see McKean 1996).[2]

The Ganges Valley is stunningly beautiful, and the religious lore that infuses both the Himalayan range and the Ganges River as well as the region's many individual peaks, streams, caves, and confluences is dense with mythic history. In particular, the Himalayas are famous as a region where devout ascetics retire to meditate, and in autumn 2000, I saw many hermit caves, both inhabited and abandoned. Legends explain that the mountains are the embodied form of Himavat, the father of the goddess Pārvatī, while the Ganges River embodies the widely loved goddess Gaṅgā, the maternal goddess who soothes earthly woes (Eck 1996). North of Hardwar, the river that becomes the Ganges is known as the Bhagīrathi, as are the three mountain peaks that dominate the landscape of the river valley.

Once only a trail, the road is now paved for pilgrim automotive traffic up to Gangotri, where a discreet temple marks the source of the Ganges. The river's glacial source, Gaumukh, is actually two days' walk further northeast, toward the triple-peaked Bhagīrathi and the equally impressive Śivliṅg Peak. Bhagīrath is the name of the king who, with relentless *tapas* (ascetic austerities), successfully implored the Ganges to descend to earth in order to cleanse the souls of sixty thousand ancestors who had been burnt to ashes without proper funereal rites. Both the river and the mountains of the region, named in Bhagīrath's honor, applaud his ascetic entreaties. Asceticism works, the landscape tells us: devotion and meditation produces earthly beauty such as this. And ascetics have returned here for their own *tapas* since.

The ways Hindu ascetics relate to space strike at the very heart of this landscape: should they wander like the river or stay solidly rooted like the mountain?[3] I heard both metaphors implied in my discussions with renouncers in the region. The texts that describe how *sādhus* should live require renouncers to move through space—renunciation means, above all, breaking attachments to sedentary householder communities. To the extent that they fulfill their reputation as wanderers, most contemporary ascetics are frequent pilgrims. Certainly *sādhus* are on the road more often than lay pilgrims, since they do not have to take time away from farm work or office jobs; renouncers are free—and perhaps duty-bound—to attend religious events. Being in the right pilgrimage place at the right astronomical time is a *sādhu*'s vocation. And yet almost all *sādhus* I spoke with had a home base that roots them spatially.

Breaking away from the spaces of householder life means that renouncers need to find alternative locations through which to articulate community, and different ways to think about space, home, movement, and mobility. The image of the wandering renouncer is powerful because it implies that *sādhus* leave places where householders live in *māyā*-infused homes. The symbolic act of wandering insists that *sādhus* have broken free from the spatial constraints of social life. Since they have no place in which they are rooted, and no location through which they are governed or socialized, wanderers live outside the social fray.[4] In what follows, I look at the ways *sādhus* wander, or move through space, while remaining social beings.

Renouncers form their community through an expanded, encompassing view of space, projected on to a cosmic level. For renouncers, the spatial experience of community is articulated through a network of pilgrimage circuits, rather than in particular locations. As an example, I use a network of pilgrimage sites in Garhwal—a mountainous area to which many millions of lay pilgrims also travel in the spirit of asceticism—to show how a region serves as an expanded spatial base for the *sādhu* community. Shared pilgrimage circuits mean that even though their home bases are dispersed, renouncers know where to go to find each other and to support and be supported by both pilgrims and fellow *sādhus*.

What does space look like for the Hindu renouncer community? What places are important, and what do they mean? This chapter is about the ways *sādhus* think about space and place, why they do or don't wander in pilgrimage, and where they live. The first part looks at wandering, the traditional way that *sādhus* train themselves to disassociate from householder space, and also at what contemporary *sādhus* say wandering teaches them. Renouncers do not fit our cultural stereotypes—consider the warrior regiments described in the last chapter—but most do still wander for some period of their lives. The second section considers how particular religious places sustain the renouncer community and shows how circuits of pilgrimage places constitute renouncers' communal view of space. The last part of the chapter turns to sedentary renouncer life. Although contrary to textual ideals, most renouncers do have a home base, and some live there for decades.

In using the terms "space" and "place," I am inspired largely by Casey (1996), who argues that while space is the larger ground of being, places are the specific locations into which human beings infuse meaning, and through which human bodies articulate culture and history. In this context, I use "space" to map larger terrain, the ground for wandering. I use "place" to refer to concrete locations, such as particular pilgrimage towns, for example, and also the kinds of places renouncers live in and return to. The ideal of wandering—moving through space—is, I argue, somewhat different from pilgrimage, which refers to moving from place to place.

The two words my informants use for these separate concepts set their meanings even farther apart. Space, *ākāś,* is the first of the five elements of matter, and is the ground in which all form manifests. For renouncers, space is the capacious foundation of the physical world. Place, *sthān,* or location, usually refers to a holy spot (as in *pīṭha sthān,* sometimes translated as a "power place" [Bubriski and Dowman 1995]) or to a renouncer's home temple. *Sthān* is derived from the Sanskrit verb *sthā*-, "to be," or to stand still, and therefore marks the physical location of a body.

In addition, my informants used yet another word, *āsan,* to refer to the specific places where they lived. Derived from the Sanskrit verb *ās*-, "to sit," or to stay or live in a place, *āsan* means "seat." Renouncers' seats—sometimes literally marked by a small portable rug or deerskin—are the places they stay unless they are traveling to festivals or moving on pilgrimage. While *sthān* implies that the physical presence of a subject's body brings into being the characteristics of place, *āsan* refers to an external seat, as well as to the internal seat or balance of the body. Physical yoga postures are called *āsanas,* because *yogīs* are instructed to use their bodies to maintain the steadiness of a pose (Desikachar 1995). Through this language, renouncers differentiate their spaces and places from those of householders: their dwellings are not "homes," but balanced seats of the body; their pilgrimages are not temporary, but a way of life.

Moving Through Space

Wandering has always been part of *sādhu* life: the excitement and freedom of travel is one of the prerogatives of what for many is an otherwise difficult life choice. *Sādhus* move often and over great distances, and some of the most frequent narratives I heard at *dhūnīs* were itineraries of journeys taken or planned. Where they had been, where they were going, and how long they had stayed were the key axes of conversations among renouncers. *Sādhus* mapped their whereabouts and their routes, compared temples from different regions, and asked each other whether they had met common acquaintances during their voyages across the subcontinent. Lay pilgrims, too, asked *sādhus* which places they had traveled to, and where they would go to next. Sitting at Rādhā Giri's *dhūnī*, I often heard renouncers talking to householders about their long and arduous journeys. Wandering renouncers were the narrators of space in communal settings—what was going on where, who was voting how—able to bring tales of far-away sacred locations and famous temples.

But what does wandering mean to *sādhus,* and why is it such an important literal and symbolic action of renouncer life? The image of wandering implies no real destination; wanderers have a mythic ability to cover all earthly terrain and encompass human space. These are precisely the concepts conveyed in the *Sannyāsa Upaniṣads,* and also in the narratives of *sādhus* who study Vedānta texts. Wandering is a religious practice for renouncers, as much a way of learning about—and detaching from—materiality as it is a means of locomotion. The wandering that texts prescribe for *sādhus*—to avoid the dangers of sedentary attachment—is somewhat different, however, from the benefits of wandering real renouncers described, and the reasons they told me they travel through space.

Traditional Wandering

The traditional texts of asceticism require that renouncers wander perpetually, and not always to pilgrimage places. The *Sannyāsa Upaniṣads* propose strict guidelines for the serious ascetic: no more than one night in a village, two in a "burg," three in a town, and five in a city, for example, for the entirety of a renouncer's life (*Nāradaparivrājaka Upaniṣad* 159 in

Olivelle 1992:187).[5] The only exception to this perennial wandering is during the rainy season (*caturmās,* the four-month monsoon when the gods are said to sleep), when a *sādhu* may, because it is so difficult to move around, retreat to an isolated place to focus on his or her *sādhanā.*

Wandering is also an isolated endeavor: a peripatetic ascetic is ideally more able to focus on religious practice because he or she lives apart from the active social settings of householder communities. "Alone indeed shall a mendicant wander," the *Nāradaparivrājaka Upaniṣad* insists, "because two form a village, three a town, and four a city" (verse 202 in Olivelle 1992:215). Social company itself counters wandering. Manu too is explicit about the requirement of solitude for the wanderer: "He should always go all alone, with no companion, to achieve success; realizing that success is for the man who is alone, he neither deserts nor is deserted" (verse 6:42 in Doniger and Smith 1991:121).

These texts demand both solitude and a very low ratio of nights per place expressly to prohibit extended social contact, which might bring about a number of damaging effects. First, a *sādhu* would potentially become attached to the people who comprise a village, town, or city. The *Upaniṣad* proscriptions seem perfectly calibrated to population size: in a small village, for instance, an extra day might mean leisurely chat, building social connections, an intertwining of destiny, and the possibility of ongoing relationships. The attachment latent in these relationships would threaten to bring the renouncer back down to the plane of social engagement, where his or her body and mind identify with emotions, desires, and other manifestations of worldly existence. Wandering is designed precisely to remove these threats of attachment.

The philosophical premise of these discussions suggests that staying in place might damage religious aspirations, by permitting worldly habits to come to fruition in the bodies and minds of renouncers. Mental habits are rooted in place, these texts suggest, and staying in place allows the mind to return to cycles it quickly becomes used to—habits of thought, habits of rhythm, and habits of identification with the body and its activities. Sedentary life keeps the body trapped in the daily spheres of time and place, and the mind immersed in a web of human desires and sufferings. Wandering as a religious practice is supposed to remove those limits from the body and the mind. The wanderer, like the divine, ideally transcends the human spatial and temporal world.

Place is one of the primary ways people become attached to one another, and staying in place is one way people become habituated to constructs of space and time. These are the very constraints from which a *sādhu* tries to break free. Being sedentary, according to the textual dictates of renouncer life, lessens the likelihood that a *sādhu* can access sacred experience. Contemporary writers who think about place and movement, like Edouard Glissant, have argued similarly, if in a very different context: "In reality, errant thinking is the postulation of an unyielding and unfading sacred" (1997:21).

Pāgal Bābā used the river to demonstrate how movement can keep the religious path clear: "You don't stay in one place so that you don't get attached to anything," Bābā explained. "Moving like the water," he added, indicating the flowing Ganges, "the Gaṅgā keeps nice and clean. When it comes to one point, it's spoiled." For the wandering renouncer, villages and towns—those places of human congregation—symbolize the locations where humans live in *saṃsāra,* the cycle of social and material life. Even for contemporary renouncers who may choose to live in one place, sedentary, socialized human activity is the metaphor for the human conditions of illusion and attachment.

In the textual examples I quote above, renouncers are supposed to wander with little regard for where they are wandering: movement is more important as a religious act than any location in particular. There is no destination in traditional ascetic wandering—the goal of the journey is rather achieving detachment from people and places, food and shelter, and the rhythms of sedentary life. Physical hardships on the body during religious travel de-emphasize the material plane, my informants told me. The dimension of space and the vehicle of the body are not to be taken literally, but as props for experiencing the true, undifferentiated nature of reality (Daniel 1984). Paying mind to where you are or how your body feels, I was told, only distracts from a glimpse of the sacred, which pervades all space and matter, and collapses all differentiation.

Renouncers at the Bābā Mastarām Āśrama in northern Garhwal told me that true wandering was one of the highest and rarest forms of *sādhu* practice in contemporary South Asia. The ashram's co-founder, Svāmī Ācāryajī, said that wandering helps produce that state of disassociation from the material world, where space and place become immaterial. "The measure of space is one's own body," Svāmījī explained. "Insomuch as there is a reality of any body, so there is a reality of other things. When realized, the body does not exist, and neither do other things. I'm saying that a *sādhu* has that much to do with space as he has to do with his own body." If a *sādhu* identifies with his body's desires, place becomes important: where he ends up, whether he eats, and where to go are meaningful questions. If, however, a *sādhu* is beyond bodily limitations or identifications, the relevance of particular places, and of space as a material experience, falls away entirely.

A Contemporary Wanderer

The figure of the wandering *sādhu* is an image both respected and mistrusted. Many stories are circulated about *sādhus'* limited involvement with those villages they pass through. Some stop to cure local patients with sophisticated medical knowledge of local herbs and roots, it is said, and some stop to impregnate the wives of sterile husbands. Many give religious lectures; some offer political propaganda. I have heard these interactions spoken of both admiringly and dismissively: some Hardwar residents thought it laughable that *sādhus* have a reputation for celibacy, while others praised their knowledge of nature and its healing capacity.

Nānī Mā, the English co-founder with Svāmī Ācāryajī of the Bābā Mastarām Āśrama, told me that local villagers venerate the wandering, lecturing *sādhu*—it is this rural population that comes in millions to the Kumbh Melā, cherishing the flower petals or coins that *sādhus* touch during their glorious processions. But they also circulate a cynical expression about renouncers: "*Rām nām jāpana, pariya dān āpana*"—*sādhus* recite the name of Rām, and they take the wealth of others.[6] The head *sādhvī* at the Nepali Ashram in Hardwar echoed this suspicion. "Those wanderers just want money," she said. "They come, then they go." When I asked Pāgal Bābā why *sādhus* had a bad public image, he too referred to wandering. "The one who leaves his original home," he quipped rhetorically, "what will happen to his reputation?"

Both renouncers and householders I spoke with agreed that a "true" wandering *sādhu,* someone who has relinquished his or her attachment to space and body, is worthy of high respect but is very hard to come by. Pāgal Bābā told me that only a few renouncers ever wandered, and fewer still wander now. Nānī Mā was sure that there remain a few who do but also that it is very difficult to meet one, since a real wanderer arrives in a village late at night, sleeps under a tree or in a temple, and leaves early the next morning. "Real wandering is a high practice," Nānī cautioned, lest I mistake all the *sādhus* walking on the road for true wanderers, "not just wandering around begging."

The closest approximation I met to the textual ideal was a young, slight *sādhu* who was passing through Hardwar. We met only once: he was sitting under a tree just south of the Nirañjanī Akhāṛā, on the western bank of the Ganges. He would stay under the tree until 7 PM, he told me, when he would pack his things (including a poster picture of Krishna tied to the tree with gold ribbon), and find a safe place to sleep on the *ghāṭs,* or the river bank. By nine the next morning, he would have bathed, washed his clothes, repacked his things, and found another place to sit for the day. After a week or so—an undetermined time—he would move to another location entirely, finding a new place to sleep each night, and a new place to sit each day.

He had come to Hardwar from Mathura by bus. I asked him if, as a wanderer, he did not have to walk? He would walk short distances, he replied, like to the nearby Chandī Devī Temple. But for journeying, it didn't matter how you got from place to place. Simply being on the road—wandering—was enough. "It's not how you go," he explained, "it's *that* you go." All his possessions were compactly packed into two bags which lay near him. The first sack contained cooking utensils: a plate, a cup, a stove, and the head of cauliflower that would be his next meal. The second contained other miscellaneous objects for daily use, which he would meticulously unwrap after removing them from separate cloth compartments. These objects included a pocket knife for slicing up and immediately offering around an apple which was offered as *prasād,* for example, and a small bag which contained a pipe, matches, and marijuana, which he would smoke with those gathered.

The two bags were tucked at the foot of the tree under which he had settled for the day. He had placed them upon a plastic sheet that kept them clean and demarcated their area, and covered them with a woolen blanket which would be his bedding that night. He was certainly not unencumbered, but he was able to live anywhere completely self-sufficiently, a quality that I frequently heard cited as a criterion for a real renouncer. He sat on a carefully placed jute mat, his *kamaṇḍal,* or *sādhu* jug, next to him, a plate lining the top where he meticulously placed all the *prasād* that was offered—his share of the apple, the peanuts I had offered, and also any small money offerings he received. He was meticulous with his few belongings, carefully tying the bag of *ganja* and replacing it, and cleaning the knife thoroughly before he repacked it. Most of the *sādhus* smoked hashish in their clay pipe *chillums,* but this *sādhu* smoked marijuana, which his onlookers explained he could simply pick in the jungle—it grew wild. I took this as evidence of how little money he lived on, and his extreme degree of mobile self-sufficiency.

I asked this young renouncer why he had chosen this particular place to sit. He told me this place was good because he was under a tree, he could see the Gaṅgā, and he was near the road, the *chai-wallah,* and food he could buy with the offerings he had received. Here he was in a "peaceful" place, he explained, a tranquil wooded area (*braj*), which was relatively easy to reach; he had access to water with which to wash and clean dishes, and to drink and serve as tea. These were practical concerns rather than exclusively religious ones. When I asked if he always faced north, he looked around, assessing his position—he obviously hadn't realized he *was* facing north, but quickly understood the significance of the question. From Hardwar, the Himalayas are due north, and the area is popularly referred to as the holy region of Uttarkhand, the North Land. But that had not been his intent. "I have to face down," he said emphatically, pointing to his eyes and then to the ground. "To the earth?" I asked, ever the student of Hinduism, ready to substitute the five elements for the four cardinal directions. He clucked at me. "Down! I have to look down! At the ground! Otherwise the stuff gets up and leaves!" If he did not pay attention to his whereabouts, his few possessions would be stolen.

In his downcast demeanor there was an element other than guardianship of possessions—an introspection that allowed very little outward connection or potential for building any kind of relationship. He offered almost no eye contact, and no information unless explicitly asked. He was socially withdrawn and solemn. Whether he deliberately engaged in a practice that kept him isolated or just had an introspective personality or disposition, by keeping his eyes down, he gave very little import to the world around him, and very little ground for continuing social contact. Although intermittently in the company of people, his wandering had effectively withdrawn him from the world of active social relationships. Or perhaps he did not wish to (or could not) engage in social relationships, and so chose to wander.

Wandering as a Learning Stage

The wandering *sādhu* I met was quite young, and it is unlikely he will continue wandering for the rest of his years. Quite a number of *sādhus* told me that they had wandered for a period, and that it had been an important preparatory period or learning stage. While renouncers studying Vedānta texts told me that true wandering was the last stage of *sādhanā,* many *sādhus* talked about wandering rather as a training period early in their *sādhu* lives, an opportunity to practice detachment from householder society and to learn about the nature of the world. Some wandered for a specific period of twelve years, the traditional period for a particular *tapas* austerity, or for part of a twelve-year *tapas* cycle.

"We did all those phases!" exclaimed Pāgal Bābā when I asked if he had wandered at any point in his life as a *sādhu.* "For nine years, I never spent more than one night in a village," he claimed. (The remaining three years of his twelve-year cycle were spent in sedentary but solitary isolation in the forest, he told me, doing *sādhanā.*) During his wandering period, a man with a new car had tried to give him a lift, but he would not accept the ride because he would travel only where his own feet would take him. He didn't know where he would end up each night, and he would eat what food he was given. Once a householder offered him a chance to cook, and he did—for himself and the householder's whole family. They wanted him to stay on afterwards, but he moved on. He had only a few clothes and a *kamaṇḍal,* and even these few possessions sometimes felt burdensome: "If someone stole something, thank you very much!" he recalled.

Dudh Bābā, a long-time and well-respected resident of Paśupati, the area he grew up in, wandered for fourteen years as a young *sādhu.* Twelve years is standard for Śaiva *bābās,* he said, but Vaiṣṇava *bābās* wander for fourteen, in accordance with the number of years Rāma was exiled to the forest. Although he now focuses his *sādhanā* in his *kuṭī* (small room) across from Paśupati's burning *ghāṭs,* he told me, "Wandering is also important. To wander the *tīrthas* [sacred places]. To have the experience. To have all the pains and joys. To know how people live." The Sanskrit-derived words that Bābā used for experience, *anubhav,* and pains and joys, *dukh* and *sukh,* refer to a complete range of human emotion. *Dukh sukh* is a term that refers not only to the pain or pleasure arising from a particular experience, but more accurately to the nature of suffering and delight in the universe. Wandering from place to place, Bābā suggested, gives *sādhus* the experiences of pain and of happiness, and also lays the ground for knowledge about the range of human experience and emotion.

Emphasizing not the destination but the movement, just like the textual sources on renouncer life, Pāgal Bābā told me, "Wandering is not to get some place—it's to get knowledge." Journeying is a religious method, but one with limited use:

> First you walk around, then you are finished with walking and looking. You don't have any longing to go and to see. If you have all that wishing, then when you're in one place, you can't make meditation and *pūjā* [ritual]—you're distracted. After you've done your wandering, all the *tīrtha* and pilgrimage places are with you. Okay, I've done it. I've finished everything. Now I stay in one place.

For Pāgal Bābā, wandering was a way to see the world, incorporate the blessings of holy places within one's own body, rid the mind of desire to wander, and, most importantly, prepare for the more difficult and higher phase of consistent *sādhanā.* His narrative echoes the sentiment I heard from many renouncers: once someone learned the lessons wandering could teach, it was more important to remain sedentary and do one's religious practice.

Wandering is an early developmental phase, these renouncers suggested, not for a senior *sādhu,* whose body has aged and whose mind has refined; it is an experience whose lessons can be used as tools. Pāgal Bābā said that his period of wandering taught him "to see things as they were. The mind projects itself, you know, but it's not like that. Next time it can be the way I want it! Few ups and downs, but it's okay. Good teaching. Preparation." From the way both Pāgal Bābā and Dudh Bābā describe their experiences, wandering is a way to see the nature of the exterior world without the projections of the interior mind. The "ups and downs" to which Pāgal Bābā refers are the difficulties and delights of travel, and, of course, metaphors for human experience in the world. *Sādhus'* wandering is an opportunity to see the world as people live in it, experiencing the extremes. As real-life renouncers tell it, wandering is an early stage of observing and learning about the material world, not a final or perpetual stage.

Destinations and Circuits

The *sādhus* I spoke to were quite consistent in their answers about why certain earthly places matter, even though devoted religious practitioners should ultimately recognize that space, place, and the outer world are immaterial, illusory concepts. For the vast majority of aspiring practitioners, however—for almost all human beings, *sādhus* told me—place still matters. Until we have moved far enough along the path to be unaffected by either the positive or negative traits of particular places at particular times, our locations—where we travel or where we live—impact our minds and bodies. We have to use specific sacred places, like holy geographical spots, rivers, and caves, to help get us to the point of realization. In the social and material worlds, space *is* place.

A *sādhu* who had chosen an inaccessible pilgrimage place for her practice explained these levels of accomplishment to me. She referred to her *guru*'s capacity to meditate anywhere, and contrasted his equanimity to her own continued need for particular qualities in a place:

> Ultimately you can be in the middle of a street and not be affected. Once I went to Ahmedabad with my *guru*, and I was very uncomfortable with all the dirt and noise. I asked him, Shouldn't we be in some place quiet? He told me how he had some devotees in Bombay who gave him a room—right on top of Churchgate Station! And of course *he* could do his *sādhanā* there. At the moment I'm not ready for it at all. I'm still enjoying peace and solitude so much.

While some *sādhus* argued that renouncers should train themselves to be able to conduct practice any place, this *sādhvī* suggested that such an ability was the effect of sustained religious effort. In her narrative, a realized *guru* could be anywhere—in a noisy city, even near a railway station—and be unhampered in meditation and spiritual awareness.

Most renouncers I talked to about whether place matters echoed the sentiments of this renouncer: *sādhus* still on the path of religious effort have to make use of the material plane and the hierarchical holiness of place. "*Sādhus* are supposed to stay in *sattvic* (pure) places," Nānī Mā told me. I asked her how certain places could be holy, if all differentiated space was illusory. She explained:

> It is illusory, but it is systematic. The three *guṇas* (qualities of the material world)—*sattvā, rajas, tamas*—are differently represented in different places. Holy places are *sattvic* places, because of Gaṅgā Mā, because of God, or because of a boon granted. Some places and times are more *sattvic,* and some are more *tamasic* (dark or inert), such as a tavern or a slaughterhouse, where there is alcohol or blood. This is the way creation is. *Sattvic* places attract *sattvic* people who do *sattvic* things. It's not so easy to meditate in a tavern or slaughterhouse as by the Gaṅgā. The purpose or intent of a place also has an effect. If you build a tavern or slaughterhouse, the work that had begun there sets that quality into action and concentrates it there. Gangotri has Gaṅgā Mā, so it's full of *sattvā.* It gets covered up by tourists and shops, but it's there. These places attract people who want to do that thing there. When people go there they want to do that kind of practice. The environment gives us help, and that's why we go to a holy place.

A young Gangotri *sādhvī* argued similarly, "Doing *sādhanā* in a holy place where lots of people have done *sādhanā,* we can get the vibrations." Holy places further benefit from the history of great *sādhaks,* or practitioners of *sādhanā,* who strengthen the sacredness of a place.

A period of wandering in their early years as *sādhus* is a way for renouncers to visit India's most prominent pilgrimage points. Wandering teaches detachment and observation, but also gathers the blessings from dispersed holy places into the body of the wanderer. Both Dudh Bābā and Pāgal Bābā refer to the idea that having wandered the *tīrthas,* the *tīrthas* will be contained in their bodies. Even for the textual *sādhu,* who is supposed to wander without a destination, pilgrimage to particular holy places is important: strict lists allow *sādhus* to spend a whole week (rather than a single night) in a "sacred bathing place" or a "pilgrimage place" (Olivelle 1992). This allowance implies that sacred locations have the capacity to enhance a *sādhu*'s spiritual practice. Pilgrimage—journeying to a holy place—remains one of the central religious acts in Hindu practice, for both renouncers and householders (see Gold 1988). Indeed, during a religious voyage, a lay pilgrim is supposed to become more like a renouncer—someone who leaves home to visit holy places, and who, ideally, in abstaining from indulgences, is able to transcend his or her quotidian existence (Daniel 1984:247).

A Community in Sacred Space

Going to pilgrimage places, unlike solitary *sādhanā* or even solitary wandering, is not a solitary venture. Nānī Mā described to me her shock, when she first arrived in Gangotri, at the number of *sādhus* who were just "hanging out" at such a holy place. Pilgrimage places are places of congregation, where renouncers can meet not only members of their own community but also lay pilgrims from all over India, knowledgeable *pūjāris,* or priests, and spiritually inclined Western travelers. Famous temples, for all the "vibrations" my informants said they emitted, are also places of social gathering. *Tīrthas* are "crossing-places," in Eck's translation (1981),[7] not only between the earthly and heavenly realms, but also between large cross-sections of humanity, where wares are for sale, *dhābās,* or food stalls, are plentiful, and entertainment is easily available. I saw Ferris wheels, prostitutes, *hijṛās,* and street performers all doing good business on sacred days in holy places.

Since wandering to holy places is what *sādhus* are famous for, pilgrimage spots are well-known gathering places for the renouncer community. The subcontinental network of pilgrimage locations (and a linked calendar of sacred times) enables traveling renouncers who are usually diffused in space to come together periodically in predetermined places. Pilgrimage destinations are the spatial nodes of a dispersed, dynamic community. Most renouncers use the multiple mythic pilgrimage circuits of India and Nepal as travel routes, where they know they will find both old friends and generous lay pilgrims willing to spend money to ensure profitable rebirths.

Pilgrimage circuits are mapped onto different geographical levels, from local to regional to subcontinental. The Kathmandu temple Guhyeśwarī is on the very large pilgrimage circuit of *śākta pīṭhas*—"power places" where the body parts of the goddess Satī fell—which includes sites in Afghanistan and Pakistan, in some accounts. The circumambulation of the Narmada River, by contrast, was particularly important in the accounts of those renouncers I met who were from Madhya Pradesh.

South Asian pilgrimage circuits serve as both a geographical (and therefore social) web and an economic (and therefore material) support system for the renouncer community. Quite apart from fulfilling a religious mandate and receiving the respects of lay Hindus, visiting pilgrimage places is an important way *sādhus* sustain themselves. Wealthy pilgrims offer regular *bhaṇḍārās*, or feasts, for *sādhus* in pilgrimage places; less well-off pilgrims offer *dakṣinā*, or small cash donations. In smaller pilgrimage centers like Gangotri, or on festival days in any sacred location, renouncers sometimes sit in lines outside focal temples, where as part of their devotional ritual pilgrims will offer each *sādhu* a helping of grain. Some larger ashrams have branch accommodations that offer traveling renouncers shelter in regional centers. Śivānanda Āśrama, for example, whose headquarters is in Rishikesh, has smaller centers all the way up the Ganges River to its source. Traveling renouncers may sometimes stay in ashram beds.

The map of sacred pilgrimage places marks the collective space (and in many cases, the collective property) of the renouncer community. Pilgrimage centers are locations where *sādhus* can both reap the blessings of place and, in turn, bestow them upon visiting pilgrims who offer alms. Gross argues that pilgrimage is different for renouncers than for lay pilgrims because renouncers give *darśana*, blessing through sight, as well as receive it (1992; Eck 1998). He suggests further that the circuits renouncers travel have significantly contributed to the popularity and prosperity of pilgrimage sites in India: circuits of holy places traveled by renouncers have been made popular in part through pilgrims' eagerness to see and be blessed by *sādhus*.

Certainly pilgrimage travel is enormously popular in India, and it is an industry that has been heavily supported by state infrastructures. An elaborate network of hotels, rest houses, and public transport is funded by the state and regional legislatures, and detailed maps and a voluminous amount of pilgrimage literature are published by the district tourist agency, as well as private tour operators. The reputed power of holy places has also meant that Hindu nationalist rhetoric has incorporated mythic pilgrimage circuits into its own definitions of space, and identified the renouncers who live in these circuits as exemplary Hindu practitioners (McKean 1996; Menon 2006). By claiming holy places as their collective home base, the renouncer community, too, claims the entire ground of sacred South Asian space as its own. Overlaying pilgrimage centers with mythic readings of landscape means that renouncers can construct a collective space-time where their community can gather, and also be collectively sustained by Hindu pilgrims who are convinced of *sādhus*' religious power in part through their association with sacred places.

Space, when differentiated, turns back into place, and a constructed circuit of places becomes collective space once again. Although renouncers are supposed to leave the physical dimensions of householder life, the nodes of South Asian pilgrimage circuits come to stand in for geographical loci of community. Pilgrimage destinations are fixed points on the cosmological map of South Asia, the places around which renouncers base their wandering. Shared spatial conceptions of the Himalayas are the mechanisms of community for Śaiva renouncers who visit these holy places not only to bless and be blessed, but also because they will be materially sustained and because they know they can find common ground. If renunciation requires both social and material departure, pilgrimage places provide both social and material sustenance.

The Pleasures and Pains of Travel

To disassociate from space, place, and body, in the model of wandering, or to amass the benefits of holy places, in the model of pilgrimage, are not the only reasons *sādhus* travel. Life as a *sādhu* begins with leaving home. The social departure that symbolizes renouncer life is made literal in the act of wandering, and, in particular, wandering away.[8] Renouncers told me that physically leaving home is spiritually important, for it requires great strength of purpose and determination to begin a voyage. One *sādhvī* whose religious practices had been emotionally and materially supported by her family told me that she left home anyway: "The experience of divine grace will not come at home. You have to go without money, without food, to have those experiences that prove divine grace." Leaving home meant becoming vulnerable to the diverse forces of the universe for this woman, and required an increased faith in her *guru* in order to support a difficult path. "If this body needs something," she continued, "it will come on its own." Staying at home, with its comforts and habits—even to meditate—would not have allowed her to believe that she could be so cared for and guided by a divine force.

Leaving the comfort and habit of home or, conversely, the pressure and unhappiness of home is a significant act, especially in the South Asian contexts of extended natal and marital homes and connectedness.[9] Although women, men, and couples are increasingly living on their own in major cities, leaving home (and leaving home alone in particular) is sometimes still not an acceptable life choice. Most people who choose to leave village homes probably become *sādhus* by default because there are very few social options available to them. Similarly, many people probably choose to become *sādhus* because they want to leave unhappy situations at home. Moving directly to a pilgrimage place in order to leave natal or marital householder life is not uncommon in the stories of how *sādhus* choose their life paths.

Both women informants I worked with became *sādhvīs* in part to leave marital homes. As a very young woman, Rādhā Giri left an unhappy marriage in Kumaon, and she told me she had not been back. In response to my question of whether she kept any ties to her family, she waved away her hand brusquely and said, "I left all that." Mukta Giri Mai, too, had wondered for a long time about what to do when her husband died years earlier—should she "go to the jungle"? For Mukta Giri, becoming a *sādhvī* was a choice that allowed her spatial mobility, some measure of social freedom, and, it seemed, psychological support through religious life that she had not felt as a widow. "The jungle," that place away from social convention to which *sādhus* go (which I discuss further below), was an option that posed both a social and a spatial escape from the restrictive widow's life (see especially Lamb 2000; Arthvale 1930).

The unhappiness of householder life may inspire departure, but wandering need not be an entirely solemn affair. Leaving a natal or a marital home in the guise of wandering may be the beginning of *sādhu* life, but it is also, for many, an introduction to travel, the pleasures of which may keep renouncers enthusiastic about their new vocations, at least for a time. Traveling on pilgrimage is a way to enjoy seeing new places and also, as renouncers come to know larger numbers of their community, old friends. Journeys open both spatial and social vistas. Narayan's informant told her, "Though we leave our families, look what happens, the entire world becomes our family!" (1989:79). Like lay pilgrims, *sādhus* travel to holy places not only to reap the blessings of sacred locations but also to see whom they will meet and for the fun of the voyage.

Traveling is exciting and freeing; visiting different places gives renouncers the sense of accomplishment that comes with covering ground and visiting famous places. Many *sādhus* gave me lists of places they had been or proudly showed me the formal government permits they had received to travel to restricted *pīṭha sthāns,* holy places of power, such as the famous temple Amarnāth, located in Kashmir. Dudh Bābā gave me a complete breakdown of eighty-four major *tīrthas* in India, Nepal, and Tibet—including four lakes, three oceans, seven cities, four heavenly abodes, twelve *jyotir liṅgams,* or self-arising *liṅgams* of light, seven cities, and so on—all of which he claimed he had visited during his fourteen-year phase of wandering, and some more than once.

Thrilling as the opportunity to travel far and wide across the South Asian subcontinent may be, after a while most renouncers get "fed up" with wandering and want to stay put. Thus, perhaps, the argument that wandering is better done earlier. When I asked the head *sādhvī* of the Nepali Ashram in Hardwar about the merits of having an ashram rather than wandering, she sighed and waved her hand away. "Oh, I did all that wandering, wandering," she replied. "Paśupatināth, Maṇikaran, Bhagīrathi," she continued, counting off on her fingers a list of holy places that spanned the Himalayas. If being a respected *sādhu* in contemporary South Asia requires a personal knowledge of pilgrimage circuits, she had fulfilled her duty. Now that she had visited all these holy places and attained her *sādhu* credentials, she could stay in one place.

Staying in Place

The Hindi month of Āśvin is known to residents of Hardwar as Bengali Month, that period over Durgā Pūjā when Bengalis have a good deal of vacation time and visit pilgrimage places in record numbers. "I don't know why, but Bengalis love to travel," explained a Hardwar landlady who rented out rooms in her house and had a solidly booked month.[10] Durgā Pūjā (celebrated in Himachal Pradesh as Dussehra and in Nepal as Daśaiṅ) also marks the last fortnight that pilgrims can travel to the Char Dham before the road closes for the winter. For these last weeks of October, Garhwali rest houses and pilgrimage tour companies operate a brisk business.

Sādhus from Bengal were among the thousands of pilgrims in Hardwar during Bengali Month—right on schedule, it seemed, with their lay pilgrim counterparts. They carried less, traveled further, and slept on the *ghāṭs* rather than in rest houses, but Bengali *sādhus* were clearly conscious of both their prescribed peregrinations and the rhythms of their native place. One Bengali *sādhu* I spoke with was very particular about which temple he belonged to in West Bengal, and the place name where the temple was located. Bengal was the place from which he began his travels, and the place to which he would return. Once his identity as a Bengali was firmly established, he told me the itinerary of his pilgrimage circuit, pointed out that he had found his red-ribboned walking stick in Amarnāth, and showed me the documents that had allowed him to visit the restricted holy place.[11]

Almost all *sādhus* I spoke with identified strongly with a particular geographic location, which was usually not their native place, but a place they used as a base from which to travel. Gross also found this to be true: he writes that many *sādhus* "are part-time itinerant wanderers having some sort of semi-permanent residence from which they make a number of pilgrimages throughout the year" (1992:126). Some renouncers I met lived in a particular temple; some lived in a small room, or *kuṭī* affiliated with a temple or an ashram; many lived at a *dhūnī*, or sacred fire-pit. This surprised me at first: were not *sādhus* supposed to wander, or at least journey as perpetual pilgrims? How could renouncers have homes? Every classic text—and every modern pamphlet—emphasizes that *sādhus* leave home and travel from place to place. But my informants made clear that home bases figure prominently in the ways *sādhus* chart their journeys. In contemporary South Asia, *sādhus* still travel in frequent and active pilgrimage, but more often stay in one place for extended periods of time.

A *sādhu*'s place was clearly not a *ghar*, however, which is an exclusively householder term for "house" or "home" in both Hindi and Nepali. Not once did I hear a *sādhu*—even a married *sādhu*—refer to his base as his "*ghar*." Renouncers' reluctance to use the concept of home to describe their sedentary bases is universal: "*ghar*" clearly refers to householder homes. On one trip through Delhi, I spoke with a sophisticated journalist householder who had been initiated into the Nāth lineage as a young man, and had spent some years living as a *sādhu*. He told me of an occasion when he was wandering with a *sādhu* friend. When they arrived in the place they would sleep for the night, they put their things under a tree and went to visit another *sādhu* who was staying nearby. After some time, my informant turned to his friend. "Let's go home," he said, "*ghar me jau*," meaning to the tree. Years later, he says, he still remembers the look of incomprehension on his friend's face—he knew no *ghar*.

Similarly, I never met a *sādhu* who lived at his or her natal family's home. Even Ramaṇa Mahāṛṣi, who is held up by many as one of India's greatest saints and who lived with his mother for much of his adult life, was joined by his mother at *his* place of *sādhanā*. Part of being a *sādhu* is leaving a natal home. Mukta Giri, who returned to Kathmandu after some years of living and wandering in India, was adamant about living at Paśupatināth even though her *maiti*, her natal neighborhood, Chabahil, was around the corner. (*Maiti* is the Nepali term for a woman's natal home, as compared to her husband's home, which is her marital home, or *ghar*.) "I'm a *sādhu*," she said forcefully. "I live here," she asserted, meaning at the temple. In place of the word *ghar*, or home, *sādhus* usually refer to their bases as *sthāns*, holy locations (especially if they live in a room at a temple, for example), or *āsans*, seats, probably in reference to the specific places where they sit to do meditation. *Sādhus'* seats are like householders' homes in the sense that they mark the places where daily life takes place: food and bath, prayer and ritual, upkeep and maintenance, and gathering and socializing. But they differ from homes in the sense that they can shift at any time, and that their primary purpose is to sustain a religious life.

Sādhus may be more sedentary in modern South Asia than they were historically (when bands of wandering ascetics were the dominant mode of renouncer life, for example), but there is still a longstanding tradition of respect for renouncers who stay in one place. Staying put means *sādhus* can do their *sādhanā* and receive and bless pilgrims; the places they live usually take on religious significance as well. Many contemporary ashrams honor saints who lived in one place, such as Ramaṇa Mahāṛṣi's ashram in Tiruvannamalai and Sri Aurobindo's ashram in Auroville, both in Tamil Nadu. Nānī Mā and Svāmī Ācāryajī told me with some pride how Mastarām Bābājī, their *guru*, never left his ashram—and rarely left his cave—even to cross the bridge over the Ganges into the main town of Rishikesh. Although he was sedentary, he adhered strictly to many requirements of ascetic life: he would eat only food that was offered by householder pilgrims, for example. Nānī Mā said that he actually became angry at a woman disciple who decided to build a kitchen at the ashram. The kitchen would feed pilgrims, *sevaks*, and disciples, to be sure, but sustaining a large group kitchen required the purchase of food and the regulation of meals.

This story was somewhat anomalous in my experiences with renouncers, many of whom used their roles as renouncers for the benefit of the communities in which they lived. Dudh Bābā supported the children of Paśupatināth, giving them small amounts of money and little tasks. Women in particular took responsibility for feeding local communities (see Ramanujan 1982; Khandelwal 1997): Rādhā Giri gave work and food to a homeless woman from the area; mothered many local children, scolding them when they misbehaved and giving them snacks; and, most notably, agreed to rear an abandoned child despite having left householder life expressly behind and having no solid or reliable income. I heard about but did not meet a *sādhvī* named Tapovan Mā, who, after many years living alone at frigid mountain heights had shifted to a slightly lower-altitude location, Harsil, about an hour's drive below the shrine of Gangotri, for the sake of her health. She had also switched her severe, isolated *tapas* into a practice of feeding people daily. Narmada Puri, a Western *sādhvī* who lived on the outskirts of Hardwar, organized a daily meal for all *sādhus* from the area. All these renouncers used their power as respected local *sādhus* to make sure people were treated well. These sorts of actions were referred to by other renouncers as *kriya yoga,* meditation by action, and were clearly seen as an appropriate *sādhanā* for sedentary *sādhus.*[12]

Where do *sādhus* choose to stay, and what does a *sādhu* seat look like? Many renouncers choose to live in pilgrimage places because these are already holy locations infused with a history of powerful religious practice, and an infrastructure that will materially sustain *sādhus* as well. When I asked Rādhā Giri why she had chosen to live in Hardwar, however, she thought it was a ridiculous question. "Where do you want me to live?" she asked back. "At the railroad station?" Any place holy and convenient could be a *sādhu* seat, and a good spot vacated by a resident runs the risk of being quickly occupied by another *sādhu.* Many *sādhus* departed on pilgrimage leaving a large padlock on a makeshift door to guard their few belongings and, more importantly, the *sthān* they left behind. Traditionally, I was told, a *sādhu* should sleep under a tree or in a temple, but the *sādhu* seats I saw varied widely. Caves, ashrams, *dhūnīs,* rooms in pilgrims' guest houses, hotel rooms, apartments, tea shops, *ghāṭs,* huts, tents, *kuṭīs* in residential courtyards or temple complexes, made of stone, concrete, straw, brick, or wood—all served as bases for *sādhus* I met.

The three most important kinds of *sādhu* seats are the cave, the ashram, and the *dhūnī*. Clearly, mobility is not the only relation to land and space that is important for *sādhus*: stability is too. But renouncers' seats do look different from householders' homes, and they have different meanings for the *sādhu* community. Many *sādhu* seats wave the small triangular red flag that also flies from temples, a public symbol of religious activity. Nānī Mā explained, "[The red flag] is to tell people it's a place of worship—it's for God. It means he's here." Renouncers' seats are outward symbols of their renunciation, representing or symbolizing different aspects of the contemplative life: they are seats of religious practice, social refuge, and earthly nature.

The Solitude of Caves and Jungles

The reason most *sādhus* gave me for staying in one place for an extended period of time was the importance of *sādhanā*, religious practice. It doesn't matter where you meditate or say your mantras, I was told again and again, you just have to do it.[13] Wandering makes religious practice more difficult, not less—all that movement was distracting, renouncers told me. One needs to stay put to do *sādhanā* properly; once a renouncer has a secure room and a steady rhythm, all attentions can be devoted to practice. Although wandering without possessions and without destinations seems like a way for renouncers to live without encumbrances, most *sādhus* said just how much easier it was to stay put. Many talked specifically about their religious practice, but my impression was that most aspects of life—cooking, cleaning, eating, and socializing, as well as ritual—seemed easier if renouncers were sedentary.

Many renouncers were actually quite vehement about how sick of wandering they were. "I don't like all this wandering and more wandering!" Mukta Giri Mai said emphatically. "Here! There! Everywhere! I don't like it. You can praise God in your own room!" The head *sādhvī* at Hardwar's Nepali Ashram first assured me that she had wandered for a time, and then pointedly asked, "But what do you do with that wandering? Here I do *bhajans* [devotional singing]. I stay in one place, so I can praise God." Dudh Bābā, a well-traveled *sādhu,* felt similarly about the ultimate requirement of *sādhanā,* if more neutral about its location: "I do my mantras and my meditation. It's all the same to me whether I do it here in my room or in other countries." For most *sādhus,* a sedentary seat provided the stability of regular religious activity and a reliable daily rhythm that allowed their actions to be directed towards God.

The renouncers I met chose places for their practice that provided isolation and a natural setting. The classic place for *sādhanā* is the cave, and even in the twenty-first century caves flying red flags still dot the Ganges Valley of the Garhwal Himalaya. In the caves I saw, the cavern of rock was supported by concrete walls, a striking combination of a natural setting and the modern, cheap building materials that characterize the architectural landscape of contemporary Indian pilgrimage places. I met a *sādhvī* who had moved out of her cave into a small concrete building down the river in preparation for the winter months. She took me back to see it, pointing out the small ridges in the rock that served as shelves. She felt nostalgic for it, she said: she missed looking out of the window on to the Gaṅgā, and she couldn't wait to go back once it got warm enough.

Caves are famous symbols of *sādhu sādhanā* because the isolation of a mountain retreat resonates with the image of anti-social solitude. Although I have argued that social connections with other renouncers are an important part of *sādhu* life, almost all *sādhus* I spoke with insisted that even if they were social when they traveled or in the places where they lived, they needed solitude to do their religious practice. Even if they did not live in literal caves, renouncers told me they must be separated from society to do *sādhanā:* only alone can a practitioner analyze the mind for what it is, observing how it behaves when unchecked.[14] In the traditional edicts of renunciation, a cave symbolizes social isolation, a place where even a sedentary renouncer is laid bare to the elements of nature and is undistracted by social interactions or concerns.

Related to the isolated cave is the symbol of the unsocialized jungle. Metaphorically (and in some cases literally), the jungle is that wild place where no social interactions can distract a serious *sādhak.* But "jungle" does not necessarily mean a densely wooded area with many wild animals (although it could); in many South Asian dialects, it simply means any place away from society. Mukta Giri told me that she had wondered, for example, if she should escape to "the jungle" when she became widowed. The "jungle" is the place most emblematic of nature and least tainted with social relationships, an uninhabited location, far from villages, away from interaction, a quiet place of no distractions. Because the jungle is a place set apart from social requirements and assumptions, Mukta Giri felt religious bliss might be attained there.

In its distance from civilization, the jungle symbolizes a place where a practitioner is theoretically exposed to the world as it is untouched by human forces and desires. In a place of nature rather than a place where people congregate, the mind has different associations, renouncers implied, and it becomes possible to remove identifications with mental thoughts or bodily urges. The jungle is ideal for religious practice: a place where the practitioner's human body is exposed to heat and cold, and required to eat very little and very simply, relying on survival instincts to keep healthy enough to practice. In these ways, desires for material possessions and luxuries are stifled, detachment is fostered, an observation of natural forces at work is permitted, and divine grace can be demonstrated.

Other metaphors spoken of as ideal places for *sādhanā* were the Himalayan "forest" (many forest goddesses are worshipped throughout these regions) and, located beyond Gaumukh, at the base of the Śivliṅg Himāl, a place called Tapovan, or Grove of Tapas. Again, this *van,* or grove, is far above the tree line—it is a grove or a meadow in the sense of its natural isolation and appropriateness for meditative action. To properly do effective *sādhanā*, the renouncer must be free from—and physically far from—social attachments, and all the attendant man-made details, events, and emotions of secular life. Legends abound about *sādhus* who take to a cave in the Himalayan range or in the deep forest in order to separate themselves from society and focus only on God, and these tales continue to inspire *sādhus* in choosing locations. The scholarly Svāmī Ācāryajī confessed to me that reading a book about *sādhus* in forests inspired him to become a *sādhu* when he ran away from his family to the then-undeveloped town of Rishikesh, at age sixteen.

The Refuge of Ashrams

As an institution of learning and place of refuge, the ashram is one of the original locations of asceticism, and has symbolized steady religious practice in South Asia for two millennia. When they needed to stop moving, the wanderers of classical texts lived in forest ashrams, as did the *munis* and *ṛṣis* who are collectively referred to as the first contemplative sages in India, the forerunners of *sādhus*. The Sanskrit word *āśrama* means hermitage or refuge, and the institutions connote a place of peace and quiet study:

> Ashrams were the dwelling places of the *rishis,* of their families and students, and also of the old, who after a lifetime of strenuous activity raising a family, retired from the world and devoted themselves to spiritual enquiry and to their religious duties . . . The ashrams of great sages became sacred centers of learning and culture, where the young sought refinement and education, and the old repaired to for peace and spiritual guidance." (Forbes 2000:220)

Like most temples, *maṭhs* (monasteries), and *akhāṛās,* contemporary ashrams are usually not sites for individual contemplation, but places of group life. An ashram can connote the residence place of a *sādhu* (so any room in a temple could be referred to as a renouncer's ashram), but more usually implies a community, or a place of teaching, where pilgrims can come to rest or to learn. In contemporary Nepal and India, many ashrams have been constructed to house renouncers, pilgrims, or both, as well as to promote charitable action: Rishikesh's Swargāśram, for example, organizes activities that "include religious education, maintenance of an elaborate chain of pilgrim rest houses, free medical aid to pilgrims, plying of motorized boats for crossing the Gaṅgā, and a host of charitable works" (Bhardwaj 1973:211). Ashrams are centers with explicitly religious functions, but they also bring in a fair amount of money to the senior swami management, especially in places where foreigners are willing to pay for religious teaching. Changing travelers checks in Rishikesh's State Bank of India, I was surprised to see an elderly *sādhu* come in. The bank manager said that he was a client and that most of their business came from wealthy swamis connected to local ashrams. Accounts with hundreds of thousands of rupees, he said, were not unusual.

Temple-affiliated ashrams are spread throughout Nepal and India, constructed by temple *pūjāris, sādhu akhāṛās,* or individual swamis with disposable incomes. Often ashrams support rooms or even caves where visiting *sādhus* may live for a time even if they have no formal affiliation with the ashram. Like *sādhu akhāṛās,* ashrams are large landowners, and publicly support both lay and monastic Hindu religious life. Ashram administrations provide places for *sādhus* to live, practice their *sādhanā,* and spread the teachings of Hinduism, and administrators often direct interested pilgrims to resident *sādhus*. A *sādhvī* I knew graciously hosted four visiting pilgrims who had been sent to her residence by the director of a popular local ashram. After they left, she sighed at having lost the afternoon. But what could she do? she lamented—if she had been rude, she'd have made the ashram look bad and undermined the shared goal of supporting Hindu devotional practice. "Members of this community have to look after each other," she explained. "We can't give each other bad reputations."

A cross between religious seminar, ritual center, rest house, pilgrims' gathering place, and old age or runaway home, some ashrams are expressly constructed as refuges for people who have left householder homes and families. Sometimes people who choose to live in ashrams become renouncers, rather than the other way around. A lay Hardwar resident directed me to a women's ashram to meet *sādhvīs*—many ashrams are sex-segregated—explaining that people "from wherever" ended up there. A communal place of refuge is a boon for many, especially women, who may feel safer living in a group, believing it dangerous to either live or travel alone (Khandelwal 1997).[15] Quite a number of women *sādhus* I met did choose to live in solitude, but the possibility of social recrimination can make it difficult. I was not allowed to stay in certain mixed-sex ashrams because I was a *lone* woman, a prohibition experienced by some Indian *sādhvīs* as well.

Some ashrams may take women "from wherever," but others are designed to provide refuge for people from a particular area. Like the state-run pilgrim *dharamśālās* (rest houses) in Hardwar, the Nepali Ashram in Hardwar was a regional haven (operating in reverse, in a sense, since *sādhvīs* were the residents and householder pilgrims were the itinerant visitors). Located in a beautiful spot near the Bharat Mātā Mandir on the northern end of the city, the ashram hired relocated Nepalis as staff and welcomed Nepali *sādhvīs* as residents: when I visited, everyone clearly felt at home speaking their mother tongue, eating rice and lentils cooked with Nepali flavors, and wearing Nepali *cholis,* or blouses.

Just before I left the ashram, I met a Nepali *sādhvī* who had moved to the ashram from Assam when the last member of her family had died, about twelve years earlier. She had clearly been left alone and become a *sādhvī* as a way of finding refuge. She found it difficult to move around—her body was not strong, she said, and she had no money. She did not think she would be attending the Allahabad Kumbh Melā, which was soon approaching and for which many *sādhus* were excitedly making plans. Clearly the Nepali Ashram was her widow's refuge, a place where she could focus on God rather than the terrible losses she had known. Her place, she said, was wherever God wanted her. Religious devotion was a way to find comfort in the world, to go on living when life had been cruel. The ashram was both a social and a physical place where she could go, and life there provided a worldview that brought solace.

What of the argument that sedentary life implies a permanence and a sense of belonging that is detrimental to renouncers' spiritual goals? Many lay Hardwar residents leveled this charge against the ashram *sādhu* community. In the Uttar Pradesh Tourist Office in Hardwar, an official said to me, "I don't like these ashram *bābās*—they are cheaters, big cheaters." Some renouncers, too, questioned the legitimacy of domestic stability in *sādhu* life. *Sādhu* life is supposed to be hard, but both renouncers and householders questioned whether living in an ashram might be even easier than being a householder. A *sādhu* who was very insistent on living in hardship conditions told me somewhat angrily that many *sādhus* enjoy the comforts of an ashram, which is the opposite of a remote, difficult life in the jungle or the Himal: "Nowadays lots of people become *sādhus* because the *sādhu* life is very easy. They have big ashrams and lots of facilities—they wouldn't get all those facilities at home."

I discussed these issues with two Western *sādhvīs,* each of whom had pursued Hindu religious asceticism for over thirty years. Both women had started ashrams in partnership (one domestic, one fraternal) with an Indian *sādhu* man partly to offer food and rest to local or wandering renouncers. Both women were aware of the poor reputation of contemporary *sādhus* with ashrams. The first woman, Narmada Puri, was German by birth, and ran an ashram with her mate, Santoṣ Puri, whom she had met thirty years earlier when he lived as a lone ascetic on the Ganges riverbank. (Rādhā Giri took over the spot when the couple moved to the outskirts of Hardwar.)

Narmada Puri felt there was no inconsistency in living an ascetic domestic life. "If you stay in one place," she argued, "the world comes to you." She was conscious of the burdens of living a sedentary life, however: as simply as they lived, she told me, and as strictly as they lived by religious principles, sedentary domestic life still meant responsibility and involvement. "We still have so much: a farm, cows, children," she said. "You can't just blow it away." But she felt strongly that what they had, where they lived, and even the circumstances of marriage and motherhood were less important than detachment, *vairāgya,* which was the underlying premise of *sādhu* life. Detachment had nothing to do with external space, she concluded. "It comes from the inside." Narmada Puri was one of a number of married *sādhus* initiated into full *sādhu* lineages and kinship structures who argued that the *ṛṣis,* the legendary ancient meditators who developed both the religious practice and the religious philosophy of Hindu *dharma,* lived with wives and children in homes. Sedentary domesticity, I was told again and again, does not necessarily detract from a *sādhu*'s goals: even the gods have homes, such as Kailāśa and Vaikuṇṭha, mythical places that demonstrate the universal importance of domestic peace and safety.

The second woman, Nānī Mā, the English co-founder of the Bābā Mastarām Āśrama in Sainj, wasn't sure it was possible to be a good *sādhu* with an ashram and all the possessions that go along with it, such as equipment to run a kitchen and rooms to house pilgrims. Nānī explicitly wondered about the sleeping bag she used as her single blanket and the kitchen blender (a gift) that she had used to liquefy food since her doctors had prohibited solid food after an intestinal surgery. Warmth and food were basic requirements, but Nānī said she was used to sleeping with a single sheet and eating what food was given. She'd heard the heads of famous ashrams defend their large cars and houses by saying that they were just external objects which had no impact on their spiritual lives, and that they could walk away at any moment. Frankly, Nānī didn't think that she believed them. "*Māyā* (the illusion that is the material world) is a very strong force," she explained, and one that works quickly.

Unlike Narmada Puri, Nānī Mā felt that ashrams were part of the phenomena of wealthy and power-hungry *sādhus.* Although her ashram was a beautiful, welcoming, and quiet place, she felt that after her *guru* died she had left behind what she saw as a legitimate *sādhu* lifestyle that, even if it was sedentary, relied on no material possessions. Ashrams themselves, she felt, were a major problem for *sādhus;* they were a place where money was accumulated, and people—men and women—came to live together and often ended up sexually involved with one another. "And with money and sex," she said, throwing her hands up, "you have a householder situation. What's the difference?" she asked plaintively. Ashrams were no more than a parallel householder society.

Although Nānī Mā's ashram was very traditional in mores—I saw no evidence of sexual or highly emotional relationships among any of the residents—and very active in its emphasis on religious study, she and Svāmījī did have a bank account. Nānī worried that despite their religious goals, an ashram was an ashram, and she had stepped away from true *sādhu* life. When she excused herself from translating my interview with Svāmījī, she sighed deeply and said that in her guise as part-*sādhu,* part-*gṛhasthī,* she had to go tend to the kitchen, which seemed to her all too similar to householder duties.

The Heat of Dhūnīs

The most common seat for Śaiva *sādhus* is a *dhūnī,*[16] a sacred fire-pit of mud or dirt, beside which a renouncer lives. There is nothing visually spectacular about a *dhūnī,* which looks like a campfire built in an earthen pit: indeed, its simplicity is indicative of an unencumbered life. A renouncer's literal seat, marked by a small platform or rug that sits right next to the fire, means that *sādhus* sit, pray, meditate, cook, keep warm, sleep, drink tea, and smoke hashish without moving far. The fire that continuously burns in the *dhūnī* is the focal point of a *sādhu*'s place; it provides warmth, a focus for meditation, and sacred ash that many renouncers rub on their bodies or wear on their foreheads.

A *dhūnī* fire is both a practical source of heat and directly symbolic of one of the five elements that makes up the Hindu natural universe. When I asked Pāgal Bābā about the significance of the *dhūnī,* he said emphatically, "It's fire! It keeps you going. Fire keeps you warm, burns dead bodies, cooks your food. The energy inside the human body is fire." His statement demonstrates the value renouncers place on the elements as a way of understanding the natural world and material bodies within it: fire maintains the body through life and destroys it after death. Fire is primary, the first element after space to be created ("How can anything more be created in the dark?" Pāgal Bābā pointed out), representing all light and warmth in the world. The heat of the *dhūnī* fire, too, plays an important symbolic role in the healthful and religious practices of renouncers: bodily levels of heat are directly responsible for the proper digestion of food and circulation of nutrients, as well as for the maintenance of religious power.[17]

Renouncers were extremely careful to point out to me that a proper *dhūnī* should include all five elements, so that a *sādhu*'s place can properly act as a mesocosmic link between a renouncer's body and the outer world. The mud that lines the fire-pit represents earth, the mantra recited by a *sādhu* represents air, and the water kept in a small pot by the *dhūnī,* used most often to moisten the *sāfī,* the cloth used to smoke *chillums*, represents water. A number of *sādhus* also emphasized the importance of the link between the elements and the way a renouncer lived: he bathed each day in water, he lived by a fire, he repeated a mantra with the air of his lungs, and he worshipped a Śiva *liṅgam* made of stone or clay, materials of the earth. Space, *ākāś,* is the fifth element, of course, both the ground for manifesting the four other elements and itself a substance, sometimes translated as "ether." The four directions are also represented at the *dhūnī,* symbolized by the four even sides of the square mud-pit. In this way, the entire universe is represented at a *sādhu*'s seat.[18]

The consonance between bodily fire and *dhūnī* fire was repeatedly asserted in my conversations with *sādhus*: the equivalence of the outer world and the inner body, the macrocosm and the microcosm of Hindu yoga, was most directly symbolized by the *dhūnī* fire. Meditation on the fire may help a *yogī* understand the consonances between the outer and inner planes of existence, the nature of the element of fire and the specific mechanisms of inner heat (Eliade 1958 [1954]:72).[19] While textual sources are clear that ascetics should internalize householder fires and never relight them (cf. Heesterman 1993; Olivelle 1992; Doniger and Smith 1991), in practice the *dhūnī* is conceptualized as an external corollary of bodily fires.

Whether or not a *dhūnī* fire is analogous to a sacrificial fire, the *dhūnī* fire is sacred. No trash must be burned in a *dhūnī,* and the ash that comes from its fire, known as *vibhūti* or *bhasma,* is a sacrament. *Sādhus* will sometimes bless a guest with an ash *tilak,* or forehead marking, or offer a small packet as *prasād.* The ash symbolizes how all matter reduces to the same gray carbon—a reminder of the impermanence of all material forms—and also reputedly keeps away mosquitoes. *Dhūnīs* are often marked with tridents and fire tongs, sometimes a great many of both, and decorated with flowers or photographs of *gurus*. The *dhūnīs* I saw were almost always treated as renouncers' altars.

Little is known about the historical development of *dhūnīs,* but it is likely that both householder and ascetic wanderers needed fires to cook on and warm themselves: a *dhūnī* is a portable hearth.[20] Certainly one of the reasons *dhūnīs* are used as *sādhu* seats is their mobile adaptability. A *dhūnī* can serve as a religious base anywhere—under a tree, outside a temple, or in an *akhāṛā*—and for any length of time. *Dhūnīs* can be stable seats for many decades (and pilgrimage destinations in their own right, if they are the seats of well-respected renouncers), but I have also seen *dhūnīs* used by itinerant *sādhus* who stayed in a place for no more than a few days. Sometimes pre-built mud-pits in pilgrimage places are left inactive when no renouncers claim them as seats, but some locations and some occasions call for the construction of entirely new fire-pits. At the 2001 Kumbh Melā, which lasted no more than a month, *sādhus* built thousands of *dhūnīs* lined up next to each other; each marked a small personal space for a *sādhu* and his or her disciples, *sādhu* family members, and pilgrim visitors.

Most *dhūnīs* have an implicit "open-door" policy and visitors are frequent (including pilgrims, service providers or *sevaks,* interested passersby, other *sādhus,* and foreigners in search of religious life or a hashish pipe), especially in popular pilgrimage places. I have never sat in a *dhūnī* where tea is not perpetually served; in many Śaiva *dhūnīs* in particular, *chillums* are also perpetually smoked. For many *sādhus* who live at *dhūnīs,* most waking hours are spent in *chillum*-smoking visitation; renouncers smoke, compare notes on common acquaintances, and gossip about the politics of different *akhāṛās.* From the social webs they weave, sedentary renouncers know who is where when, and who might soon be coming to visit.

In most cases, a *dhūnī* is built by and belongs to an individual *sādhu.* Disciples may live at their *gurus' dhūnīs,* and sometimes a group of *guru-bhāīs* live together at a *dhūnī* if their *guru* is no longer alive. The person whose seat it is sits by the *dhūnī* and is the unquestioned director of *dhūnī* life, in charge of monitoring the logistics, the dynamics, and the seating arrangements around the *dhūnī.* At both Kumbh Melās I attended, *sādhus* lived in close quarters and members of the same renouncer family shared responsibility for their collective *dhūnī.* In these cases, the senior-most *sādhu* present at the *dhūnī* at any given time would sit on the primary seat next to the fire—the *āsan*—and monitor the *dhūnī*'s communal social life. Seniority among *guru-bhāīs* was determined by the number of years spent as a *sādhu*, the number of initiations taken, and administrative rank in the *akhāṛā*. A presiding *sādhu* would offer the *āsan* immediately if a more senior *guru-bhāī* arrived, a gesture of respect and deference. At the Allahabad Kumbh Melā, I saw a *sādhu* angrily kick a foreigner off the seat by his family's *dhūnī*—the *āsan* is clearly not to be sat upon by outsiders.

Sitting on the *āsan* puts a *sādhu* in charge of mediating the ever-changing social dynamics of the *dhūnī*. This includes delegating work and accepting donations—and also the more subtle tasks of asking disruptive people to leave, protecting or reassuring someone in a precarious situation, and defusing any potentially volatile discussions. On one occasion at the 2001 Kumbh Melā, I arrived at a *dhūnī* where upwards of ten *guru-bhāīs* lived together; I was looking for a particular *sādhu*—one of their *guru*-brothers—who had gone out. The *sādhu* sitting on the *āsan* asked me to stay for a few minutes, served me tea, sent a helper out to look for the *sādhu* I was to meet, and made polite conversation to make me feel at ease. When my friend was nowhere to be found and other *sādhus* started asking too many questions of me too eagerly, the *sādhu* in charge gently suggested I leave and come back later in the day. A renouncer has to maintain some degree of control over social events and behaviors at his or her *dhūnī*. Some *dhūnīs* are known as places that reflect the character of their residents—where *chillums* are always available, for example, or where political discussions or religious teachings are active.

Much of the research for this book was conducted at *dhūnīs*, because they are renouncers' spatial bases and because they are welcoming places for lay guests. The *dhūnī* I came to know best over the course of fieldwork was Rādhā Giri's. Rādhā Mai was unabashedly queen of her roost, running her *dhūnī* with certainty and efficiency, delegating to *sevaks* the purchase of milk and vegetables, arranging to have food cooked for visitors, sweeping up, disposing of garbage, and caring for the child she had agreed to raise. There were always a few people performing service at Mai's, as well as a steady flow of respectful *sādhu* and pilgrim visitors. All visitors were required to follow her rules for social conduct, which she did not hesitate to make clear. At the 1998 Kumbh Melā, a policeman in full uniform joined the congregants at Mai's *dhūnī*, coming to pay his respects and to see who had gathered. Out of deference to Mai and the ethos of her *dhūnī*, he calmly passed an illegal hash pipe between two pilgrims, without comment or explicit judgment.

Rādhā Giri's *dhūnī* was located on a small Ganges island just a few meters north of Har-ki-Pauri, the "footprint of God," the most sacred part of the Ganges' run through Hardwar. Her seat was a holy place in microcosm, popular with visiting *sādhus* partly because Hardwar is such an important thoroughfare and partly because Mātājī's *dhūnī* was, after twenty-five years, almost an institution. Without fail, when visiting *sādhus* arrived at her *dhūnī*, she would greet them with a cup of tea and the question, "Where have you come from?"[21] When asked of householders or foreigners, those people who belong to a particular place, the question takes on a standard global meaning: Where are you from? But when asked by resident renouncers of journeying renouncers, it means, Where are you coming from *now*, so as to arrive here in this *dhūnī* at this time? Which pilgrimage place have you just descended from?

Mai's *dhūnī* was built between two *pīpal* trees, each worshipped in its own right, beneath which were two attractive and well-kept altars. These were *pūjā* places worshipped by Mai, local residents, her disciples, and visiting pilgrims who found the spot spontaneously worthy of reverence. In between the two holy trees and on the banks of the sacred river Gaṅgā, Mai's *dhūnī* was itself treated as a sanctified place of the community. Every dusk a neighborhood man offered incense to the steps of the Ganges right in front of Mai's seat, to the tree altars, and to the small altar next to Mai's *dhūnī* itself. Every evening, Mai herself made a ritual first to the river and then to the *dhūnī*, the center of her religious efforts. And then she blessed all present with ash from the sacred fire.

Moving Forth and Staying Put

If wandering represents for scholarly renouncers of Vedānta texts a complete disidentification with space, place, and body, it poses for the vast majority of contemporary *sādhus* mechanisms to leave home, to connect with other renouncers, and to keep their bodies sustained. On the plane of divine reality, Vedānta scholars told me, all places are the same and there is no differentiation in space. But completely detached wandering, when a renouncer becomes aware of the illusory nature of space as the ground for physical reality, is a final step in the hierarchy of advanced *sādhanās:* it is too difficult, they suggested, for most practitioners. Wandering may be a tool of religious practice—a way to learn detachment and clear observation—but most renouncers have to wander to particular places.

In place of wandering at all, however, many renouncers I talked to were altogether tired of traveling—they had wandered the circuits for years, in many cases—and wanted to stay put. Until a renouncer is sufficiently realized, most of my informants insisted, human places really are important. Holy places can enhance religious practice and also further a sense of renouncer identity: *sādhus* play an important role in distributing blessings to pilgrims and, in return, they are materially sustained. As a result, pilgrimage circuits are the spatial ground of renouncer community. Mythical links between geographically distant sites establish a coherent, communal experience of space.

If, following Casey, we understand space as culturally articulated through the specifics of place, a circuit of places becomes the way a community projects its collective space. A South Asian network of pilgrimage places creates a social geography for a community that is not limited in space, just as the sun, the moon, and the stars of the heavens create an astral calendar for a community that projects itself as not limited in time. If pilgrimage circuits give the renouncer community their shared locations, where *sādhu* life begins and is collectively regenerated, festival cycles give the renouncer community their shared sense of time, and it is to the greatest festival of all that I now turn.

4 ❁ *Allahabad*

THE COMMUNITY IN TIME

Every Kumbh Melā in India's history has probably been an enormous religious gathering,[1] but the 2001 Melā in Allahabad was the first Kumbh to receive massive international press coverage. The BBC ran nightly specials about the festival every day for a month, and the number of foreign and local reporters trailing around microphones, wires, cameras, and photography equipment was itself no small spectacle. The main bathing day during the 1989 Allahabad Kumbh recorded 15 million people in attendance—after which the *Guinness Book of World Records* started listing the festival as the largest-ever gathering of human beings for a single purpose—as did the main bathing day at the 1998 Kumbh Melā in Hardwar. The numbers rose much higher for Prayag's 2001 Mahā Kumbh—to about 25 million on January 24, the main bathing day, and possibly as many as 70 million over the course of the month-long Melā.

In 2001, Kumbhnagar, or "the city of the Kumbh," as the constructed city is named, was erected alongside the Ganges on a plot of land that measured more than thirty-five square kilometers. The event required staggering administrative prowess, which was amply displayed by the Uttar Pradesh government (which has reputedly been solicited for other major world festivals, like the Berlin Love Parade). The Mahā Kumbh Melā *adhikhār*, or administration, planned and constructed Kumbhnagar with all the public works and planning accorded to any large city in the world—roads, bridges, latrines, and water pipes—on a site that is normally a non-arable riverbank. The Melā administration staff numbered about twenty thousand (*Times of India* 2001a), and the manual labor staff must have numbered many tens of thousands more, although I saw no reporting on this total. As a rule, every administrative body keeps and updates detailed written manuals on how and when to construct, facilitate, and maintain the structures that provide food, accommodation, water, light, and hygiene to millions of temporary city residents for the entire length of the gathering.

Kumbhnagar was constructed on the sandy bed that flanked the length of the Ganges, just south of the confluence of the Ganges and the Yamuna Rivers. The *saṅgam,* the primary site of ritual activity at the Melā, is really the central location of the festival because it marks the confluence of not two but three rivers: the Ganges, the Yamuna, and a mythical, "invisible" river, the Sarasvatī, which Pāgal Bābā called the "river of knowledge." (Sarasvatī is popularly known as the goddess of knowledge.) Bathing at the point where the rivers join is the whole point of the Kumbh, Bābā told me, because when a supplicant is submerged in the confluence of the three rivers, with their myriad mystical qualities, true knowledge "enters his heart."

The layout and administration of Kumbhnagar allowed for maximal pilgrim traffic and relatively easy access to the bathing places in the sacred rivers. Nine pontoon bridges spanned the Ganges, and parallel to these ran thirteen administrative districts, or "sectors," of the newly created city. Each sector was managed by an administrative headquarters that had elaborate lists and maps of residents. To find the Nāth Akhāṛā, for example, which I knew to be in Sector 7, I arrived at the Sector 7 administrative block and waited for the Sector 7 chief administrator, who could direct me to the appropriate row and column of the ground plan. Large roads were laid out more or less in a grid system, so by walking perpendicular to the bridges—parallel to the Ganges—on the central road, steel plate after steel plate, pilgrims could traverse the sectors. Construction at all levels continued throughout the month of the Melā, as new religious organizations arrived and built cloth and bamboo façades announcing their camp, and as new pilgrims arrived to occupy the tents that burgeoned in number.

Despite the enormous organizational effort and the remarkable facilities that were constructed for the unique event—water pipes laid and taps constructed throughout each camp; electric lines wired and fluorescent bulbs affixed to each tent; a team of several thousand latrine-cleaners who twice daily disinfected hundreds of toilets in each camp—living conditions at the Melā were difficult. The steel-plate roads could not prevent enormous gales of dust from being churned up into the air by the vehicles that plied them, the smoke from thousands of *dhūnīs* and thousands more pilgrim fires filled the atmosphere, and, as a public-health measure against the spread of epidemic, a highly noxious disinfectant—Flit mixed with kerosene—was sprayed through the camps at least twice a day, and hourly on the more heavily populated days. And as everywhere in South Asia, the number of vehicles trundling over the roads, even the makeshift steel-plate roads of Kumbhnagar, had risen exponentially over the past decade, kicking up sand, dust, and diesel. By the end of the first week, every Kumbhnagar resident had irritated lungs and a bad cough. Melā doctors were on duty every few days at the Nirañjanī Akhāṛā, and the lines of patients waiting to be treated were long.

Prelude: Preparation

Pāgal Bābā had not really planned to attend the 2001 Allahabad Kumbh Melā. In the months prior to the festival, he had developed a stomach infection, and as he convalesced in Hardwar, he thought he might not have the energy to rally for the enormous event. Having been a *sādhu* for forty-five years, and having attended numerous Kumbhs and other Melās all over India, he did not feel he would miss anything new.

I very much hoped that Bābā would attend the Melā, however. At the Hardwar Kumbh in 1998, he had introduced me to members of the Nirañjanī Akhāṛā, his home institution, and two and a half years later, back in Hardwar, we spent quite a bit of time together while Bābā recuperated from his illness. He insisted on cooking for himself while he recovered, and he often fed me, too, as we sat on carefully folded newspapers that covered the floor of his small hotel room. While he rested after his meal, or in the evenings while he sat by the Ganges, I would ask him questions about *sādhu* rituals and *sādhu* rankings, about Śaṅkarācārya's teachings, and about holy cities and sacred times. Bābā's understanding of—and articulateness about—the details of *akhāṛā* life, the symbolic meanings of religious practice, and the textual guidelines of *sādhu* tradition was unmatched among my informants. Participating in the Kumbh in Allahabad with Pāgal Bābā as a guide was the closest I would get, I felt, to having an insider's experience.

I was not the only foreigner who hoped Bābā would attend the Melā, and as a result both material and social incentives to attend the Melā increased for Pāgal Bābā in the months just before the Kumbh. A small number of Bābā's long-time friends from Slovenia and the U.S. wanted to participate in the Melā, and together the group was willing to sponsor the costs of constructing a tent for the duration of the Kumbh. The pooled money would cover renting the land from the Melā administration; renting the material for the tent itself; constructing a twenty-person, three-compartment tent complete with electrical wiring and a sheltered patio area; making a contribution to the Nirañjanī Akhāṛā, which would be our formal sponsor; buying enough firewood to keep a *dhūnī* alight for the month; and providing enough extra cash so that Bābā could in turn sponsor a *bhaṇḍārā,* or public feast, for the officials of the *akhāṛā,* in part to thank them for agreeing to host, feed, and protect a small number of European and American participants. With money available and foreign friends and fellow renouncers encouraging him, Pāgal Bābā decided to go. He would arrange for the construction of a tent for us, and for his own health and comfort he would live in one of a few rooms at the Nirañjanī Akhāṛā headquarters, a permanent structure beautifully situated on the banks of the Ganges, about a kilometer away from the tented camp.

In Hardwar during the autumn before the Kumbh in Allahabad, (whose ancient name is Prayag, referring to its site at the confluence of rivers), Pāgal Bābā and I began talking about the dates of the Melā. Bābā explained that the holy days of the Kumbh were determined astronomically, "according to the confluences of the stars." The holiest day in Prayag was always Maunī Amāvasyā, the "Black Night," or the new moon of the Hindi month Māgh, but, as with any lunar calculation, the solar date for the event would vary by Kumbh cycle. Trying to understand how sacred dates and times were calculated by and for members of the *sādhu* community, I asked Pāgal Bābā directly if space and time were different for *bābās* than for householders. "Not really," he answered. "For some maybe. But most *bābās* do live in space and time—it is not easy to come out of that. You can't say all *bābās* live out of it. Maybe a few, but they are hard to find." Real sacred time, Bābā seemed to be saying, transcends astral calculation.

At the 2001 Prayag Kumbh, Maunī Amāvasyā fell on January 24 on the Gregorian calendar. On that morning I sat with Pāgal Bābā at the *dhūnī* the Nirañjanī Akhāṛā *sādhus* had built outside our tent. It was exactly four months after my original query, and as we sat at the fire on the holiest morning of the festival, the energy of the camp at a palpable high, I asked Bābā a different version of the same question: whether time at the Melā was different from normal time. "There is no time at the Melā," he replied emphatically. "It's beyond space and time."

Remembering his assertion about how difficult it was to get beyond time, I was surprised by his certainty that we had somehow done it, or that being together in this place on this carefully calculated day had spontaneously propelled us there. "If it's beyond space and time, it's a very high place," I suggested. "Yes!" he cried. "You're there! And if you keep this with you," he continued, implying that the effects of the Melā would be enduring ones, "you will be a changed person. Anywhere, anyplace, people will see. And say this girl has found God." There at the holiest of times, Bābā was saying, we were beyond time.

Pāgal Bābā's exuberant declaration to me that we had arrived in a place beyond time points to the Kumbh as a particularly powerful event in the experience of *sādhus.* In this chapter, I use the Mahā Kumbh Melā, the Great Festival of the Nectar Jug, to look at the construction of the renouncer community over time, and also at the construction of time by the renouncer community. The Kumbh is the pivotal festival cycle for *sādhus* in South Asia, and the occasion for the ritual regeneration of renouncer society. Grounded in space and time, the Kumbh ritual mediates between renouncers' collective history and a collective experience of transcendence, or timelessness. By overlaying detailed attention to the configurations of the stars with the potency of a myth about immortality, the Kumbh combines visions of time in such a way that it produces an experience that is "beyond time," which is renouncers' ultimate religious goal.

Central to the enormous festival are the *sādhu akhāṛās,* both spatially and socially. The Kumbh serves as both a fixed point on the map and a fixed point on the calendar around which renouncers base their travels and their pilgrimages: the festival reproduces a collective space-time for renouncers. Just as geographical landscapes articulate renouncers' communal locations, the Kumbh festival articulates *sādhus'* communal history.

The bodies of the earth and sky—landscapes and stars—determine when and where collective ritual action should take place, and act as the ground for communal experience. Astral configurations and transitions determine the ritual activities of the Kumbh Melā: by refracting collective events against the cycles of the natural world, the *sādhu* community asserts that its own construction of time is aligned with the forces of nature, beyond average human experience.

The festival experience also raises the question of being "beyond time," or transcending time, and suggests that *sādhu* time is itself transcendent. As powerful as natural forces are, I heard renouncers say, and as worthwhile as it may be to perform rituals on certain days at certain times in order to derive the maximum benefit from those forces, time is still a projection of human thought. Built into renouncer philosophy is the idea that although we try to use the time that is built into nature to our benefit—like when the sun moves into reverse on the horizon or when the moon becomes new—the ultimate experience is to move beyond the concept of time altogether. The Melā is an opportunity for religious knowledge, but it is also an intense collective experience, when a community that rarely meets does so for a brief moment.

The sociologist Emile Durkheim suggested that a collective ritual event can produce something called "collective effervescence," meaning that the experience of being together during a powerful ritual creates a transcendent state which forms the ground of culture. Pāgal Bābā's suggestion that we were in a place beyond time may have been as much a product of Durkheim's collective effervescence as it was a collective ability to realize oneness in the Hindu sense. Whatever it is called, the experience of transcendence is a powerful one for *sādhus* at the festival. If each Melā is both a unique event and part of a cycle, the combination is a transcendent ritual that propels a community forward in time.

The Kumbh Melā

The myth of the Kumbh Melā's origin centers on a bitter battle between the gods and the demons of the Indian heavens. The fight was over the possession of a precious Kumbh, a vessel, which contained *amṛta* (literally non-death) the nectar of immortality. The story of exactly how the gods manage to wrest the jug away from the demons varies, but in all tellings, the gods escape with the vessel and fly to heaven, where they can exclusively consume the magical liquid. In one version of the story, the god Viṣṇu takes the form of the beautiful Mohinī, a woman so lovely that the gods and the demons actually agree to share the liquid if it is she who apportions it. They sit in two rows, facing each other, and Mohinī dutifully moves down the row of gods, giving each his cupful. Just before she turns down the row of demons, she takes flight, the vessel in hand, leaving the demons to exist in mortal time.[2]

During Viṣṇu's flight to heaven, which took twelve divine days, four drops of immortal nectar fell from the jug and on to the earth. And eons of human years later, four cities in contemporary India mark the spots where the nectar fell: Nasik, Ujjain, Hardwar, and Allahabad. These four holy places cyclically celebrate the Kumbh Melā, the Festival of the Jug. When the stars in the sky move into the exact configuration they were in when Viṣṇu made his original flight, the myth tells us, the rivers in human cities become *amṛta* once again. Those who bathe in the nectar-infused rivers are cleansed of their sins, it is said, and freed from the cycle of birth and death. Using the twelve-year cycle, which corresponds to the twelve days it took Viṣṇu to get to heaven (and also to the twelve-year orbit of Jupiter), the contemporary Kumbh Melā circuit rotates among these four cities every three years, and each city hosts the festival in its fullness every twelve.[3] This cycle also resonates with the twelve-year *tapas* cycle that many renouncers recounted in their histories of wandering.

If pilgrimage circuits and festival cycles serve as meeting places for renouncers from distant locations, drops of nectar form the pre-eminent circuit and the twelve-year Nectar Jug Festival forms the pre-eminent cycle. By using the Kumbh cycle as their communal gathering, renouncers publicly align themselves to the temporal cycles of the gods, rather than to those of their fellow humans. This ritual adherence to the time of the gods, rather than to seasonal lay rhythms (cf. Berreman 1972[1963]; Babb 1975; Eck 1982; Kumar 1988), means the *sādhu* community projects itself as a class of divine beings whose temporal reckoning revolves around holy configurations in the skies and *amṛta* in the rivers.[4] The Kumbh Melā is the public arena where *sādhus* can show householder Hindus that their community lives on sacred circuits and in divine cycles: renouncers, as the pre-eminent participants of the Kumbh, claim a closer link to godly time than lay pilgrims.[5]

For months leading up to the Kumbh, I would hear *sādhus* describe their forthcoming routes, and they almost always culminated in Allahabad in January. The Kumbh appeared in *sādhus'* narratives as an event that had to be planned for and that must be attended. In Hardwar, a pilgrimage place where many *sādhus* gathered on their way up to and down from the Char Dham, the Kumbh was almost always identified as the next place they would meet. In Garhwali pilgrimage places, I heard pilgrims asking *sādhus* when the *bābās* would descend from the mountains, and in the detailed itineraries renouncers gave in response, the Kumbh was the inevitable end-point, the non-negotiable destination, the fixed point in time. Some *sādhus* raised their voices as they talked about the upcoming festival, to mark both its import and their excitement about the event. Others raised their hands as if in submission to divine will: as *sādhus,* they had been summoned to Prayag for the month of Māgh.

Meeting at the Melā

In 2001, Kumbhnagar was built close to the village of Jhusi, located a few kilometers away from the town of Allahabad and the shade that trees by the flowing rivers could provide. This had not been the case twelve years earlier when the Ganges flowed much farther from the city itself, and much closer to Jhusi: in1989, Kumbhnagar had been built up against Allahabad city limits, under the trees and alongside Allahabad city's fort. But the Ganges unexpectedly changed course, and plans for the Melā city had to be redesigned for the far side of the river as late as October, Pāgal Bābā told me, just three months before the Kumbh began (*Times of India* 2001c). Bābā thought that because Kumbhnagar was placed well into the desert, far from the tree-lined border of Allahabad town, the levels of dust were much higher than twelve years earlier. Every Kumbh has its own character, one pilgrim told me; even the route of the Ganges fluctuates over time.

The renouncer camps were built right in the center of the constructed city, as close to the Ganges as possible. Probably half a million *sādhus* attended the Kumbh, including members of all seven *daśnāmī akhāṛās,* as well as the Nāth, Vaiṣṇava, and Udāsīn *akhāṛās*, and other independent orders. The *daśnāmī sādhu* camps, their orange flags flying, were placed right on the main road, which emerged directly from the central bridge.

The Melā city planning staff had given the renouncer community star billing, spatially, in accordance with their status as the honored guests of the Melā. Renouncer processions on primary bathing days would be the visual pinnacles of the entire festival; *sādhus* were the kings whose astrologers would determine the holiest dates and times for the millions gathered, who would bathe in the holiest places first and foremost, and who, in turn, would dispense blessings to the crowds.

The Jūnā Akhāṛā, with about ten thousand registered *sādhus,* occupied the largest amount of space. A separate camp for women renouncers was constructed adjacent to the main camp, occupying a small corner on the plot of land allocated to the Akhāṛā. (Rādhā Giri refused to stay in the women's camp, however, opting instead to live with a *guru-bhāī* in the men's camp for the two days she and Gaṅgā Giri attended the Melā.) Small alleys separated the fifteen parallel rows of *sādhu* tents. Each tent housed one *dhūnī,* and by each *dhūnī* lived about three or four *sādhus* who were related by lineage (usually *guru-bhāīs*), as well as their devotees, or *bhagats,* who came to the Melā from their host *sādhu*'s home part of the country. The *bhagats* working in each tent helped keep the *dhūnī* running as a viable, active, and sociable location: they set up tents, kept the reserve of firewood high, cooked on a daily basis, and served tea to *sādhu* and pilgrim visitors.

The Nirañjanī Akhāṛā camp, almost immediately next to the Jūnā enclave, was much more open and grander in style. Large and immaculate tents were laid neatly alongside one another on the wide boulevard that was the main walkway through the *akhāṛā.* Fairly strict hierarchies of seniority dictated which *sādhus* would run to get tea or distribute coupons for the daily *bhaṇḍārā,* the feasts hosted by each *akhāṛā* to feed its resident *sādhus* and their attendant pilgrims. Lay devotees lived not with *sādhu* families but in smaller tents behind the walkway, perpendicular to the tents of the *sādhus* they came to visit and serve. Some tents were constructed for pilgrims from a particular village where a Nirañjanī *sādhu* lived or had supporters: rotating groups of pilgrims would occupy the tent for a few days or a week at a time and then return to the village, leaving room for the next group to attend the Melā.

The pilgrims who remained at Kumbhnagar from one full moon to the next were known as *kalpavāsīs,* or residents for the entire *kalpa,* a period of time which denotes a single full day in the life of the deity

Brahmā (Forbes 2000). Special camps were constructed for the *kalpavāsī* pilgrims, who undertook the spiritual challenge of living in Kumbhnagar as a particular form of *tapas,* refusing to eat until guests had and only eating food cooked under the proper conditions in their own camp. The use of one of the longest temporal measures—one *kalpa* lasts 4,320,000,000 human years—to denote the single month of the Kumbh Melā signifies that the Melā was itself a complete age, encompassing all of time. Although only a human month in duration, the Melā contained more time than any human could otherwise experience. Experiencing the fullness of the Kumbh was to experience time at a divine level—a day of Brahmā—as well as the compression of time, from an age that normally lasts millions of years into one lunar month.

The tent Pāgal Bābā arranged for his foreign guests was in the Nirañjanī Akhāṛā proper, under the jurisdiction of a senior *mahant.* Our tent was constructed and looked after exclusively by members of the Giri lineage, Pāgal Bābā's family. To eat elsewhere, or to join members of another *akhāṛā* for one of their *bhaṇḍārās,* would have undermined our loyalty to the Nirañjanī crew who prepared food for us twice a day and delivered pots of tea every few hours. This strict rule, which Bābā repeated a number of times to me (perhaps because I worked with members of other *akhāṛās* and had lived for a time with the Jūnā Akhāṛā during the Hardwar Kumbh), reflected the sensitivity around commensal relations between two *akhāṛās* with different caste codes, as well as the ritual antagonism between the rival *akhāṛās* over which regiment should be the first to bathe at the *saṅgam* spot at the sacred time.

True to its name, the Melā served as a "great gathering" of *sādhu* families, lineages, regional affiliations, and *akhāṛās.* Despite the large area over which the Melā sprawled, the *sādhus* themselves rarely left their camps, especially since pilgrims from all over Kumbhnagar came to see them. Some younger *sādhus* were out and about all day, to the extent their *gurus* and *dhūnī*-bound duties would allow, seeing what was for sale, who was wandering the boulevards, and where they could meet their friends from other *akhāṛās.* The *sādhu* camps were the centers of an astounding range of people from all over the country (and the world), the places where all the visiting groups attending the Melā came to pay their respects and hustle for hand-outs. There were *jaṅgams* wearing bells and plumed turbans who came to sing the stories of *sādhus; hijṛās* who stopped to dance and taunt groups of celibate *sādhus;* television crews who traipsed through camps to film the famous Amar Bhārti, whose right hand had been raised in *tapas* for over a decade; troops of Bhairavis whose arms and chests were wrapped in thick *rudrākṣha* beads, and who marched through the camps chanting Śaiva mantras; cops, doctors, beggars, and performers; backpacking foreigners who sat beatifically at the feet of renouncers, hoping for spiritual guidance or a hashish pipe or both; and red-and-silver-caped *koṭvālas*—up-and-coming young *sādhus* in each *akhāṛā*—who vigilantly paraded the camps, wearing pale yellow turbans and holding silver scepters, charged with maintaining order amid the chaos.

Regenerating Community

As the family gathering that happens once every three years, and in its fullness every twelve, the Kumbh acts as a religious summit where both ideological and political discussions can take place between orders and between cohorts. The festival allows renouncers who live in diffuse locations to meet, re-meet, and put into place the formal structures for the administration of each *akhāṛā* and each *daśnāmī* lineage. Many *sādhus* told me, "Oh, if you're going to the Melā, you'll meet so-and-so," or "At the Melā, look up such-and-such." More importantly, the Kumbh is a gathering where the entire community—the extended families—can take stock: the community collectively establishes who has died, how the elders are faring, how the young have grown, and how new leaders have taken on their positions of responsibility.

For the 2001 Melā, the *sādhu akhāṛās* formally arrived a few days before the beginning of the Kumbh, marching into Kumbhnagar from Allahabad city with great pomp: painted elephants, gilded parasols, and marching bands accompanied each order (*Hindustan Times* 2001). Ever mindful of keeping peace among the regiments, Melā organizers scheduled the *akhāṛās* to process into Kumbhnagar on successive days, so they would not come into contact with their rivals. The Nirañjanī Akhāṛā, for example, processed into Kumbhnagar on January 5; once they were safely settled, the Jūnā Akhāṛā processed to their allotted camp, just next door, on January 7.

The Kumbh Melā serves a classic role of cyclical regeneration for the renouncer community, when *akhāṛās* replenish their ranks with new initiates, promote their flourishing members, and revitalize themselves through grand processions and prominent ritual bathing. In the non-procreative world of a *sādhu akhāṛā,* continuity over time must be ensured through creating new members by formal induction, and the Kumbh serves as the formal forum for *akhāṛā* initiations. Each *akhāṛā* gives over one day to initiations (the Jūnā Akhāṛā, which accepts women, has two separate initiation days, one for women and one for men), when initiates strip naked, bathe in the *saṅgam,* and sit, closely guarded, for many hours around large fires in the *akhāṛā* grounds, where they are given new mantras to recite and practices to perform.

When I would ask my informants how long they had been renouncers, many counted the number of Kumbh Melās that had elapsed since his or her initiation. Even if initiation into renouncerhood had not taken place at the festival itself, the timing of the event might have corresponded with the Kumbh. I met one renouncer who did not attend Kumbh festivals, believing them to be little more than showy political events, but when I asked her when she had been initiated, she said, "Only at the last Kumbh." I was confused—had she gone to the Melā after all? No, she clarified, she had been initiated while the Kumbh was going on, in a different location: "The Kumbh is an auspicious period for initiation." The Kumbh was point zero, the beginning of life as a renouncer, and subsequent Melās were birthdays.

The Melā also provides the opportunity to promote last cycle's initiates to positions of seniority in the *akhāṛā* and to assign up-and-coming young renouncers administrative posts in the regional headquarters. Each *akhāṛā* holds elections and high-level official meetings during the course of the festival. Officials of the Nirañjanī Akhāṛā are elected directly after the Melā at the *akhāṛā* headquarters in Varanasi. New officers are immediately relocated across the country in administrative posts. By using the Melā as a sacred period to initiate new members and rejuvenate the ranks of old members, the Kumbh serves as a cycle of time for the *sādhu* community as a whole.

On a smaller and less formal scale, the Melā is also the opportunity to renegotiate the dynamics of each renouncer lineage, since the rankings, the friendships, the political jostling, and the personalities are all on display. The public can see the hierarchy among a group of *guru-bhāīs,* for example, through who wields authority in a family's *dhūnī* and who sits on the *āsan*. Moreover, paying homage to the elders of each lineage is one of the most important practices of the festival. The members of each *akhāṛā* pay daily respects to the most senior members of the institution: at dusk in the *akhāṛā*'s central location, senior *mahants* watch each member as he files through and offers *praṇāms,* gestures of deference, visibly assessing each *sādhu*'s demeanor and progress.

Finally, on each of three main bathing days, the renouncer *akhāṛās* participate in ritual processions to the confluence of rivers where they are the first to bathe. At both Melās I attended, the *akhāṛā* processions were the crescendos of the festival, and quite literally millions of people crowded the procession route—and were beaten back by state policemen—to catch a glimpse of the *sādhu* parade. The *nāgās* of each *akhāṛā* began the renouncer processions with high energy: naked, ash-smeared, and garlanded with marigolds, some rode on horseback and brandished swords as a testament to their history as military regiments. Even on foot, they charged out of their *akhāṛā* camps with a rush of power, hair flying, yelling praises to Śiva, largely unrecognizable from the sedate, saffron-robed, highly administrative figures they presented during the other days of the Melā.

The *sādhus* returned to their camps having been the first to bathe in the cold early morning water, having refreshed their spirits and the honor of their *akhāṛā,* and having renewed their ties to their *gurus, gurubhāīs,* and lineages. In this heightened, ritual state, warfare has sometimes broken out between the *nāgās* of rival *akhāṛās* (see *Independent* 1998). In 2001, Allahabad officials tried to time the processions of respective *akhāṛās* so that no two would even cross each other on the procession path to and from the bathing area. It worked, for all three bathing days. The Nirañjanīs were back, safely in their camp, before the Jūnās even left. There were no battles, no bloodshed, and all were bathed in the river of bliss.

Collective Space-Time: Circuits and Cycles

Just as holy places mark locations of transformation, particular astral configurations mark potential moments of transcendence. "The planets are like a giant clock," Bābā told me. "Not with three hands, but with planet hands. They clock auspicious moments, these meeting spaces where flows of information can happen." The movements of the moon, the sun, and the planets, and their locations in relation to the stars—twelve constellations of the zodiac—together constitute the astral calendar that *akhāṛā jyotiṣīs,* or astrologers, use as determinants of ritually auspicious time. As in Euro-American astrology, both planets and zodiacal signs are symbols with particular characteristics. Apart and in consonance, they are thought to exert particular effects on human mood and behavior. Popularly available *tithi* (lunar) calendars describe the positions of the sun, moon, and planets in relation to the stellar constellations, and also counsel for or against particular actions on different days. Varied revolution times of each astral body combine to create different configurations in the sky, and renouncers told me that these combinations affect human actions differently, heightening certain conditions and qualities, and mitigating others.

Through carefully charting the movements of astral bodies, the renouncer community articulates its collective time. The job of the Melā astrologers, Bābā explained to me, was to ascertain precisely when renouncers should collectively bathe—using the moon as the finest variant of time, since it has the shortest cycle—for the most powerful results. With its twelve-year revolution cycle and its status as the largest and most powerful planet, Jupiter (or Bṛhaspati in Indian astronomical nomenclature) is the astral body that determines the cycle of the Kumbh Melā. The Allahabad Kumbh takes place when Jupiter is in the constellation of Aries, the first zodiacal sign.[6] Many renouncers told me that wandering ascetics had "always" known when and where to go to the festival because they followed the path of Jupiter in the sky: when Jupiter entered the constellation Aries, they knew it was time to go to Prayag.

The formal period of the 2001 Allahabad Kumbh lasted one lunar month, from one full moon (in the Hindi month Pūs—in this case January 9) to the next (in the Hindi month Māgh—in this case February 8).[7] The daily activities of renouncers during their month in Kumbhnagar were fairly consistent except for the three major bathing days known as *śāhī snāns,* or royal baths. The two successive full moon dates (*pūrṇimās*) were important pilgrim bathing dates, since bathing on the full moon is an important ritual anywhere, any month in India—at Prayag, the holiest bathing place, during the month of the Kumbh Melā, the holiest bathing time, they would be more auspicious still. They were not, however, *śāhī snāns,* bathing dates when the *sādhu akhāṛās* would royally process to Prayāg Rāj, the king of confluences, early in the morning for their communal bath, leaving behind traces of their own holiness, so they said, for the householder pilgrims who would follow.

At every Allahabad Kumbh, the three *śāhī snāns* correspond to annual, solar, and lunar events: Makar Saṅkrānti, Maunī Amāvasyā, and Basanta Pañcamī. The first *śāhī snān* occurs on Makar Saṅkrānti, January 14, or the solar transition into Capricorn,[8] which is also when the sun begins its motion northward, or *uttarāya,* from the Tropic of Capricorn.[9] "The starting of the sun to the north is quite a significant change, of course," explained Bābā. "The transit of the sun has an effect on our mind and also on our soul. The sun is the symbol of our soul." In Bābā's interpretation, the transition of the sun marks a liminal threshold for our own souls. Using language inflected by Greco-Roman metaphors, Rām Puri, a knowledgeable Western *sādhu* explained, "The sun has gone through the passage to the underworld, and during the Makar Saṅkrānti *snān,* facing east at sunrise, we're seeing the sun emerge from Hades." On the first royal bath, he was suggesting, our souls have the opportunity to move from the south (the direction of death) toward the north (the direction of creation), and from darkness into light, or a heightened state of knowledge.

The second and third *śāhī snāns* are lunar dates, not solar ones. Once Jupiter is in Aries and the sun is in Capricorn, the highest moment of the Prayag Kumbh arrives when the moon becomes new. Maunī Amāvasyā is literally translated as "silent new moon." "It's good to be silent once a year," Pāgal Bābā told me, implying that looking and listening, observing rather than asserting, could teach practitioners about the nature of the world. Rām Puri described this bath as the period when esoteric knowledge is passed down from *guru* to disciple: the silent moon symbolizes knowledge of the inarticulable. (Taking a vow of silence is not an uncommon austerity among renouncers; I met quite a few *maun sādhus,* or *maunīs,* but most had taken a vow that lasted longer than a single day.) Basanta Pañcamī falls on the fifth day after the new moon and heralds the arrival of spring. Most of North India celebrates Basanta Pañcamī as Sarasvatī Pūjā, the day when students, teachers, and other householders propitiate the goddess of knowledge. Although the third bath was much less important than the first two—quite a number of sādhus left Kumbhnagar after Maunī

Amāvasyā—the theme remained the same: winter was over and spring had arrived; with Sarasvatī's blessings, knowledge could spread.

Astral bodies articulate time for the renouncer community, much as earthly landscapes articulate space. The festival cycles and the pilgrimage circuits that cohere and sustain the renouncer community are based on the movements of the stars and the shapes of the earth. Moments of transition in the sky—such as when the sun moves into a new sign or the moon moves into a new cycle—are coded by renouncers as ritual periods for their community. Astral transitions are like liminal periods in nature, renouncers argued, and they correspond to ritual moments when the community can collectively accumulate knowledge and regenerate power. The two rivers which come together in Allahabad, the Ganges and the Yamuna, each articulate their own circuit, and the power of the Allahabad Kumbh derives in part from the layering of the two circuits into one ritual occasion. The Kumbh festival shows how the renouncer community uses the natural forms of the earth and sky to articulate collective space and time: they are a community whose dispersion requires a space-time of a cosmic order.

Combined with mythic readings of space and time, the Hindu astrological calendar determines where and when the renouncer community should meet. When the stars are configured as they were when nectar drops fell from the sky, renouncers explained to me, earthly rivers follow suit, spontaneously reproducing the sacred liquid. The cycles of nature are so regular and so powerful in this interpretation that when the stars repeat their configurations, the earth too reinhabits the physical form it had at the moment of Viṣṇu's flight, and the *amṛta* reappears. The entire natural universe—and also the entire social universe, with its numerous but invariably recognizable political dynamics—finds itself in the same configurations, again and again, cyclically.

The Ritual Mediation of Time

Although, ironically, the religious goal of the Melā is to transcend time, form, and nature altogether, using the tools of nature is one of the most important parts of the ritual practices of the Melā. Like using the human body to transcend materiality, the renouncer community uses the physical forms of the earth and the sky—rivers and stars—as the ground for practices that can ultimately liberate. Just as bodily practice mediates between worldly experience and metaphysical knowledge, ritual practice mediates between the earthly collective experience of time and the collective transcendence of time. The ritual processions and baths of the Kumbh Melā demonstrate both the renouncer community's very worldly history—its militarism—and also its goal of religious transcendence.

The Experience of Time

In renouncer thinking, the experience of time is both linear and cyclical. Each Kumbh Melā is at once a unique event, marked by particular characteristics that constitute *sādhu* history, and also a node on a never-ending cycle. This replicability is what allows the Kumbh to be the place where the *sādhu* community is regenerated. The Kumbh is the event renouncers return to again and again because it marks a specific moment of time in communal history (not to mention mythic history), and because it reproduces that history every time it comes around. Each individual festival has its own characteristics, renouncers told me, with its own stories and a particular place in Kumbh history. The Ganges changed course in Allahabad between 1989 and 2001; the fears about *akhāṛā* rivalry increased after Jūnā-Nirañjanī hostilities in Hardwar in 1998; the international press corps practically outnumbered the *nāgā* ranks in 2001. Just as each Kumbh location has its own flavor—Hardwar is a city, Kumbhnagar a flood plain—each Kumbh event has its own quality.

When, after the Melā, our small camp repaired to Varanasi, Bābā tried to describe the feeling of this particular festival: "This Melā was . . . what's the word? Soft. Silky." Bābā's feeling that this Melā was a gentle one came from the peace that prevailed between the *akhāṛās,* and also, I suspect, from the continual respect that people showed him because of his age, experience, and capacity to deliver religious teachings to people from many different backgrounds. "This Melā," as Bābā talked about it, was a unique historical event that had its own character and effects—a point on a cycle that has looked slightly different every time it has come around for the past two millennia.

But at the same time, "this Melā" was the latest in a very recognizable series. The Kumbh is a testament to communal longevity and a loud public demonstration of structural continuity, a cycle of regeneration, when *akhāṛās* revitalize themselves through grand processions and prominent ritual bathing, and also refill the ranks with new initiates. Rādhā Giri came to the Allahabad Kumbh for two days only, for Maunī Amāvasyā. I asked her how this Kumbh was for her, and she characteristically waved her hand away to downplay its importance: "It's a Melā," she replied, like any other. The festival experience is eminently familiar, a repeated series of political intrigues, initiations, promotions, and spectacles. If you've been to one, you know the drill. The very nature of the festival's repetitive quality reproduces renouncer history, in place, over time.

The cyclical nature of time in Hindu thinking applies to all natural systems, earthly and divine alike. All of human history comes in cyclical form, renouncers told me, just like the cycle of birth and death. The sun rises daily, the moon waxes and wanes every fortnight, and each planet charts its revolution cycle through the constellations of the sky. These natural rhythms determine renouncers' actions throughout their lives, in the pursuit of knowledge and as part of their practice—and not just in festival settings. During my fieldwork in the Himalayas, one *sādhvī* used the same metaphor I heard at the Kumbh about the correlation of natural light to knowledge: "It's important to get up before the sun rises," she told me, "because Sūrya (the sun) is the Lord of Knowledge." Also, she went on, "night is when nature sleeps"; by being awake when nature, too, is waking, at the daily point of transition between light and dark, a practitioner can reap the most intense power of the natural world.

Cyclical action is a natural law. Renouncers expressed all sorts of collective concerns to me in terms of the *yuga* cycle, for example: the four *yugas,* or ages, run through their courses and start again. The *yuga* into which we are born irremediably impacts our social world and our collective behavior: the reason *sādhus* have a poor reputation, renouncers told me, the reason *sādhus* behave badly, and the reason so few householders can accurately identify a wise *sādhu,* is simply because it is the Kālī Yuga, the final, degenerate age of time, when few humans are capable of acting well or seeing clearly.

Cyclical time, like circuited space, is a feature of nature and form, Prakṛti. The material world—even the places where gods and demons live—is marked by constant change and flux, and an unending cycle of birth and death. Time, change, nature, and death are of a singular system for renouncers, and *amṛta,* the nectar of immortality, is the potion that can supersede them all. Conquering death for the gods means eternal play, but conquering nature for religious aspirants means rather eternal liberation, *mokṣa,* from the natural cycle of *saṃsāra. Saṃsāra* is an endless cycle not only of birth and death, but also of attachment and illness, or social and material suffering.

Renouncers strive to break the twin cycles of nature and *saṃsāra* in order to re-merge with the absolute plane, Puruṣa, where sacred knowledge exists in a formless, changeless—timeless—state. A scholar of Śaṅkarācārya's scriptures explained to me:

> When nothing is growing or decaying, there is no need for time. We think, "It's like this in the past; it will be like this in the future." When the object is going through a process of change, the time factor comes into being. Anything that goes through any kind of change is not reality. Reality is something that is unborn, that does not go through any change, is immortal.

The religious knowledge to which the renouncer community collectively aspires at the Kumbh Melā means release from the natural cycles of time and repetition, and of birth and death. The dominant ritual practice of the festival—bathing in the confluence of rivers where immortal nectar briefly flows—clearly articulates renouncers' religious goals and ideology. The nectar's ability to overcome death translates for the deities who drink it into an ability to live forever. For the community of renouncers who bathe in it, however, the nectar translates into an ability to attain religious knowledge freed from the circuits and cycles of space and time.

The Transcendence of Time

Rituals everywhere mark specific moments in time even as they mark the repetitive nature of existence—astral bodies, which move into the same configurations cyclically, are particularly well suited to the determination of ritual periods. Each Kumbh Melā festival hovers between being a repeated event on a recognizable cycle and generating a particular historical event determined by the reality of temporal shift and the dynamics of social structures. The performances of the renouncer community during these occasions integrate the particularities of the Kumbh with the cyclical nature of the Kumbh, just as they mediate between the experience of time and the experience of transcendence.

The ritual of the Melā derives its power from its ability to encompass and articulate all these variants of time and experience. The communal transcendence of time, in Pāgal Bābā's narrative, supersedes both linear time and cyclical time. "Reality doesn't travel in time and space," Bābā told me. "Reality is beyond time and beyond space. If you put it between time and space, it's not reality, it's creation. The more you go inside," he continued, "the more you don't need these outside things." By describing the Kumbh Melā as "inside"—it was located at Prayāg Rāj, the king of confluences, and occurred when Jupiter was in Aries, the head of the zodiac, thereby serving as the very center of the universe, the calm at the center of a cyclone—Pāgal Bābā suggested that the festival acted as a kind of centripetal point in space and time. At the holiest place during the holiest time, he was suggesting, we had a point of collective access through which we could slip inside space and time, and transport ourselves beyond them. The more we attuned ourselves to the cycles of time, the closer we could come to leaving time behind altogether.

I heard renouncers refer to different ways of being beyond time—as immortal gods, as realized *yogīs* cognizant of the illusory quality of time, or as members of a collective without past or future. For Pāgal Bābā, the experience of being beyond time at the Kumbh was clearly a product of collective effort:

> Flows of exchange have happened. Everyone made a change in their life to come here. The Melā is people coming together. It's people meeting together and discussing, about all the things in life. About religious, social, personal problems, physical problems, and trying to find solutions.[10]

The metaphors for collective experience in Bābā's narrative were the converging flows of the three Melā rivers: the two real, visible rivers, whose confluence symbolized a "meeting of energy," and the invisible Sarasvatī, who symbolized "what's going on invisibly between us." Bābā elaborated, "When two people come together, there is energy. If I am between, I get a little bit." For Pāgal Bābā, the collective gathering had a kind of exponential ripple effect, where each exchange was reflected by hundreds of thousands of *sādhus* and millions of pilgrims. The literal exchange of money, goods, medicine, and food, and the metaphysical exchange of energy sparked a collective reaction that was powerful enough to propel all of us beyond our everyday lives, into the expansive realm of sacred existence, beyond space and time.

Through collective rituals like the Kumbh Melā, Durkheim suggests that religious communities achieve "collective effervescence," a communal experience that transcends the bounds of what he calls profane daily life (1995 [1912]). In the narratives I heard, renouncers' experiences of the Melā sound very similar to the boundless transcendence that Durkheim describes. But I would add to Durkheim's social model the capacity of the material world to mediate between the experience of effervescence on one hand, and the experience of history on the other, both produced by the collective space-time of the Melā. Even as renouncers march to the bathing areas to experience ritual transcendence, they wear the medals of army decoration and carry the weapons of warfare as symbolic tributes to their military history. Grounded in the rivers of Allahabad and guided by the planets and stars, renouncers perform a bathing ritual at the Kumbh that at once replays their unique history and transports them "beyond time" altogether.

As soon as the Maunī Amāvasyā bath took place, younger *sādhus* began planning their next meeting point, deciding which upcoming Melā would provide the same level of energy and spirit. On the evening of January 24, only hours after the holiest bath in twelve years, I heard *sādhus* planning to go to Kathmandu for the Śiva Rātrī Melā, a month later, at Paśupatināth. Indeed, at Paśupati during Śiva Rātrī, a few weeks after the *sādhu* camps of the Kumbh had closed down, I saw an exchange between two *sādhus* that confirmed for me the role of the Kumbh as a seminal event in renouncers' experiences. A young *sādhu* saw an older woman renouncer he knew, and his face lit up. They were obviously pleased to see one another, and it had clearly been some time since they had last met. His first question to her was, "Did you go to the Kumbh?" She had not, she said; she had been ill and had stayed put in Bengal. But he had been to Allahabad at the ritually auspicious time, and his face was animated as he told her so. His question, her response, and his ensuing energetic account of the festival showed how the Kumbh Melā was a pivotal point in space and time on this renouncer's pilgrimage routes, an event in time around which he had organized his travels.

5 ❀ Kathmandu

THE BODY IN PLACE

Renouncers physically depart from the spaces of householder social worlds by leaving. Festival occasions provide an opportunity for collective transcendence, temporarily. But in everyday life, breaking away from the material world is more complicated because renouncers cannot just leave their bodies behind. The body is the source of paradoxical experience in *sādhu* narratives: on one hand, it is the most personal symbol of the deluded world of form; on the other, it is a precious vehicle of religious practice and a tool of perception. Balancing these conflicting views of embodiment is at the core of renouncers' bodily austerities. Keeping the body at bay, while at the same time using it to further religious experience, is the dominant mode of practice in renouncers' lives.

Scholars writing on space have convincingly argued that space becomes place through the articulation of bodily experience (Casey 1996; Harvey 1996, 2000). Scholars writing on embodiment have come to a similar conclusion, but from the other direction: bodily experience articulates meaning in the outer world (Csordas 1994). The renouncers I spoke with partly agreed with these scholars: the physical world of form, they told me, is perceived through bodily cognizance. The body is the marker of space, landscape, and indeed, all external matter. But my informants did not discuss bodily experience with the appreciation of phenomenological theorists.

On the contrary, bodies (along with space, time, and the social worlds that embodiment produces) are, in renouncers' views, illusory

« Sādhu with armful of jaṭā

fragments of a dualistic plane. The more an embodied person is unconsciously affected by his or her experiences, my informants implied, the farther he or she is from reaching his or her religious goals. From *sādhus'* perspectives, undisciplined bodily experience can be distracting and deceptive. The discipline of renouncers' religious practice is to restrict or overcome body-mind activity and thought, which, they argue, are deluded identifications. The epithet for accomplished sages in Sanskrit literature, *jitendriya-*, translates as "conqueror of the senses."[1]

Māyā

During the first months of my fieldwork, I was unable to have a conversation about the experience of embodiment with a renouncer that went any further than a basic oral version of Advaita hypotheses on the nature of illusory matter. The body was nothing, the body didn't matter, the body was just an outer form, the body would die: I heard all these phrases repeatedly, from men and from women (Khandelwal 1997). I took this consistency seriously, surmising that this position reflected a fundamental aspect of renouncers' religious philosophies, but I also felt frustrated, like I was hearing the party line over and over again. How was I to explain renouncers' very visible bodily practices? Although renouncers insisted that their bodies were immaterial and irrelevant, they bathed (usually meticulously), they ate (sometimes with great ritual), and they took great care to adorn themselves (always with clean and symbolically appropriate clothes and ornaments). Even if the body was nothing, it also clearly meant *something*, and maintaining it properly was a large part of what renouncers did all day.

Mukta Giri Mai, the poor, elderly Nepali widow, was the first *sādhvī* I met who talked to me at length; she also discussed ideas about embodiment with me without automatically resorting to classic explanations of bodies as external casings. She was at the very fringe of society, too much of a burden for anyone really to care about. I met her at Paśupatināth Temple in Kathmandu, soon after Mahā Śiva Rātrī, the annual festival in honor of Śiva. As one of the central sites for Śiva worship on the subcontinent, Paśupatināth hosts thousands of renouncers during the festival every year.[2] Most dutifully stay only three days, in accordance with their peripatetic status. Mukta Giri was one of very few renouncers to stay on at Paśupati after the holy night, because, she said, she had fallen ill and could not travel. Her body had given way—her joints ached, her breath was strained, and her skin was cracked and painful.

At sixty-seven, Mai was an elderly *sādhvī* when I first met her in February 2000. She planned at that time to return to her base at the Nepali Ashram in Hardwar, but within half a year she had moved back to Paśupatināth for good, choosing to live out her last years in her native Nepal. "Moving this body here and there and back and forth! I don't like it anymore," she explained to me. "I just want to stay in one place." Her age, her illness, and her conscious decision to stop moving—to give her body a rest from the difficult circumstances of *sādhu* life—meant that I met her during a period of active reflection on the nature of embodiment and the inevitability of death.

Rather than speaking about her body as a gross external form that would undoubtedly decay, Mukta Giri's language about her body referred to emotions and circumstances. "There is no love [*māyā*] for a *yogī*'s body," she told me as we sat together one afternoon. "We live in the jungle."

Her construction certainly reflected a view that I had heard from others: There *should be* no love for the body, since the body was nothing and should be consciously denigrated. But she also invoked an emotional state, love—or rather, its absence—in the context of embodied *sādhu* life. Love, *māyā*, is also the word for illusion, and refers to the attachment that grows in a web of social connections (Lamb 2000). Being a renouncer requires detachment from the body, Mai implied: to let emotions and caring actions take over would be indulgent and unwise. Attachment to material forms is precisely what *yogīs* are supposed to renounce, because they belie social and emotional involvement in the physical plane of *saṃsāra*.

But Mai's choice to refer to herself as a *yogī* also revealed a respect for the uses of the human body.[3] A body is the only material form a *yogī* is required to possess, and in turn, attaining divine knowledge is possible, many renouncers told me, *because* we possess human bodies. They are the vehicles of our human lives. Even if the human form is nothing but a material, sense-obsessed object from which a *yogī* must detach, Mukta Giri could not speak of her body with scorn. Her tone as she spoke of *yogīs'* bodies was almost one of sympathy, or regret, that the body was the fall-out of a *yogī*'s lifestyle, apparent in her use of the word "love," and in the way she stroked her ailing knee. *Māyā* carries sweet connotations of indulgence—babies and children are loved, as are close girlfriends, people who are slightly indulged because of the degree of affection. Because of her *sādhu*'s lifestyle, she was unable to give her body the care it deserved.

Mai called herself a *yogī* in part because *yogīs* are respected figures who engage in physical hardship and sacrifice, *tapas*. A *yogī*'s wandering lifestyle contributes to the aches and pains of the mortal body, she argued, because being a *yogī* requires a willingness to live in challenging material conditions which will take their toll. The "jungle," as discussed in chapter 3, symbolically refers to that place away from physical luxuries as well as social encounters and emotional entanglements. Even in the large city of Kathmandu, Mukta Giri Mai assuredly told me, *sādhus* live in the "jungle," meaning not a literal location but a place for the isolated, uninterrupted pursuit of religious austerities. The discipline to live in defiance of bodily obscurations, such as sensory indulgence and mental disturbance, is the *tapas* of yogic life. The physical hardships that renouncers require of themselves (symbolized by—and made literal in—the jungle) bring about a higher state of awareness, renouncers told me, and with it, detachment from the material plane.

The three perspectives on embodiment that I have interpreted in Mai's statement—antagonism towards the body, respect for the potential of the body, and a practical refusal to indulge the body—make up the core of this chapter. In most *sādhus*' narratives, as in Mukta Giri's comment, these three models were not so much separate worldviews as different approaches that were seamlessly combined in the realities of lived experience. Finding a mid-point between thinking of the body as a burden and thinking of the body as a divine tool was the heart of discussions I had with *sādhus* on the nature of embodiment. For the *sādhus* with whom I spoke and lived, *tapas* was not so much a singular action as the discipline of living that mid-point. *Tapas* is that practice of *yogī* life which maintains a tenuous balance between abhorring the body and indulging it.

In my discussions with renouncers, the body was never discussed with abject horror, even if it was a burdensome way to negotiate experience. Rather, if properly trained, the human body was a means to higher religious knowledge. I see renouncers' bodily disciplines as a way of mediating what Parry calls an "ideological tension" between denigrating the body and glorifying the body (1992:501). Through bodily practice, renouncers find a lived balance between regarding the body as filth, pollution, and a sack of impurities—something that will inevitably decay and die—on one hand, and a treasure to master or know—a tool that can reach high levels of religious achievement—on the other. Ascetic bodily disciplines both control the body's obscurations and support the body's revelations.

The Model of Nature

My conversations with Mukta Giri took place on the top of the Paśupatināth hill, in the Śaiva temple complex which celebrates the generative organs of divine forces. Named for Śiva in his peaceful and productive mode (the literal translation of Paśupati is "Lord of the Animals"), the temple glorifies nature, creation, fertility, and the manifestation of form. The main object of worship at the central temple is a five-headed *liṅgam*, which represents the phallus of Lord Śiva in all its aspects. Each head corresponds to a direction, a natural element, and an aspect of Śiva (Dangol 1993): one face celebrates his enjoyment of the material world, for example, another his status as a *mahāyogin*, a great ascetic.

Of the many faces of Śiva, the Paśupatināth Temple honors not Śiva the ascetic or Śiva the destroyer, but Śiva in the gentle mode of nature and creation, a divine force choosing to manifest in embodied form.[4] Other translations of Paśupati might be "Lord of Embodied Souls" or "Lord of the Noose of Materiality." Numerous ithyphallic—that is, with phallus erect—representations of Śiva sprinkle the temple grounds (Aran 1978): the complex is filled with symbols of creation, and even in the center of dense urban life, the compound forests are still heavily populated by monkeys, deer, bulls, and cows. The frequent negations of the body in both textual and oral Hindu parlance are belied by temples like these: worship of form and nature has a place in Hindu practice as well. Locations where divine bodies lie are important holy places for *sādhus* to come do their *sādhanā*, or religious practice. Dudh Bābā estimated that about one hundred resident *sādhus* live on the temple grounds, perhaps evenly split between men and women. Many thousands more visit on pilgrimage every year, particularly during Śiva Rātrī.

Upriver, the Guhyeśwarī compound is one of the most sacred goddess temples in the Kathmandu Valley. The goddess herself is represented only by a *kumbh,* the open pot or vessel thought to represent the torso of the body in yogic texts,[5] and the sacred divine *yoni,* or vulva, in the context of a popular goddess temple. Guhyeśwarī, the Goddess of the Secret Part, is worshipped in the form of a hypaethral open shrine. As the Ganges River and the holy terrain of India itself are respectively called Gaṅgā-Mā and Bhārat-Mā, Guhyeśwarī is explicitly referred to as the Great Mother, she who creates and protects. (The Newār tradition venerates "eight mothers" of the Kathmandu Valley, each exceptionally powerful). I saw a number of young couples from various Nepali ethnic groups and religious traditions elope here, having developed illicit "love marriages." My friends in the area explained that they came to Guhyeśwarī because she was "Mā," a mother goddess who could bless an otherwise unsanctioned union: she is thought among Kathmandu residents of all religious traditions to be one the most important *śakti pīṭhas*—places of power, usually where Satī's body parts fell—in the valley (Pal 1975; Dowman 1981). The active worship of Guhyeśwarī at the Paśupati compound clearly shows the popular reverence for the sacred maternal figure who gives form and life and who, in her infinite wisdom, both cares for her offspring and metes out what her children deserve.[6]

The *liṅgam* of Lord Paśupati and the *yoni* of Mā Guhyeswarī iconographically represent the divine sexual organs of creation: they are gods whose genders matter. The word *liṅgam* actually translates as "sign": bodily sex is that which differentiates or marks. The two temples are partnered as a procreative couple—Nepali religious architecture dictates that each Śiva shrine should have his consort (Slusser 1982)—and together they birth the world of form. Each deity fulfills his or her role as mother or father: many renouncers explicitly spoke of themselves and the entire material world as the offspring of the two great deities.[7] When I asked Mukta Giri why *sādhus* came to Paśupatināth specifically, she said, "They're our father and mother! We're just like Paśupati's children." As she spoke, she rocked her arms, as if holding a baby, "Pārvatī is our mother." These divine parents together symbolize fertility and creation, birth and form, and the sacred nature of embodiment.

The temples of Paśupati and his consort are revered by Hindus throughout the subcontinent, despite their location outside Indian borders. They are a point of Nepali pride: both Paśupatināth and Guhyeśwarī are constructed in traditional Newār architecture styles, where the main deity resides in the center of a large courtyard. The image of Lord Paśupati is housed in a Newār pagoda, with detailed carvings on the roof struts. The symbol of the goddess Guhyeśwarī sits in an open-roofed structure with only four carved brass snake deities as her ceiling.[8] The temples are covered in gold and silver plating, carved by world-famous Newār craftsmen; the site is one of Kathmandu Valley's seven UNESCO World Heritage Sites. An exact replica of Paśupatināth is one of Varanasi's prominent pilgrim attractions, and the Newār architecture stands in stark contrast to the other temples on this circuit (Eck 1982). The Paśupati Area Development Trust has been generously funded by royal coffers, a symbol of Nepal as—until 2006—the world's only Hindu monarchy. That famous Hindu temples are located on Nepali soil translates into nationalist pride among local shopkeepers, too, who told me that Indian pilgrims were pushy and cheap and that, unlike authentic Nepali *sādhus* who came to Paśupati, Indian *sādhus* just came to the temple to beg.

The twin temples, separate structures linked through geography and myth, sit coupled on the same river, the Bagmati, the site of Kathmandu's main cremation *ghāṭs*. The site of these temples of the body aptly symbolizes the predicament of existence for Hindu renouncers: Paśupatināth may be a temple of origin and birth, but it is also a site of decay and death: the smell of burning flesh permeates the grounds, and the dead and the mourning congregate on the same river that would have mythological maternal qualities if it were not so filled with garbage. For the renouncers I spoke with, nature (meaning both Prakṛti and earthly materiality) encompasses the dimensions of form, matter, differentiated space, and change and dynamism. That which has form, Prakṛti dictates, must change over time: birth, growth, decay, and death are all qualities of nature and embodiment.

Mukta Giri sometimes compared her body to the natural features of the temple compound in which she lived: the new spring leaves that grew on the trees in the courtyard would, like her own frail frame, decay and die. As the leaves grow and fall, she gestured, so too do our bodies.[9] Her physical form, like the forest, could only subscribe to the processes of nature. For Mukta Giri as for other renouncers, making analogies between the human body and cycles of nature helped produce neutral observations on the body's decay and a detached acceptance of death. Death as a part of nature's cycle is prominently visible at Paśupatināth, a place where generation gives way to cremation, and the symbols of fertility sit alongside the rituals for the dead.[10] The body is ephemeral, the symbols cry out. Do not be too attached to your living form, for it cannot endure.

The image of burning bodies turning to ash on the Paśupati cremation pyres clearly suggests a final mode of interpreting the mechanics of nature, as the material body's return to the elements (see Parry 1992). The five organic elements—fire, water, earth, air, and the ground of them all, space—are the irreducible building blocks of matter, my informants told me, the stuff which makes up the physical bodies of people and places. Substance exchange with the earth (Alter 1992) is possible precisely because the earth and earthly creatures share the same organic elements. As we see in the story of Satī's decomposing body sprinkled across the Himalayas, bodies, places, and earthly landscapes are connected through the shared elements of matter. The bodies of every living creature, the forms of mountains and rivers, the characteristics of holy places (and even homes, in Daniel's [1984] account), and the aspects of renouncers' *dhūnīs* are reducible to the same five qualities of materiality, the five lowest common denominators of nature. When bodies so obviously reduce to gray carbon and flowing water, renouncers ask, how can we mistake them for our true selves? Religious life requires that we view our bodies as ephemeral, mutability being the true nature of all material elements, and thereby more easily detach from bodily emotions, passions, and obscurations.

The Obscurations of the Body

The dominant textual view of the body in Hindu thought is as a transient casing of the higher soul, or *ātman*. The *Laws of Manu* and the *Sannyāsa Upaniṣads* are quite vehement in their denigration of what they call putrid outer matter. If the body is the shallow form of the internal "Self" which the renouncer wishes to liberate, embodiment stands between a renouncer and his or her true, liberated spirit. Manu is not gentle, therefore, in his opinions of the human body:

> a foul-smelling, tormented, impermanent dwelling-place of living beings, filled with urine and excrement, pervaded by old age and sorrow, infested with illness, and polluted by passion, with bones for beams, sinews for

> cords, flesh and blood for plaster, and skin for the roof. (verses 6.76–677 in Doniger and Smith 1991:124–125)

Sections of the *Upaniṣads* are no kinder: "If a man finds joy in the body—a heap of flesh, blood, pus, feces, urine, tendons, marrow, and bones—that fool will find joy even in hell" (*Nāradaparivrājaka Upaniṣad* verse 144 in Olivelle 1992:179).

Living renouncers were not as disgusted by their physical forms as are these texts. But they did often and in many ways emphasize how *difficult* their bodies were, and how consistently challenging it was to live in embodied form, in the grip of the illusion of reality, at the whim of emotion, and with the physical discomfort of illness. Bodies were external and illusory, decaying and distracting, physical annoyances that had to be accommodated. Renouncers emphasized to me again and again that the body is superfluous at the level of religious experience and action. The real work of religious knowledge and liberation happens *despite* the body, on interior and subtle levels of experience.

Mukta Giri very clearly pointed to her heart when I asked her about the body: inside was what counted, her *ātman;* outside, peripheral to her religious enterprise, was her body, her *sarīr.* A Hardwar *sādhvī* told me simply, "There are physiological elements to the body—*nadīs* and such—but they are not important. In this body there is *ātman.* And *ātman* is holiness." For these renouncers and for many others, the body is nothing but an ephemeral sheath that is consistently misinterpreted as real, that will grow old and wither, and that, in its fragility, is the ground for imbalance and disease.

Renouncers on the *jñāna mārga,* or path of knowledge, spoke of the body not as a horrid mass but as an illusory product of the mind, and as such, a potential trap. The renouncer's goal, I was told, is to "eliminate identification with the body. It's a weakness you identify with. On this *jñāna mārga,* we say that initially we are absorbed in material forms, and we need to get away from that level." The difficulty of living as humans in embodied form is that we confuse our bodies for our selves—we "identify" with our bodily needs and states. Bodily experience is not, in this model, a source of knowledge or being, but a distraction and an occlusion of knowledge. Differentiated bodily forms are illusory manifestations of a unitary reality, and bodies mask or obscure the divine force that equally pervades all physical nature. Renouncers spoke of the body not as terribly impure, but as dangerous in its ability to trick our higher consciousness. By producing mental distractions and false emotions of identification, the body takes over.

As discussed in chapter 1, *sādhus'* desires to distance themselves from physical and mental phenomena in order to liberate their souls sound very reminiscent of a Cartesian split between spirit and matter.[11] Some renouncers suggested that matter is the form of spirit (in the model of Prakṛti molding form out of Puruṣa), an idea which I take up more fully below. But even these *sādhus* insisted that the human experience of having a body is powerful; as a result, bodies and bodily experience take on disproportionate import. I heard a number of renouncers praise their *gurus* for being able to live with a minimum of sustenance, eating only what fit into their two hands, or wearing very few clothes in frigid climates. Their *gurus'* bodies no longer distracted them, renouncers told me; food and clothing took up no mental space. "He was completely beyond body identification," one *sādhvī* said of her *guru*. The illusion had been broken—he saw through bodily delusion—and he was living on the plane of divine reality. But for most renouncers, physical embodiment and emotional obscurations still presented obstacles.

Illness and Decay

The most obvious burdensome quality of embodiment for *yogīs* was the enormous amount of attention that had to be paid to illness. Poor public health in South Asia[12] is particularly pronounced in the *sādhu* community: renouncers by and large live in extremely difficult physical conditions, often sleeping outdoors or on stone, and with limited nourishment. Almost without exception, every *sādhu* I met had health problems, and most spoke to me at length about them. In part this was because I was someone who might be able to provide Western medicines or money to buy local ones. But the renouncers I spoke to were also clearly undergoing a great deal of physical suffering, and the burdensome nature of illness gave rise to much spontaneous discussion. When Mukta Giri told me there was no love for a *yogī*'s body, she was also commenting on how many renouncers suffered from serious health problems.

Mukta Giri was often preoccupied with her own physical ailments. She spoke often of her two cataract operations, comparing which was better done, the one in India or the one in Nepal (in a nationalist moment, she eventually decided that Nepali medical care was better than Indian). She showed me bad skin on the heel of the foot, frequently and absentmindedly squeezed her thigh in discomfort, and complained of the dark blotches and the heat of illness. She was not particularly interested in going to see a doctor, although at times I encouraged her to and offered to pay. These pains were for her part of aging, and part of life as a renouncer. Her illnesses marked her as mortal and reminded her of the fragility of the human body.

Pāgal Bābā was fighting a stomach infection when he was living in a Hardwar hotel in autumn 2000. It was the first time he had taken medicine in his life, he told me, and he was highly frustrated by the intrusion of illness and medication in his daily practices. He had never eaten breakfast, but now he had to buy bread every morning, "just for this damn medicine!" Being old and ill were reasons to be sedentary for Bābā. When we spoke about his days as a wandering *sādhu,* he would invariably sigh, "Now I'm old. I'm tired of traveling. I just want to stay in one place and meditate." The body was tired and sick, and so he needed to rest, heal, and stay in one place.

Rādhā Giri, too, was unwell for most of the period I knew her. She had lived in a small tent on the banks of the Ganges for over two decades, and was a heavy *chillum* smoker as well. My standard greeting to Mai, "How are you?" was invariably greeted with a long litany of aches, pains, and bodily troubles. She insisted on sticking her tongue out to show me just how unwell she was—it was orange and pockmarked from years of smoking—and she touched each part of her body as she described her hip problem, her throat problem, her aching joints and extremities. Like Mukta Giri, she seemed unwilling to go to a doctor—these were the troubles of an aging body—but life was negatively affected nonetheless.

The child Mai reared, Gaṅgā Giri, also had physical problems that troubled Mai. The little girl had fallen off the small temple platform beneath the two trees near their tent and broken her arm, which had required an operation and the insertion of a steel rod. Mai's focus on the child's illness was certainly a plea for money for medicine, especially for Gaṅgā's doctor's fees. (When she insisted that I accompany them to the doctor for Gaṅgā's appointment, I was terrified that I would have to witness a medical procedure, but it was only a checkup, which the doctor performed in a tea shop. My role, I think, was to add some legitimacy to their claims for medical attention.) These maladies were also an indication of how much trouble the body could be. While Rādhā Giri fed the child medicine and took her to a doctor, she was uninterested in treating her own ailments. Aches and pains were simply the nature of embodiment, she implied as she waved her hand away to my questions. How am I, she retorted, as she touched each part of her body: my body is unwell. But such is the nature of bodies. Bodies fall ill, from when they are very small, until they are old. They shall never be any other way.

Gender and Emotion

Gendered bodies are the most obvious example of dualism on the material plane, and are no doubt the referents for the paired forces of creation, Puruṣa and Prakṛti. *Sādhu* rhetoric emphasizes that renunciation is able to overcome the limits of gender, since the disembodied state of divine liberation knows no differentiation, least of all gross physical distinction (Khandelwal 1997). In my conversations with Mukta Giri on top of Paśupatināth Hill, amid the sculptures of *yonis* and *liṅgams,* she insisted on the irrelevance of gender distinctions: "Bodies are all the same. Men and women are no different." Every time I broached the subject of women's bodies, she repeated, "Everything is one. One!" As Khandelwal puts it, renouncers speak of gender as "a mere attribute of the body" (1997:80). Gender might be understood as one manifestation of a person's *karma*, whereby past actions determine the nature of bodily form for subsequent rebirths.[13]

Khandelwal shows, however, that in spite of this rhetoric renouncers are treated very much on the basis of gender. My women informants, too, told me that their gender made renunciation more difficult, both logistically and emotionally. Khandelwal documents the physical risks and sexual threats the *sannyāsinīs* she met experienced, and also the struggles some women encountered to be accepted as renouncers (1997). One *sādhvī* laughed at me when I told her how frustrated I became when, as a lone woman, I was not allowed to stay in a Hardwar ashram. *Sādhvīs,* she said, experience such discrimination all the time.

In my informants' narratives, women's bodies were particularly prone to producing emotions.[14] Early in my relationship with Rādhā Giri, I asked her what the differences were in men's and women's experiences of renunciation. She told me that renunciation was more difficult for women than for men because women became more attached to people they cared for, especially children. Male renouncers, she argued, could be carried away by lust and not feel the same degree of responsibility, emotionally or otherwise. Much later I discovered that the child she raised was the product of a sexual relationship between a male renouncer and a householder woman. As a woman renouncer, she suggested, Rādhā Giri felt responsible for the needs of both the renouncer community and the local community she lived in, and had stepped in where she was needed. She clearly felt the burden of raising a child that was not hers even though the father's child, a fellow renouncer, did not.

Similarly, the only area where Mukta Giri allowed for difference between men and women was in the sphere of emotion: men experienced less. For both *sādhvīs,* the female body perpetuated worldly attachments through its production of emotional bonds. Ironically, their view resonates with a common perception that the female body provides a natural ground for renunciation, because women are born with the love and mothering instincts that characterize great renouncers (Khandelwal 1997). Women saints are thought of as a natural phenomenon because of—or in spite of, if we consider *sādhus'* own accounts—their capacity for maternal emotion (Ramanujan 1982).

Despite her rhetoric about the bliss of renunciation, Mukta Giri acknowledged that leaving her children was emotionally painful. "How could it not be hard?" she asked. Although Mukta Giri had left her children in order to become a renouncer and Rādhā Giri had adopted a child many years after becoming a renouncer, both women referred to their relationships with children as a source of emotion that had to be dealt with. Both also implied that negative experiences around sexuality, marriage, and sexual roles had influenced their decisions to renounce. Leaving householder life, I surmised, allowed the renunciation of gendered, emotional life.[15] Renunciation was for these *sādhvīs* an explicit attempt to depart from the social role of womanhood and the sometimes physical experience of painful emotion.

In my conversations with these women, emotions and passions appear as mental activities that keep us trapped in dualist reality; as features of the mind, they are produced and experienced by the body.

The body produces sensations and emotions that sway us, my informants told me, and these must be kept in control. Experiencing attachment is a "weakness," one *sādhvī* told me, but with practice, she said, emotion gradually dissipates. The point of religious discipline is to train mental activity to a point where a practitioner can discriminate between experiences that obscure and experiences that reveal. My informants talked about emotion as a bodily experience that is distracting and deluded; with proper training and discipline, however, bodily experience can become a tool of religious knowledge.

The Revelations of the Body

Despite renouncers' negative narratives about their bodies and their arguments that organic matter obscures formless spirit, *sādhus'* thoughts on embodiment were not always derogatory. The poor reputation of bodies in some textual examples, and in some renouncers' experiences, reflects the religious goal of splitting the material body from the immortal soul. But the body is also our only hope. In an alternative view of embodiment in renouncer narratives, human bodies reflect the nature of the cosmos. The model of the five elements, for example, translates into praises for the glories of nature. The physical world is sacred, and our bodies are the most precious forms of all, the means through which we can perceive the world and experience life. Prakṛti, the Sanskrit term for the force of change and form, is also the Hindi and the Nepali word for physical nature. From this viewpoint, there is no difference between nature and body.

To help me sort out what seemed like contradictory views on the body, I spoke to Narmada Puri, a Western *sādhvī* of thirty years. "On one hand, it's illusory, nothing, decrepit," I began. "On the other," she continued for me, "it is a temple and it is your duty to keep it as proper as you can. It's a boat for meditation, a vessel. It's what you do *sādhanā* with. If you have no body, you cannot sit [for meditation]; if you have no *prāṇa* [or breath] you cannot do *prāṇāyāma* [breathing exercises]. This body is your lifetime. It's what you have been given in this life to pass the time." Religious practice—indeed, *any* practice—is impossible without a body. "God gave us bodies," Mukta Giri told me emphatically. "Without them, how would we exist? Breathing, walking, living—how would we do it?"

The capacity of the body to contain, reproduce, and mirror divinity shows us another dimension of embodiment in the Hindu worldview. While many classical texts and textual analysts emphasize the fundamental impurity of the body and bodily processes (and women's bodies in particular), most come around to arguing that the body is the living manifestation of transcendence. The worldly body is not only a source of illness and emotion, desire and misery, but also a representation of divinity and a way to experience it. Even Manu—the lawgiver from whom so many arguments about the impurity of the Hindu body are drawn—emphasizes the use of yoga not as the way to escape the body but as the way to see divinity in the body: "Through yoga [the ascetic] should meditate on the subtleness of the supreme Soul and its presence in the highest and lowest bodies" (verse 6.65 in Doniger and Smith 1991:123). Olivelle points out that, as a collection, the *Sannyāsa Upaniṣads* describe the body of the renouncer as having a particularly "sacred nature": the renouncer's body is the "visible image of god," or the embodied form of the absolute (Olivelle 1992:69).[16] Both Manu and the *Sannyāsa Upaniṣads* suggest that the body is uniquely capable of attaining religious knowledge.

Contemporary practitioners also refer to the positive potential of the body. Parry's ascetic informants insist on the authority of the *Gauda Purāṇa* text, which states, "The wealth of the *yogī* is his body. There is nothing more precious than this." After fully elaborating Hindu views of bodily impurities, Parry argues that the body has an inherent "capacity for transformation, refinement, and even perfection" (1992: 501). Gold's lay informants insist that the deity is ultimately to be found within their own bodies, not in any external shrine or image visited on pilgrimage; they describe their bodies as the manifestations of their souls (1988). The parallel between the human body and the physical construction of a temple is an extremely common image in traditional texts, contemporary descriptions, and poetry across the subcontinent.[17]

In my fieldwork, too, some bodies were very publicly treated as manifestations of the divine. Lying on gold-threaded couches, well-respected *gurus* were often given massages by their disciples; during processions they sat under red- and gold-tasseled umbrellas and were gently fanned by junior members of their orders. Even at a crowded *dhūnī*, a *sevak* might massage a ranking *sādhu*'s calves after a meal or during a public discussion; disciples tended to the bodies of their *gurus* as they might a religious image. Renouncers are supposed to revere the spiritual and the "physical perfection" of their *gurus;* the body of a *guru* is seen as the perfectly refined substance of divinity (Alter 1992; Babb 1983, 1986). Even feet, physically and symbolically the lowest part of the body, are worthy of devotion if they belong to a high enough being. The most common gesture of respect to a senior *sādhu* is for supplicants to touch his or her feet with the right hand, or even the head. The sandals of patron saint Dattātreya lie on a high platform in a central courtyard of the Jūnā Akhāṛā Hardwar headquarters, poised to bless both visitors and residents.[18]

Many renouncers suggested that all bodies were equally divine, not just those of *gurus.* Rādhā Giri told me that the human body, like all bodies, was a manifestation of Bhagvān, or God. When I asked her about the meaning of the human body, she pointed to a cow wandering by, and to a dog barking. "These too are the forms of God," she answered, in a rare conversational response to my question. "Those creatures also have bodies: they're all forms of God." Rādhā Giri's claim that all bodies are forms of divinity argues against a gradation of holiness in materiality. Matter itself—Prakṛti, and all the forms she produces—is sacred. Even as renouncers told me that bodies consisted of ephemeral matter, they insisted that their human forms were also sacred vessels, divinely granted gifts through which to experience creation. Like participating in communal structures in order to split apart from society, using the body as a source of divine knowledge was a method of negotiating material reality.

The only way to know reality is to live it, renouncers repeatedly told me, and the only way to live it is to be embodied. Thus is the blessing of a human body: being embodied provides an opportunity to understand the nature of the divine. I asked Vedānta scholar Svāmī Rādhā Raman Ācāryajī why human bodies come to exist if the point is to dissolve again. First he chastised me for asking such a query, saying, "That question is not asked." But then he agreed to answer:

> The human body is valuable because we can find its root. This is what the body is for: to go back to the Self. And this is why the human body is so wonderful, because it has the ability to find the Self. In truth we can say there isn't any creation, but the snakes are still biting us. Like in a dream you're still screaming. You have to wake up before it's okay. So that's the way out. And if it's not here at all—if it's just a collective illusion—well, then, that's fine too.

Once the cosmic play has begun, having a body is the condition of participating at all: no spirit is possible without nature.

Renouncers' bodies are the tools they have to understand the cosmic system of which they are a part. If the body is nature, appreciating its wonder can be one of the most salient metaphors and most important teaching tools of life, as renouncers tell it. The laws that govern the material world—the breakdown and interaction of the elements, the inevitability of the cycle of growth, death, and regeneration, the responses to actions that create reactions—are divine processes, with an inexhaustible internal logic. By understanding their bodies through yoga practices, renouncers suggested, and by using their own bodies as teaching tools, they could come to understand these laws of nature, and in turn develop such a degree of physical awareness that they could heal other people's bodies.

Yoga Practices

The philosophical and practical systems of yoga rely directly on the potential of the body to facilitate religious understanding. Few Śaiva *daśnāmī bābās* practice *haṭha yoga* as a full-time way of life, but many *sādhus* do have a personal meditation practice, and yogic interpretations of the body ground most renouncers' approaches towards their bodies. Physical *āsanas,* "seats" or postures, were described to me as part of a daily regimen and as a way of maintaining and preparing the body for meditation (*dhyāna*). Although less important than meditation, *āsanas* are probably a part of most renouncers' practices, but they are usually conducted early in the morning and in private. The most important part of physical yoga exercises for most renouncers is *prāṇāyāma,* techniques for the control of *prāṇā*, or breath, the body's "life-force."[19]

Sādhus who proudly announce or demonstrate their yogic prowess are not uncommon. A number of *sādhus* I met made a point of telling me that they engaged in yoga practice, as they invariably straightened their backs, inhaled strongly, and insisted on the impressive levels of strength and power they had attained. I came to the conclusion that *sādhus* who conduct yoga practices publicly tend to have ulterior motives, such as winning Western (and, in particular, female) disciples. A *sādhu* I met through Rādhā Giri volunteered the information that he did half an hour of yoga every day. "It keeps me strong!" he bellowed, as he flexed his bicep. One *yogī* I met on the Hardwar riverbank led me to his *dhūnī* and performed an elaborate ritual of breath, or *prāṇāyāma*. A good body reflected a good *ātman,* he said after standing on his head, while a body that wasn't strong couldn't properly sustain a soul. Apart from his obvious inclination to show off (and a rather odd insistence on calcium as critical to his yoga practice), his words countered the exclusively negative representations of the body I had heard from a number of *sādhus*. This renouncer's inner *ātman* could only flourish if the outer body was hearty.

Even if a minority of Śaiva *sādhus* engage in lengthy or rigorous *haṭha yoga* practices, almost all renouncers I spoke with had some knowledge or use for yogic views of the body, which make clear how the *yogī* aims to attain liberation physiologically. In addition to the vital winds, the human body contains seven *cakras,* or metaphysical wheels of energy, and many thousands of *nadīs* (literally, rivers), or energy channels in the body. The seven *cakras* are located on the spinal column, and with proper realizations of different levels of consciousness, these can be pierced by the serpentine *kuṇḍalinī* energy of the body that usually lies dormant at the base of the spine (cf. White 1996; Varenne 1976; Eliade 1958[1954]). Next to the central spinal channel, two primary lines of energy run up and down the right and left sides of the body. The two sides are respectively associated with moon and sun, coolness and heat, *tamas* and *rajas,* keeping the body wet and moist on one side and able to burn negative elements on the other (cf. Johari 1987; Desikachar 2000). If the *yogī* practices correctly, the energy of the body is properly directed through all these points and channels, and religious power and knowledge can awaken.

Renouncers laid out for me detailed symbolic equivalences (not always consistently) between the *cakras* of the body (particularly the belly, heart, and brain or mind), the elements of the earth, and the deities of the pantheon: these seven discrete physical locations constitute an explicit guide for religious experience.[20] The *cakras* are mnemonic devices for linking different aspects of experience, providing clear ways for a practitioner to connect his or her physical being with the outer world; the entire universe can then appear as an ordered system that lies within the physiological grasp of a human body. Through a system of equivalences, each body encompasses all aspects of the earth. Techniques for the control of *prāṇa,* too, teach a practitioner to bring all the vital energy within the confines of the body, rather than let it dissipate outside the bodily periphery (Desikachar 1995). This instruction ensures a symbolic encompassment of knowledge, and brings it within the grasp of the practitioner.

Renouncers were very explicit with me that their bodies were tools for learning about the cosmos. Knowing the nature of the material world would develop not through watching the outside world, *sādhus* told me, but through learning the nature of the body. "You can't see it from here," a Hardwar *bābā* said, pointing to his eyes. "You can only see it from *here,*" he stressed, first touching his heart—the body point most often correlated to the *ātman*—and then the point between his eyes, meaning his "third eye" or mind *cakra.* He then described to me a series of detailed divine activities at each *cakra:*

> This is Viṣṇu's lake [navel center]—a lake of strong power. And then it goes up to where Śiva and Śakti are together [heart center]. And this is where Brahmā and Śiva are together [mind center], where there's fire! A lot of fire! A lot of fire, and a lot of heat! And this is the Himalaya [fontanelle], where Śiva lives. It's very big and very cold.

This *sādhu*'s associations of deities, temperatures, movement, and activity in these metaphysical centers show how *yogīs* use their bodies as places to chart different ways the world manifests and different levels of experience. Divine forces are linked to sites on the body, and the process of spiritual realization can be mapped onto (or into) the physical form. "See from your own inside," this renouncer encouraged. Meditation had an explicit anatomy, and the body could serve as a spiritual guidebook.

The system of equivalences between the inner body and the outer world at the core of yogic philosophy—the "microcosm" and the "macrocosm," as often cited in English translations (White 1996; Danielou 1985)—means that bodies are the material link to both spatial knowledge and religious understanding. With the clear articulation of channels (or rivers) and centers of energy, yogic models establish an explicit map of the human body as analogous to the sacred geography of the earth. Both circuits and centers—routes of movement and specific locations where transformation can take place—are significant in renouncers' practices, individually and collectively. If the universe can be mapped on to renouncers' bodies, the dispersed nature of the renouncer community does not, in symbolic terms, detract from collective experience. Instead of communally articulating a single location over time, renouncers share a view that every practitioner's body is an equivalent location of knowledge that, if accessed properly, can articulate the universe.

Healing

As people who ideally understand the qualities of nature more clearly, talented *sādhus* are also thought of as people who can cure bodies. Both renouncers and lay Hindus suggested to me that mastery over one's own body and knowledge of the physical environment provide an ability to cure others. Healing, in this construction, is premised on the consonance between the nature of the body and the nature of the world. Because *yogīs* are reputed to have higher levels of experience of the workings of inner and outer natures, they are known as talented healers.

Legends persist about *sādhus* who live high in the Himalayas, surrounded by roots and herbs with natural curative powers, and who are able to use them for the benefit of householder communities. A Hardwar tourist officer described the classic *sādhu* to me in these terms: "He is devoted to God, doing yoga and other things to get power himself . . . He will serve such people who are sick, giving holy, not [bio]medical, treatment. The *sādhu* who lives in the Himalayas knows many *jaiv* or *dhuti,* treatments with roots and herbs." His description suggests that a *sādhu*'s attention to nature provides a therapeutic knowledge base (and a religious power) that can positively (or, presumably, negatively) affect the outer world in order to right its imbalances. It also suggests that living outside normative society ("in the Himalayas"), as renouncers do (more often in a ritual sense, perhaps, than in a literal or spatial sense), provides a kind of insight and power on how to right social ills.

Whether or not there are living renouncers who collect Himalayan botanical cures, many *sādhus* I knew were approached for medical advice. For example, Tyāgī Nāth Bābā, a renouncer in the Nāth lineage and an extremely well-respected Ayurvedic physician, comes to Paśupatināth every Śiva Rātrī from his base in Dang, western Nepal, the primary seat of the Nāth order. He comes both to preside over the main Aghori *dhūnī* at Paśupati's cremation *ghāṭs* during the annual festival, and to treat the hundreds of patients who come to see him. Each year I attended the festival, a steady stream of pilgrims crammed into the small *kuṭī* on the *ghāṭ* for the week he was in residence. They came to receive blessings, food that was offered them as *prasād,* and medicine and medical advice from the talented *yogī*-physician. "All these people want medicine! Medicine!" Tyāgī Nāth said to me, bemoaning the amount of illness he saw in front of him, and almost sad that his most coveted ability was medical advice.

Impressed with Tyāgī Nāthjī's combined professions, I pressed him on the question of the materiality of the body, asking if the body wasn't a product of the mind? He was explicit about the premise that the body can be understood—and cured—through models of nature. "The body *is* nature," he told me. "In the cold, the body gets cold. In the warm, the body gets warm. Disease comes from nature, just like the body." Temperature, he suggested, was the most salient feature of the body; like the five elements, temperature effaced the difference between human bodies and other material forms. Using foods that were either heating or cooling to adjust the temperature of the body was the most common way Tyāgī Nāthjī prescribed behavior change. Teaching his patients how to properly maintain their bodies so that they could function productively in society was more important than teaching them how to achieve transcendent knowledge: "Health is wealth!" he announced.

I experienced renouncers' abilities to heal personally, on a visit to Rādhā Mai's *dhūnī* when I wasn't feeling particularly well. She looked at me, made a pacifying gesture with her hand, and started to prepare tea for me to drink. At first, I resisted her implicit proposal of treatment, saying I should just go home and return the next day. But everyone gathered in her *dhūnī*—other renouncers, lay pilgrims, local community members, and service providers—insisted that I stay and just let Mai do her work. (Her own forcefulness was such that it was hard to resist her plan anyway.) She prepared my tea with *methī* (fenugreek) and salt, and handed it to me. "It will make you burp and you'll feel better," she said, which was true. She massaged my forehead briefly by squeezing my temples with her forefinger and thumb, and then she blew a quick, short breath at my *agni cakra,* the place between my eyebrows. She repeated the gesture three times, in an obvious—and effective—ritual of healing.

Sometimes renouncers' curative capacities extended to other domains, as when they were approached for psychological, social, or financial advice (see also Narayan 1989). Kathmandu residents often visited Dudh

Bābā, the Paśupati renouncer, to ask for help with personal matters, such as when a member of their family or community was troubled or was causing trouble. A Nepali friend of mine brought me to meet an Aghori renouncer he knew on the outskirts of Kathmandu, who had helped him and his family in innumerable ways, by anticipating problems and suggesting prescient and straightforward solutions. From their religious knowledge, their understanding of the mechanisms of nature, and their vantage point outside normative society, renouncers are known as people with the capacity to heal social and physical ills.

The Practices of the Body

How does the body negotiate experience in renouncers' narratives and how does a contemporary renouncer use his or her body in religious practice? In the range of religious interpretations that I have outlined, experience can help or hinder, reveal or occlude, and the body can provide or prevent access to transcendent knowledge. Religious discipline, *tapas,* mediates these various interpretations of the body and delineates between experiences that obscure and experiences that reveal. Practice, I suggest, makes use of the body while simultaneously keeping it in its place.

Renouncers' religious practices, *tapas,* translated variously as austerity, asceticism, discipline, penance, or heat, include those ascetic mortifications for which *sādhus* are most famous. The classic image of renouncers in both Western and Indian popular imagination emphasizes extreme forms of *tapas*—keeping one hand raised until it atrophies, walking on fire, sleeping on nails, and remaining standing on one leg, even while sleeping—as the most common way *sādhus* treat their bodies (Narayan 1993b). Colonial accounts are filled with descriptions of *sādhus* who engage in death-defying physical acts (cf. Wilson 1861; Tod 1920; Bunton 1935; Oman 1984 [1905]). Popular contemporary photograph books emphasize the amazing physical feats advanced *sādhus* can and do perform (cf. Bedi 1991; Hartsuiker 1993).

Popular Indian comic books, too, highlight *tapas* as the way mythical heroes and heroines gain their powers—*tapas* is a way to win the favors of the divine. The goddess Pārvatī sits alone in the forest for thousands of years before the gods think favorably enough of her to grant her a boon, and she successfully wins Śiva as her husband. Performing *tapas* is often a test: sacrificing or challenging the body to its limits demonstrates unfailing commitment worthy of a divine response.[21] South Asian *siddha* traditions are heavily sprinkled with myths of *yogīs* who win boons from the gods—including physical immortality, extreme bodily powers, and the ability to change their shape at will—through very severe and prolonged *tapas* (see Svoboda 1986).

Some literatures methodically lay out the physical practices that produce superhuman powers (White 1996). Even Manu states that if a renouncer "abandons" his body, and conquers his senses through the right use of discipline, he will achieve immortality:

> If his sensory powers are being seduced by sensory objects he should turn them back by eating little food and by standing and sitting in solitude. By obstructing his sensory powers, destroying passion and hatred, and doing no violence to living beings he becomes fit for immortality. (verse 6.59–60 in Doniger and Smith 1991:123)

As Manu tells it, senses are capable of "seducing" or obscuring a renouncer's clear knowledge: conquering the senses means that a renouncer is able to function in the material world without being affected by it. It is precisely because he lies beyond the confines of matter that the legendary renouncer is capable of all sorts of bodily tricks. These seemingly contradictory instructions are intentional: as Cohen writes, becoming a renouncer "involves a ritual death of the body and the creation of a 'deathless' body" (1998:132). The body becomes a plaything to a successful renouncer, because he or she has achieved the body-soul split. His or her consciousness sees materiality and sociality for the illusions that they are, and is no longer beholden to the physical plane. Such a "conqueror of the senses" is able to manipulate, rather than be manipulated by, the world of form.

The senses here are equated entirely with the material plane, indulgence, desire, and sexual pleasure. As if they were themselves prospective sexual partners, senses seduce a renouncer onto the slippery slope of enjoyment, attachment, desire, and the inescapable wheel of *karma*.[22] Since sexual pleasure is the pre-eminent metaphor for sensory or bodily indulgence, celibacy is a powerful symbol of renunciation (cf. Sobo and Bell 2001; Phillimore 2001).[23] The symbolic act of renouncing sexual activity indicates the restraint, power, and non-worldly status of the renouncer, who is ideally free from desire, pleasure, and the attachments of children: celibacy most clearly marks the separation of renouncers from householder society. The proper control of semen—the precious "sap" that is the "distillate of other body fluids"—is a metaphor for renouncers' control over the physical world (Alter 1992:129).[24]

The images of *sādhus* accomplishing advanced physical feats effectively cross-cut the two approaches to the body which I have outlined. In subjecting his body to radical discipline, the legendary *sādhu* both demonstrates the hollowness of the physical form—this arm has atrophied because it is nothing to begin with; desire is irrelevant because it is illusory—and also the capacity of the body to gain superhuman powers—this body has accumulated enough *siddhis* (divinely granted powers) or enough heat (the literal translation of *tapas,* accumulated through retaining semen, for example [see O'Flaherty 1973]) to walk through fire and manipulate matter. By seeing the body as ephemeral and by understanding all the qualities of nature, the *tapasvin* rises above the physical plane on which most bodies live, and gains powers over the ephemeral world. Successful detachment from—and therefore power over—the body effectively leads to detachment from—and power over—the world, and vice versa, in that power over the world is symbolized by power over the body. In renouncers' narratives, there is no difference between the world and the body. Having conquered his or her own body, a successful *tapasvin* or *tapasvinī,* can play with the outer world—by taking on other forms or manipulating nature—as if it were part of him- or herself.

Extreme acts of self-mortification and complete sexual renunciation are probably the most famous characteristics of Indian *sādhus;* renouncers with atrophied extremities were certainly the most popular among both the Western press and Indian pilgrims at the Kumbh Melās. But the renouncers I came to know best understood and engaged in *tapas* differently, referring neither to body poses nor to body heat. They did not speak about testing their bodies, publicly proving their detachment, or accumulating physical power. Almost all renouncers I spoke to did choose to experience some degree of physical hardship, either for a particular duration or as part and parcel of ascetic life. Ascetic life is not supposed to be easy, I learned: I heard the word *tapas* used to mean living in extreme conditions, pushing oneself to physical limits, maintaining a singleness of religious purpose, developing an ability to focus or refine mental activity, and sustaining tireless devotion. Even if a renouncer did not spend years in a particular posture or following a particular austerity, he or she was engaging in *tapas* if devoted, purposeful, and single-minded.

Renouncers I spoke with also defined *tapas* as much broader than severe physical austerities. One *sādhvī* who explicitly told me that physical yoga practices were not her path said that *tapas* could be applied to the speech and mind as well: "To be silent, to recite mantras, to do meditation, or to eat only once a day, *tapas* builds your willpower." Referring to the *Bhagavad Gītā* (although she herself was a scholar of Vedānta texts), she explained:

> There are three kinds of *tapas*. First, *tapas* of the body: controlling or living in heat or cold, no fancy clothes or decorating the body with perfumes—you don't need all those things. If the body is clean and nice, it's enough. Second is speech: *maunam*, or silence, or speaking the truth, or not using your voice in idle chit chat, or not speaking anything that would harm. Also *svādhyāya*—study of scriptures of chanting.[25] Third is *tapas* of mind, withdrawing from the world. It's the final kind of *tapas*, which restricts all thoughts. It's the silence of the mind. As Ramāṇa Mahāṛṣi said, 'Where there is no mind, there is no world.'

For uneducated renouncers, too, restraining the mind was one of the most important forms of *tapas*. In response to my asking whether she did *tapas*, Mukta Giri exclaimed, "You've got to do meditation! You've got to do *tapas*! Otherwise what's a *yogī*'s work for?" Training the mind in meditation was Mukta Giri's definition of *tapas*. Both physical and mental disciplines constituted *tapas* for the renouncers I worked with: practices included both ascetic restraint and emotional detachment. *Tapas* keeps a body in its place.

The Tapas of Physical Discipline

Tapas is a renouncer's discipline of maintaining a balance in relation to his or her body. The renouncers I met tried to find a point of practice that allowed them to mediate between resisting the body (as an ephemeral form and a source of emotion) and worshipping the body (as a location of knowledge and a potential tool of great power). *Tapas* was, for these renouncers, a method that at once harnessed the powers of the body and disallowed its clamoring, a process of putting the material world to the service of the transcendent plane. Renouncers tried to use their bodies to find a middle ground between the polarities of experience. Eliade defines *tapas* as "bearing the 'pairs of opposites,' as, for example, the desire to eat and the desire to drink; heat and cold; the desire to remain standing and the desire to remain seated; the absence of words and the absence of gestures that could reveal one's feelings or thoughts" (1958 [1954]:51). In this translation, *tapas* is the literal mediation of dualism.

Renouncers tried to cultivate a tentative relation with their bodies, where they could both resist the urges, drives, and unwitting emotions of the body, on one hand, and cater to bodily needs, on the other. Most renouncers I met had a measured, self-conscious approach towards their bodies, and even those *sādhus* who did not speak of a daily physical regimen clearly devoted time and energy to maintaining their physical forms. Since we are embodied creatures, they argued, bodies must be appropriately cared for and tended to. Maintaining the body is the only way to practice *sādhanā* properly, I heard often: the body is a tool of religious knowledge, and it is the only one we are offered. In much Hindu discourse, one hears that bodies are the vessels required to navigate what one *sādhvī* called the "ocean" of experience.

Being physically active had always been important to Pāgal Bābā. He had fallen ill only on returning from Europe two years earlier, perhaps, he thought, because he had gotten "lazy" when he came back. He liked treating his body properly, he told me—even in Europe he'd been busy, cooking for scores of people, giving lectures, and attending conferences. Bābā felt that his illness was in part due to a slowing-down that came with age and a lessening of activity. "I don't like laziness, and I don't like lazy people," Bābā told me. "These infections—these ghosts—they get you if you're lazy. They see you're a good person [to infect]." In Bābā's narrative, a body used in daily activity keeps itself maintained and healthy, while a body uncared for or unproductive was exposed and vulnerable. Even while recuperating, Bābā tried to walk twice a day, in the early morning and at dusk, and as soon as he was able, he insisted on cooking for himself.

Nānī Mā referred to the body as "a machine which has to be oiled," a metaphor with a double meaning, given the importance of rubbing oil on holy images in Hindu religious practice. Even *sādhus* who firmly believe that the body is based in illusion must bathe and eat regularly, she said—bodies that exist on the material plane must be sustained. She needed to bathe, for example, since she lived with a community and wanted to set a good example and live peacefully among others. (Her *guru,* she noted, did not have to bathe since "he always smelled like perfume.") Another *sādhvī* told me she believed in a daily bath in order to keep the body very pure and *sattvic,* in a state, she said, that was worthy of and more likely to grasp Śaṅkarācārya's Vedānta teachings. Both women believed that renouncers should keep their bodies "pure" and socially functional.

While caring for the body was appropriate, renouncers stipulated as little care for the body as possible. *Tapas* meant living with a minimum: renouncers should cultivate no indulgence for or attachment to their bodies. A *sādhu* should eat in moderate quantities, for example, accepting what is offered or given. Food is a meant of sustenance, not necessarily a source of pleasure. Many renouncers I met ate only one meal a day. Pāgal Bābā always said as he cooked or ate, "Simple food. Nothing fancy." Nānī Mā explained further, "You can't do without food, but you can do without taste." Her *guru,* Bābājī, only ever had one cloth to wear or sleep under, she told me, with no cover on his cave; she and other disciples would sometimes try to sneak a blanket or curtain while he slept but he always resisted. Nānī Mā felt quite guilty about the extra blankets and sleeping bag she had used since her illness. She felt that undue care for the body led to—or resulted from—a disproportionate identification with the body.

In practice, *tapas* means a lifetime of relative hardship: most of the renouncers I met lived with few possessions, minimal food, minimal sleep,[26] and a great deal of travel. Some described a particular period where they chose to live in extreme conditions as a phase of difficult *tapas* that could heighten religious experience. Nānī Mā described a number of extreme bodily acts she undertook when she first became a *sādhvī* and was living at Bābājī's: she had sat outside all night in pouring rain; she had chosen not to use a blanket even in the extreme cold of a Himalayan winter. She used to bathe three times a day in Gaṅgā Mā; when she moved to the frigid heights of Gangotri, she reduced the practice to once a day. She had always wanted to do this or that *tapas,* having heard about it in some context or other, but by the time we met she no longer included such extreme tests on the body in her religious practice—now she consented to treatment for a stomach illness, for example, something she had refused two decades earlier. (She may have embraced the extreme of the classic model of Hindu renunciation when she first became a *sādhvī* in part because she was a young foreigner.)

Pushing the body to a physical limit, *sādhus* said, breaks through normal bounds of perception and experience. Sometimes these experiences can be maintained. "Slowly, gradually, your whole life becomes a vow," a renouncer who engaged in many hours of daily practice daily told me. Paśupatināth renouncer Dudh Bābā drank milk as his only source of protein for fourteen years, but after his planned period of *tapas* ended, the discipline had become "just part of life," and he never returned to a normal diet. Besides, he continued with a grin, he'd already eaten a lot of rice and *chapattis* in his lifetime, and didn't feel like he was missing much. His *tapas* was no longer a hardship, but had become a habit: he had integrated an extreme practice into everyday life.

The Tapas of Mental Discipline

Most renouncers I spoke with said that they needed to maintain their bodies in terms of food and hygiene, to preserve a degree of religious purity or social acceptability or both, but that maintaining the body should not be confused with overindulging the body. Nor should the body be taken as the primary way of relating to the world, which happens easily because the physical body and the mental habits it produces are immediate and demanding. Indulging the body even slightly gives it full permission to produce emotions, sensory perceptions, desires, attachments, all of which cloud and obscure clear consciousness. Some renouncers felt that even physical austerities could be extremely self-indulgent: Narmada Puri pointed out that someone who wanted to stand on one leg for reasons of glory or pride would surely fail. *Tapas* includes both physical and mental practices of neutral, ego-less restraint.

Experience can be either a source of knowledge or a source of delusion, but proper bodily practice clarifies the distinction. The practices of *tapas* were for "mind control," one *sādhu* explained to me. "*Tapas* is to do something with a force: it is the action if the mind is moving in a certain direction and you are trying to get away from it." Disciplined renouncers, I was told, are able to detach from the sensations and emotions of the mind, because their *tapas* cultivates emotional restraint as well as detachment from social and material worlds.

To achieve religious knowledge, renouncers told me, practitioners need to remember that the body is *only* a material form, a product of shallow perception, and they must discipline their bodies and minds accordingly. The body must be maintained, but it must also be recalled as deceptive. The body is not impure *per se,* but it is the source of deep misrecognition; the potential clarity of our perception is obscured by our own embodiment. Since most people radically misunderstand the nature of embodiment, renouncers explained, disparaging the body can be a way to keep the mind at bay. Careful religious practice can confine the damaging effects of identifying too strongly with the material body and the mental disturbances it produces.

In his account of a Tamil pilgrimage, Daniel describes how the difficulties of an arduous journey help a pilgrim disassociate from his or her body, "so that ego is obscured or snuffed out" (1984:268–269). In his telling, the physical experience of pain progressively transforms into love for the deity that is the focus of the pilgrimage. Repealing the illusion of a separate self (which is how I interpret a snuffed-out ego) is certainly the point of much Hindu religious activity, but in the interpretations of my informants, this is achieved by consciously distancing from physical experience, rather than by merging with it. A renouncer ideally becomes more detached from the experiences of the body, feeling physical and emotional pain less sharply, observing sensations rather than immediately experiencing them.

"*Sādhus* do have bodies," Narmada Puri told me. "They experience pain and pleasure; they eat; they wear clothes; even a *sādhu* has to go to the bathroom. But it doesn't matter so much to a *sādhu.*" The physical world does not cease to exist for renouncers, she was arguing, but through practices of mental discipline, it does have less influence. The renouncer controls his or her own mind and is no longer controlled by the material world. Ideally, *sādhus* observe pleasure and pain as ephemeral states of being, rather than being swept up in experience.

Tapas is living with a focus of purpose and a focus of mind. More than heat or even power broadly stated, *tapas* means living unhampered by the emotions and distractions of worldly existence. A number of *sādhus,* especially women, suggested that the real challenge of renouncer life is emotionally maintaining the detachment that is the foundation of religious practice. Yet while many women told me how difficult detaching from relationships was, I never met a *sādhu* who regretted or went back on her decision to renounce, and many insisted that even while it was hard, renunciation was also a source of bliss. The practice of detachment ideally translates into the experience of divine peace.

Mukta Giri lived among women householders, and she spent much of her time sitting in Paśupatināth courtyards and wandering through its temples. Although she engaged in no visible bodily austerity, she could discuss *tapas* with me simply by virtue of being a renouncer. "*Tapas* means bliss," she told me, "once you go alone to the jungle. Here the mind darts hither and thither, and what's that? That's not *tapas. Tapas* is the bliss of having found Bhagvān." In Mai's construction, *tapas* is the action of stilling the mind and is synonymous with renunciation. Leaving householder space, where the mind is too fraught with emotion in her narrative, is the act of renouncing and the source of equilibrium. *Tapas* for Mukta Giri was not about accumulating power, but about the bravery of renouncer life and the blissful union with Bhagvān that it assured.

When Mukta Giri insisted that there is "no love for the *yogī*'s body," she was referring to the hardships of wandering, but she was also emphasizing that *yogīs* are supposed to withdraw from emotional responses to the world of experience. Disciplined *sādhanā* is a conscious attempt to remove the effects of social interaction from the body and to remind a *yogī* of his or her ultimate solitude. *Tapas* is a series of practices designed to isolate the body and mind, and ultimately to prepare for the solitude of death, whereupon a renouncer, free from social connections, hopes to be permanently liberated from materiality and sociality. "We are born alone and we die alone," a *sādhu* from western Kathmandu told me. "There is nothing to take."

The Renouncer's Body

It was with Mukta Giri that I first explored renouncers' ideas about their bodies, the meaning of *tapas,* the difficulty of illness, and the blessing of embodiment. Mai appears throughout this chapter as the person whose narratives consistently pointed me towards the practical reality of living in a renouncer's body. Although she was an example of someone who became a *sādhu* in large part because it offered her the best social option (unlike, say, Pāgal Bābā, who had been reared a *sādhu* and who represented a very different social stratum of renouncer life), her reflections on embodiment were rooted in classical Hindu thought and were often quite nuanced. Her age and illness meant that thoughts on the human body were uppermost in her mind, and attempting to make sense of the world of form and the nature of embodiment were a large part of her religious goals.

As often cited, many passages in Hindu scriptures are extremely antagonistic towards the body, in order to cultivate in practictioners a distance from its loud, clamoring demands and the clouded perceptions of the world it can produce. The textual ascetic is expected to disdain the human body and its impure processes, to perform extreme austerities, and to rise above the bonds of the material world. But Mukta Giri's demeanor fills in that stark image of the renouncer and her body. Certainly she wished to detach from the *saṃsāric* state that her body was born into, and certainly she agreed with the general principles of textual derogations, although she was uneducated, in that she thought of the body as ephemeral and impossible to hold on to. She wanted to use that knowledge to assist her in her religious goals, as the texts advise. But she never spoke of her body as a weight or as a travesty; she never approached her body with disdain, but rather with acceptance. The aches and pains that were the combined effect of old age and illness were for her an opportunity to remember God, illusion, ephemeral nature, and the permanent state of bliss that lay ahead once she left her body. Perhaps in part because she had grown old, she accepted her body even while she saw its limits and tried to detach from its hold.

Mukta Giri's placid attitude with her body—mirrored by Lord Paśupati's gentle manifestation as a deer-like creature in the forest still called Mṛgasthalī, or "place of the deer," in his honor—reflects the perspective of most renouncers I met. They wanted to detach from the whims and desires that come as part and parcel of having a human form, but their mode was acceptance, not severe mutilation or manipulation. Perhaps this view is that of aged or elderly renouncers, who were by and large my informants: the embodied form must be seen for what it is, the only way to practice, in daily life and in religious effort toward the permanent, liberated state of union with God.

Many *sādhus* I spoke with told me that their bodies were manifestations of divine grace, and that every bodily act was inspired by divine action rather than individually willed. Asking how *sādhus* live in and think about their bodies turned out to be much more a question on the nature of detachment than on the nature of embodiment: how could renouncers remain equanimous about the very form into which they were born? Having a body required of renouncers a delicate balance between detachment and maintenance, between denigration and glorification.

Rather than approach their bodies with the stark horror that is sometimes the tone of Indian texts on embodiment, *sādhus* tried to overcome the sensations and emotions of their bodies, while understanding that they were part of the human experience. Speaking of their bodies as vehicles, vessels, and tools for religious clarity, they articulated a perspective that usually came across as an acceptance of embodiment as a sacred gift. And the *tapas* that is so famous as bodily mortification or severe penance was thought of more often as simply the renouncer lifestyle: bearing the burdens of renunciation was in itself *tapas. Tapas* is the harnessing of bodily power, the simultaneous rejection of the body and exploitation of the body, not a particular action but a way of life that calls for restraint, clarity, and balance, and that, more than any other practice in *sādhu* life, represents what it means to live in body and in place as a renouncer.

Conclusion

THE CULTURE OF HINDU RENUNCIATION

Renouncers' religious thought articulates a coherent system for interpreting the world, and posits a thorough and complicated model through which to grasp human reality. *Sādhus* described renunciation to me as both a social and a physical process: in discussing their distance from householder social life, they referred both to the social world of attachment and to the linked physical and mental worlds of the body and emotion. The connection between society and the body is explicit for renouncers, who consciously equate splitting apart from the normative social realm with leaving behind the material body. In *sādhus'* narratives, the body is the mechanism that gauges the contours of space, and the rhythms of nature serve as the measuring tool of time. Ultimately, the practices of the body are intended to distill knowledge from experience, and to distinguish between bodily distractions and bodily revelations.

This book demonstrates the parallels in the social, physical, and religious dimensions of life for renouncers. Most anthropological analyses use social life as the base for studying the body (see Turner 1980; Douglas 1970) or studying religion (see Geertz 1973); I have tried to reverse the terms somewhat, and show how social and bodily practices look through the lens of a religious worldview. Renouncers insist upon the split between soul and body because it is a powerful metaphor for the split they enact from householder society. Like anthropologists who argue that society is reflected in the contours or the clothing of the material body, renouncers draw a clear parallel between the gross physical body and normative

« Posed portrait on wall at Asi Ghat at Varanasi

society: they view the body and society as mutually constitutive and fully co-symbolic.

The Power of Transcendence

Through the language of religion, *sādhus* use the institution of renunciation as a refuge from oppressive, unforgiving, or inadequate social structures, and also as a ground from which to assert communal power. By renouncing householder society in favor of religious lives, renouncers argue that they transcend quotidian concerns and material reality. Ideally, this religious transcendence translates into social power in the South Asian context—being socially and spatially outside normative society means that renouncers at once inhabit a position of marginality and a position of power. Renouncers are thought to have influence over the material world and are approached for medical, spiritual, and social assistance. They assert themselves as aligned with the space and time of divine beings rather than with humans, and they use this oppositional status as a way to transcend householder society, in both social and religious terms.

Renunciation offers both social solace in a non-discriminating community and a deliberate inversion of the dominant power structure, expressed through religious language and experiences of faith. From an anthropological point of view, renouncers are liminal figures in relation to the normative caste and family structures of Hindu society and, as such, they claim transcendence over that which they leave behind (V. Turner 1969; T. Turner 1977). The classic symbolism of liminality precisely applies to the image of renouncers: as wanderers, *sādhus* are not affiliated with particular spaces or locations; being naked or covered with ash, *sādhus* conjure the image of death; owning no possessions, *sādhus* represent a defiance of social expectation and the false pursuits of wealth and upward mobility.[1]

Victor Turner argues for understanding the properties of liminality in part as "the powers of the weak," given that liminal communities (including "monastic orders and holy mendicants") usually fall "on the margins" of society or "occupy its lowest rungs" (1969:109,125). In the case of South Asian renouncers, a low status may encourage people to join a monastic order whereby social weakness may be transformed into social strength. Renunciation offers a reappropriation of the power that was denied to many *sādhus* in their former householder lives. The power of the renouncer community lies in its structural resistance to dominant social control and in its deliberate break from the wholeness that Brāhmanic society considers itself, and would like to perpetuate. By splitting away from caste and householder society, the renouncer community offers an "outside" to Hindu social life, as Dumont puts it, which breaks apart a system that claims itself as complete.[2]

The powers attributed to liminal groups over the dominant social structures from which they have broken away are usually quite extreme. Terence Turner explains that liminal groups occupy a position of ritual transcendence by encompassing multiple social dimensions. Those people occupying a "higher level of structure [in this case, *sādhus*]," he argues, "will be seen from the standpoint of the lower levels as standing to them in a relation of becoming to being . . . dynamic to static, and transcendent to immanent" and also as "a source of powers of a higher order, and at the same time as a domain of relatively uncontrollable and therefore dangerous powers" (1977:56). In Eliade's translation of yoga texts, the renouncer's ideal project is to understand the natural universe in order to transcend it, or "assimilate" it (1958 [1954]:58)—that is, be able to identify with nature so completely that the material world is at the disposal of (and under the power of) the advanced *yogin*. As one *sādhu* explained it to me, "The individual thinks the individual body is his body; the knower of *brahman* knows the whole universe is his body. Others see his body as his body, but from his point of view his body is the whole universe."

This theme of encompassment is core to *sādhu* constructions of body, space, and time: successful renouncers are supposed to be able to manipulate the world at will, they live not in one place but on an entire circuit of holy places, and they function on the plane of divine time. Even in Vedic traditions, renouncers were supposed to have transcendent bodies that could internally perform symbolic ritual duties and comprehend the nature of reality cast to the farthest reaches of the universe (Heesterman 1982:269). Renouncers "interiorize" the Vedic sacrificial fires: the fires of the renouncer's body replaced the householder's hearth in a detailed system of equivalences (the bodily *prāṇa* represents the *garhapatya* sacrificial fire, the bodily *apana* represents the southern sacrificial fire, etc. [Heesterman 1964]).[3]

If the renouncer's internal bodily fires serve as the fires of homage to deities, proper bodily austerities serve as the bellows:

> The renouncer's internal fires are permanently lit; he kindles them with every breath. His eating becomes a sacrificial offering. His body and bodily functions are transformed into a long sacrificial session. The renouncer's body thus becomes a sacred object; it is equal to the fire altar where the Vedic rites are performed. (Olivelle 1992:69)[4]

Renouncers are supposed to understand on a visceral level the system of equivalences that exists between their inner bodies and the outer worlds, and incorporate the most salient symbols of the outer world within. Consider the importance of heat and fire—that which can consume or literally take within itself illusion, illness, or the world—in renouncers' bodily practices, and in their views of the five elements and the balance of nature. In defiance of her father's rigid position on social distinction and propriety, Satī spontaneously consumes herself in flames.

Living in a transcendent body is a radical cultural critique of all that embodied society poses. In the context of caste, the Varanasi wrestlers who were Joseph Alter's informants argued that "worldly [caste-conscious] persons are unhealthy," suggesting that the body that transcends social structure is the healthy, spiritually sound, and politically radical body (1992:119). In *sādhus'* narratives, the ostensible ability to encompass the world and see through the illusory bonds of materiality and emotion is an ongoing effort demonstrated through the presentation of the body. But more than one renouncer warned how important it is not to become attached to mere matters of presentation. "Sādhus are supposed to be a higher order of people," I was told by a *sādhvī*. "But they don't realize that they're supposed to be a higher order because of the *sādhanā* they do, not because of the outfits they wear!"

The real-life capacity of renouncers to transcend the limits of householder social reality is enhanced through their communal dispersion: they do not reside in a particular place and cannot be identified or categorized as a singular, sedentary group. *Sādhus'* peripheral and peripatetic status contributes to their reputation as powerful religious people. The British frustration with wandering renouncers partly lay in the impossibility of governing a community that had no spatial limits. In the narratives of contemporary lay Hindus, wandering *sādhus,* in their evasive tactics and marginal status, have knowledge and power over sedentary communities: they have seen the world, they have incorporated the blessings of far-away pilgrimage destinations into their bodies, and they have collected cures from all over the subcontinent. Even as they denigrated renouncers, many lay Hindus told me that they feared *sādhus'* unpredictable powers. Renouncers had no homes and therefore no accountability, I was told: who knew where they had been, what they had seen, or what kinds of magical powers might be accrued from such an unrooted lifestyle?

The religious language that renouncers use to explain their separateness is based on an ideology that material and social life is illusory and damaging. Renouncers argue that they cannot live on the material plane, in normal homes, but must strive towards divine transcendence, in space and beyond. Renouncers told me they wished to leave both illusory sentiments and attachments behind, through what they described as partly physiological and spatial processes. They would try to achieve a transcendental state of *ānanda,* bliss, where they could come into contact with Bhagvān, God. In renouncers' language, *māyā,* the illusion of materiality, was opposed to Bhagvān, the reality of transcendence, and to *ānanda,* the bliss of transcendent knowledge. By renouncing *māyā*—both the illusion of the material world and the social web that produces it—*sādhus* claimed religious knowledge and also the capacity to transcend the concrete axes of householder social life.

Renouncers expressed their efforts to provide an alternative to householder caste society in the language of religious dualism, whereby the social, material world is lived by householders and the transcendent plane is experienced by *sādhus.* Renunciation was the social act of breaking apart from—and gaining reputed power over—householder society, and the body is the symbol of separation. As the metaphor for the material world, the body—or at least its experiences—had to be transcended, *sādhus* explained, its worldly passions and its social inclinations cleared from the religious path.

The Ineffable Essence of Experience

The Hindu renouncer's body poses an undeniable quandary, in that the body is the meeting point of the material world and transcendent experience, the "terrain where opposed terms meet," as Csordas puts it

(1994:20). Like the society of renouncers, who, in departing from socialized life, must remain in a social context, the Hindu religious attempt to split the soul apart from bodily processes cannot but remain within the confines of embodied experience. Through the vehicle of the body, the renouncer attempts to reconcile dualism, but in embodied form, dualism must exist.

As one *sādhu* explained it to me, an accomplished renouncer still has a body which others perceive, but s/he no longer experiences it as such. Embodiment is thus a paradoxical Hindu experience: the body is both a tool of practice and a trap of worldliness, both the site of perception and the only available mechanism with which to transcend the subject-object divide. In ideal terms, being a renouncer mediates between these two poles; the renouncer's body is the link between the spatial-historical plane of social and material process and the transcendent, unified plane of knowledge.

Contemporary anthropological emphases on bodily experience as a way to analyze culture can help us understand Hindu renouncers' perspectives, but also point us toward questions of how religious thought challenges the social and embodied dimensions of lived reality. The anthropological project to understand the cultural variability of embodiment goes back to Marcel Mauss' argument that bodies, though seemingly natural, are as culturally manipulable as any other set of signs (1973[1935]). Very simply, the experience of embodiment—the way a person lives in his or her body and experiences the world—varies in different social, cultural, and institutional contexts. The body is a precious subject in anthropology because, as Mauss argued, culture may show itself most clearly in the variability of so-called "natural" bodily practices.

Phenomenological approaches to embodiment have moved toward comprehending the material body as the ground of experience and perception (see Csordas 1994). Inverting the terms, theorist Talal Asad suggests that experience is a particularly good way of understanding the question of embodiment, specifically how the body mediates culture (1997).[5] People live in the world primarily through experiential practice, Asad argues: culture *trains* a body, just as religious philosophy, for example, may train desire.[6] Bodily experience can also be a way of understanding questions of location and place.[7] Interestingly, the tenets of the Indian Sāṃkhya philosophical school similarly argue that social life and cultural locations affect the body-mind complex, and also that the body, through sense organs and mental processes, is the ground of experience.

But unlike phenomenologists, my informants argued that experience cannot always be trusted. The ultimate state—in dualist Sāṃkhya and non-dualist Vedānta philosophy, and also in the narratives of my informants, informed to varying degrees by these schools—is something very different from what we perceive in our everyday lives, through our everyday bodies. Physical and mental experiences produce illusion to at least the same degree as they produce knowledge. To invert Levi-Strauss's oft-quoted dictum, the body is not always good to think with (1969b). Religious discipline is required precisely to distinguish between experience that clarifies and experience that obscures.

The world of experience, or the distinct but interconnected realms of body, space, and time, as Hindu *yogīs* expressed it to me, is perpetually shifting. Experience is affected by the people with whom and places where we spend our time, and the eon in which we live. We are not static beings but products of our social and spatial environments. Our physical bodies reflect our social interactions, much as our social practices derive their content from the locations in which they are formed, culturally and spatially. For these reasons, my informants patiently explained, it is critically important to find the right kind of instruction and to surround ourselves with the right kind of people, in the right place and time.

The Definition of Culture

Hindu renunciation is an isolable variable, a thing apart, a cultural unit. It is not a bounded unit, however, since its members come from and interact with members of householder society, the very group to which renouncer society defines itself in opposition. Both in bodily practice and in spatial location, renouncers conduct themselves differently than householders do. These self-conscious differences create an alternative culture, across space, through which renouncers function. They know how to recognize one another, and they place themselves into a social order that intricately defines hierarchy, fraternity, and orientation. This is the definition—or at least one definition—of culture, a binding experience that is not limited in space. Culture is the means through which members of a self-defined community articulate and practice the terms through which they engage.

As with any definition of culture, this one poses immediate paradoxes. From the material in this book, we can see very clearly that culture is not coterminous with location. Indeed, in the case of *sādhus,* a reinterpretation of space precisely defines culture. But, further, everyone knows that *sādhus* are supposed to be alone—isolated while they practice their *sādhanā*—and ideally in a high mountain cave, interacting with no one. Can singularities together constitute a culture?[8] As contradictory as it may sound, I argue that *sādhus* do indeed form a community, even when in isolation. Their commitments to their *gurus,* first and foremost, initiate them into populated and reproduced lineages. Their names codify them as having been recognized by their teachers as holding certain attributes. The rituals of initiation in which they participate are exchanges that encode them in social orders. Certainly part of a *yogī*'s practice is to focus on the illusory quality of that name, those attributes, the rituals, and any thoughts, perceptions, or desires that may arise. These elements are part of the play of *saṃsāra,* not real entities to be taken literally or with meaning.

The shared commitment to viewing the apparitions of the world this way—as illusory delusions that must be navigated—is part of what makes the renouncer community a cultural unit. In this book, I have sought to combine Durkheim's emphasis on sociality with Dumont's Weberian distinction between worldliness and asceticism. By showing how renouncer life is premised on a social religion that is also distinct from householder Hinduism, I reinsert Durkheimian principles into Dumont's useful model. Dumont calls renouncers individuals because they pursue liberation or salvation rather than explicitly social aims. While soteriology is an individual or solitary pursuit at the ideological level, renouncer life is actually a social experience. Durkheim's emphasis on collective life and the social uses of religion applies equally to the South Asian community of renouncers, just as Weber's distinction between worldliness and asceticism and Dumont's binary between householders and renouncers do. Dumont's model of relations between renouncers and householders holds in contemporary South Asia, as long as we recall the socially connected dimension of renunciation.

If we take the split between worldliness and transcendence, as posited by Weber, as the operative division in South Asian Hindu society, ethnography can only legitimately assess the former. Confined to the material plane, how, then, can we ascertain the divide? The material aspects of culture, according to many worldviews—including both the Hindu worldview and the Einsteinian worldview—rely on the triad of body, space, and time. Taken together, these three aspects of existence form the ground of *sādhu* culture. In renouncers' worldviews, each of these units in turn transcends: space constitutes whole landscapes; bodies encompass universes; time is counted in *kalpas*. At the core of wandering is a vastness, the ocean of bliss, to which we can only aspire. The *sādhu* community may be in perpetual motion, but in the Hindu religious model, it also stands still.

Coda: Departure

After that first summer of research, it was time to return to graduate school. I had spent much of the summer with a spirited young *sādhu* named Rāju Bābā, who lived in a small room above the Bagmati at Paśupatināth. He was a fascinating man: born in Africa of Indian parents, he had returned to the Indian subcontinent in his twenties, to find his roots. He had met a *guru*, whom he decided to follow, and he took initiation into *sannyāsa*.

We spent many relaxed afternoons together, but our friendship did not stand the test of time, in part because all our conversations invariably ended up at the same point: he felt I needed to be taught sexual *tantra* if I was to understand anything about embodiment, and he was willing to appoint himself my tutor. I was not interested in pursuing this line of research with him, and so opted to spend significantly less time in his room, visiting only in daytime hours when many people—including local policemen, who often came to enjoy a break from their Paśupatināth beat—were present. He was eventually run out of town altogether—I never saw him again after that summer—because his *tantric* tutorials included not only a Japanese tourist who had become pregnant and was planning to return to Kathmandu to be with him, but also a young Nepali girl in the neighborhood, whose family became furious at his licentiousness and would not abide his presence in their community.

I harbored no ill feelings toward him personally—and knew little of the range of his exploits during the time I spent with him—and I went to say goodbye to him before I left Kathmandu with genuine gratitude for the many cups of tea and afternoons of conversation we had shared. "You're leaving tomorrow?" he asked. He was himself a world traveler and knew the mechanisms of international air travel. "Make jet set meditation," he counseled in English. "Open like the sky." Meditation, I learned that morning, like wandering, comes in many forms. There are many ways—jets, and also jet sets—to navigate the skies and oceans of being and becoming, each traversing space, transcending time.

APPENDIX: LITERATURES ON RENUNCIATION & EMBODIMENT

The Anthropological Literature on Renunciation in South Asia

Over the past few decades, the Indological literature has only indirectly addressed the question of whether Hindu *sādhus* see the material world in the same way as Hindu householders. The social relationship between the renouncer community and the householder community was a prominent question in South Asian studies in the years after 1960, when Louis Dumont published an article arguing that this structural relationship offered a fundamental tool for understanding Hindu social life (1980[1966]). As Dumont's structuralist theories were gradually overthrown in the 1970s and 1980s, a number of rich ethnographies about Hindu India explicitly de-emphasized the differences in religious worldview between renouncers and householders (cf. Marriott 1976; Gold 1988; Daniel 1984; Mines 1994; Lamb 2000). My ethnographic discussions draw heavily from the nuanced understandings we already have of Hindu householder concepts of space (cf. Beck 1976; Bhardwaj 1973; Das 1974; Eck 1996; Gold 1988), time (cf. Babb 1975; Berreman 1972[1963]; Cohen 1998; Lamb 2000), and the body (cf. Cohen 1998; Inden and Nicholas 1977; Marriott 1976; Daniel 1984; Parry 1992, Alter 1992).

« *Author and Pāgalānanda, Kathmandu, circa 1976*

Theoretical Models: Louis Dumont and a Defense of Dualism, from an Emic Perspective

Structuralist thought argues that social systems are based on oppositional or dualistic relationships. The basic split in Hindu society, Dumont argued, was that between caste society—the hierarchical, interdependent units of Hindu social structure—and the individual renouncers who broke free of it.[1] The world of Hindu thought and practice could for Dumont be broken down into two discrete and non-overlapping categories: the this-worldly householder and the other-worldly renouncer. The renouncer and the householder form the two poles of a complementary yet entirely oppositional relationship. The binary is total.

Dumont's model was influenced by both Durkheim and Weber (1958[1920]), although he was more obviously descended from the Durkheimian school that gave rise to structuralism as a way of understanding collective social life (see Levi-Strauss 1969[1949]). In his insistence that renouncers alone live apart from social realms, however, Dumont relied on Weberian sociology. Gellner reminds us that Dumont used Weber in his emphasis on the division between "this-worldly" and "other-worldly," which Dumont equates to the orientations of the householder and the renouncer respectively (Gellner 2001:86; Dumont 1980[1966]:401). Dumont also relies on Weber's distinction between "social religion" (which was Durkheim's exclusive interest) and "soteriology," or the practical "discipline of salvation" (Gellner 2001:95). For Dumont, the religion of the group could be used to explain the relations of householder society, while the practices of salvation could be applied to the individualistic renouncer. Dumont does explicitly disagree with Weber on a number of points, however, including that "the ultramundane tendency" lies with the class of Brāhman priests rather than with renouncers (1980[1966]:273).

Dumont has been correctly criticized on many counts including that the individualism he attributed to the renouncer is steeped in Western notions of will (Marriott 1976); that householder Hindus have nuanced relations and three-dimensional notions of self or personhood, and are not simply units in a system (Das 1982[1977]; Trawick 1990); that his structuralist conceptions of society are too static and therefore insufficiently historical (Gellner 2001); and that theoretical models of hierarchy, or stark divisions between sacred and profane, eclipse the multiple variations of social reality, and the frequent ways people act against systems or combine elements of opposing structures (Raheja 1988). In this book, I have suggested that renouncers live very communal lives, and are no more "individualistic" than members of caste society; on the other side of Dumont's equation, recent ethnographers have convincingly argued that householders have well-developed senses of individuality (see especially Mines 1994).

While Dumont has been widely critiqued, his basic contributions to South Asian sociology are undisputed. My inclination to reclaim Dumont's position on Hindu renunciation responds in part to a recent call by Gellner, who argues that Dumont's contributions to South Asian social analysis may be unsurpassed, and that his "achievement is still important and impressive and one that should be built on rather than destroyed" (2001:11). Dumont may be wrong about the nuances of Indian social life on a number of counts, but the ideological relationship that he posited between householders and renouncers is consistent with renouncers' own views of their social relations. Although the opposition he posited between householders and renouncers is too stark, Dumont opened up the idea that the state of being inside the social world and the state of being outside the social world must be defined in relation to one another, and that householders and renouncers fulfill these structural roles. The two stages of life, or the two states of being, inform the parameters of each other.

Mine is not a whole-hearted defense of structuralism, nor of the stark ideals that separate Dumont's householders from his renouncers. Renouncers' livers are not confined by the static, structuralist, or antihistorical residue of Dumont's argument, but they do generally adhere to the basic dualistic principles for which Dumont argued, and which he based in part on the Sāṃkhya school of Indian philosophy. One caveat, however: the dualism that is clearly reflected in the narratives of renouncers is not quite the same as Dumont's dualism. Dumont posed a static system of social relations that marked people as belonging to one category or another. Renouncers talk about the opposition as an active, communal, and perpetually re-created break, which reflects the intention and the participation of its actors. What Dumont failed to acknowledge is the intentionality or the causality of the social breaks that renouncers effect, and the Durkheimian depth of community that emerges as a result.

Theoretical Models: A Disagreement about Renunciation and Caste

One of Dumont's earliest critics was Jan Heesterman, who argued that rather than pose a relationship of structural opposition, the values of Brāhmanical Hinduism were taken to their logical extreme by the practices of renunciation (1964). The relation between Brāhmanic society and renouncer society was misunderstood, Heesterman argued, if they were pitted against one another. Because the symbolic systems used by the two communities largely overlapped, and the ritual practices of one social sphere were explicitly referred to and adapted by the other, renunciation and Brāhmanical householder societies were not competing or mutually exclusive systems in this model, but steps along a continuum in which renunciation put into practice many of the extreme rules of Brāhmanical society. Renouncers were the ultimate Brāhmans for Heesterman, who called renunciation an "orthogenetic, internal development of Vedic thought" (1964:24).[2]

But Patrick Olivelle has more recently suggested that the institution of renunciation developed as a social movement that actively challenged Brāhmanic rule (1992). Rather than demonstrate how similar the renouncer worldview is to the householder worldview, which was Heesterman's approach, Olivelle shows how the symbolic and ritual overlap in the two canons can be explained as a deliberate appropriation of renunciatory models by a Brāhmanic caste society that was fundamentally challenged by the growing ascetic movement in the sixth century. "In every case the value system of the Vedic world is inverted," Olivelle writes, "wilderness over village, celibacy over marriage, economic inactivity over economic productivity, ritual inactivity over ritual performance, instability over stable residence. Both in ideology and in life-style these reversals clearly represented a radical challenge to the Vedic world" (1992:46).

Olivelle explicitly returns to Dumont's arguments to show how Brāhmanic institutions appropriated the counters to caste society that renunciation offered as a way to encompass both social power and the sacred or ritual dominance claimed by renouncers. "I believe that Dumont is right in viewing [renunciation] as a 'new' element that at least initially challenged and contradicted many of the central premises of sacrificial theology," he writes, and he goes on to argue

> that when the evidence is examined completely it does point to a profound conflict between the two, a conflict that cannot be adequately explained if renunciation was in fact 'an orthogenetic development of Vedic thought.' The claim frequently made in later sources that the Brāhman householder is the ideal renouncer far from supporting Heesterman's position appears to reflect the incorporation of renunciatory values into Brāhmanical institutions and theology; often it is mere rhetoric. (1992:21)

So Dumont may not have been far off when he hypothesized the antagonistic relationship between renouncers and householders: "We may imagine the reaction to this creature [the emaciated renouncer with the begging bowl] of the typical Brāhman . . . represented in a carving on the north gate at Sanchi . . . a round bellied figure, expressing an inimitable blend of arrogance and avidity" (1980[1966]:274). If Olivelle, following Dumont, is right, the split contemporary renouncers make from householder society is a complete and self-conscious one, arising from a deliberate political history as well as from religious ideology.

Theoretical Models: Victor Turner and Liminality

Victor Turner's famous work on liminality as a social model of "anti-structural" ritual and community has a special resonance for Hindu *sādhus*. Turner argues that, broadly speaking, renouncer societies establish themselves as permanent buffers from—or counters to—householder society. Monastic orders, he suggests, are liminal communities that do not resolve back into social structure but rather take the form of institutions. "Nowhere," he writes, "has this institutionalization of liminality been more clearly marked and defined than in the monastic and mendicant states in the great world religions" (1969:107). Ethnographer Robert Gross succinctly applies Turner's model to the Hindu renouncer community:

> [U]nlike other rites of passage where liminality is but a temporary condition leading to the incorporation into another recognized status in the social order, ascetic initiation, or ordination, establishes the *sādhus* in a *perpetual* liminal phase. . . . [The] entire life style of renunciation transforms the transitional phase of initiation into a more or less permanent state of liminality. (1992:301; italics in original)

Rather than be incorporated back into dominant social structures, *sādhu* society is reproduced as an alternative, parallel community. The permanent liminality that Turner and Gross apply to renouncer society also reflects the intended duration of ritual or religious activity. For a renouncer, ideally, religious practice—and the religious knowledge it produces—never ends.

Turner argues that the liminal state is one of *communitas,* a term which he differentiates from community by arguing it refers to "a modality of social relationship" that transcends the normal boundaries of communal life in its open-ended and non-hierarchical style. *Communitas* is for Turner "a matter of giving recognition to an essential and generic human bond, without which there could be no society" and through which a challenge to daily social relations is openly stated (1969:96–7). I suggest that Hindu renouncer society does occupy a liminal relationship to Hindu caste society, but also that it fully constitutes its own community. While the communal dynamic of *sādhu* society means that renunciation acts as a social alternative, renouncers do not live in an entirely ethereal or structure-less society. Renouncers' lives challenge householder society through the creation of parallel structures—such as the alternative lineages, families, and institutions which I outlined in chapter 2—rather than in the absence of structure. We might say that renunciation is counter-structural rather than anti-structural; *sādhus* live in an alternative community that displays hierarchy, discipline, and recognizable modes of social interaction, just as householder society does.

The Ethnographic View

Dumont's renouncers are idealized creatures, not contemporary living *sādhus,* just as Turner's liminal institutions sometimes end up displaying the characteristics of structured societies in light of real social dynamics. But the separation that Dumont identified as constitutive of Hindu society and in which Turner finds the capacity for transcendent knowledge is consonant with renouncers' own perspectives: no matter how they articulate their departure from householder life, they say they are *different.* This alterity is part of the meaning of renunciation. When Dumont describes renouncer life as "a social state apart from society proper" (1980[1966]:273), he identifies a fundamental and symbolically intentional split between renouncers and householders in Hindu society. In both the social role of renunciation and the public presentation of the renouncer, *sādhu* society is loudly and visibly proclaimed as oppositional.

The ethnographic literature on Hindu renunciation has tried to round out the idealized picture of renunciation presented by social theorists and textual scholars. Burghart insists on looking at social structure within *sādhu* orders (1983a; 1983b), a project upon which I try to build. Gross devotes himself to exhaustive description of Vaiṣṇava *sādhu* society based on over a decade of fieldwork, and shows how renouncers' lives at once occupy a permanent liminal place in South Asian social structures and interact with householders in mutually sustaining ways (1992). Narayan gives a portrait of an individual renouncer, who, with his own personal idiosyncrasies, uses stories to explain his philosophies to householders from all over the world (1989). And Khandelwal, expanding upon preliminary work on women renouncers by Ojha (1981; 1985; 1988) and Denton (1991; 2004), explores how gender identity remains a salient category of experience despite renouncer rhetoric on the irrelevance of the material body (1997; 2001; 2004).[3]

The Phenomenological Literature on Embodiment

Contemporary anthropological thought on the body has moved slowly towards phenomenology, or the study of lived experience. As a way to analyze both processes of perception and cultural interpretations of experience, recent scholars suggest, the body might provide information about acculturation itself. In the contemporary phenomenological literature, understanding the variable experiences of embodiment has productively explained cultural practices, values, and meanings (cf. Csordas 1994; Turner 1994; Asad 1997; Stoller 1997). Aided and abetted by feminist theory (cf. Grosz 1994; Jaggar and Bordo 1989; Suleiman 1986), which has insisted for much longer than anthropology that the body could be thought of as the ground for and source of knowledge, anthropology has turned its sights toward questions of bodily practice, processes of perception, expressions of emotion, and systems of sense as ways of understanding different cultural approaches toward the body, and of using bodily experience to explain culture.

The Mind-Body Split in Anthropology and Feminist Theory

After Merleau-Ponty (1962), who is largely cited as the father of contemporary phenomenological thought (and is one of the authors who most convincingly deconstructs a Cartesian dualism), Csordas in particular makes a useful distinction between the body as an object of study, or an empirical thing, on one hand, and embodiment as the ground of experience, or the state of being in the world, on the other.[4] He complains of the number of anthropological ventures that use the body "as a synonym for self or person" (1994:4), or break apart the body to study different aspects of the person "with the number of bodies dependent on how many of its aspects one cares to recognize" (1994:5). Studying embodiment, rather than studying the body, means that people's bodily experiences come to have meaning and force.

The body as an object of inquiry seems only to receive systemic or cultural influences, and never itself responds to, interacts with, or acts upon larger systems. The objective body reminds us of the problems with structuralist thought, which argued for all-powerful systemic structures that swallowed up human agency.[5] The trouble with cultural analyses of the body is that they tend to regard the body as an object, encasing an agent in the world at times, but remaining an objective rather a subjective experience.[6] The body, as it has predominantly been studied in anthropology, is itself a victim of the body-mind split.

Both recent anthropological and feminist approaches to the study of the body in the last two decades have tried to heal this split, calling for "a mindful body" (Scheper-Hughes and Lock 1987:7). Feminist theory in particular has insisted on using the body as a way to ground experience (cf. Bordo 1993; Gallop 1988; Irigaray 1985; Cixous 1981), looking for a more holistic, organic, or integrated psychosomatic dimension to mind and body matters.[7] The origin for some of the body-as-experience work began as a feminist critique of objectivist scientific method, which relied upon so-called objective "transcendence" and seemed to reinstate very starkly Descartes' duality (see Keller 1985).[8] Male attempts at transcendence (the "god-trick") in the methods of science, for example, were simply not embodied enough (Haraway 1988:587). Feminist scholars' insistence upon subjectivity and location could counter "the Cartesian fantasy of the philosopher's transcendence of the concrete locatedness of the body in order to achieve the God's eye view, the 'view from nowhere'" (Bordo 1993:39). Knowledge must be grounded in embodied experience in these critiques. The emphasis on phenomenology, or the experience of the subject, further counters a split between consciousness and physicality by arguing that embodied practice constitutes matter.

The Soul-Body Split in Indology

As I have discussed in the main text and above, dualism is not a uniquely Western system of thought, and it is not, therefore, as McKim Marriott argued, "a Western philosophic burden" (1976:109). In an attempt to find a system of explaining social relationships in Hindu society that did not rely on what he believed were external theoretical concepts, Marriott argued for an understanding of Hinduism that followed a single, or monist, code; his work gave rise to much subsequent thinking on the body in India, but also grounded the claim in the '80s and '90s that Indic thought was free from body-soul dualism.

Following the work of Marriott (1976), Inden and Nicholas (1977) and Carman and Marglin (1985) showed how Indian bodies could be seen to carry, transmit, and codify caste. Marriott's argument that Indian concepts of embodiment should be understood within a "monistic" model responded to Dumont's structuralist dualism in particular and to Cartesian dualism in general, which Marriott argued "pervades both Western philosophy and Western common sense" (1976:110). This monistic model does not hold to a split between action and body, culture and matter, or body and mind, and, for Marriott, reflected a "belief in the nonduality of all such pairs" (1976:110).

Marriott understood all Hindu Indian social interactions through his definition of the way bodies are lived, experienced, and interpreted in South Asia. In his model, any giving or receiving transmits a person's substance. Because part of the substance's code is related to the hierarchical code of caste, different social groups need to attend to how much they take in and how much they give out. According to Marriott's followers, the sharing of bodies in Hindu experience is not only a metaphor, but a physiological reality (Inden and Nicholas 1977).

The possibility of a continuum of purity and pollution and the idea that a religious practitioner can move up and down on the scale of refinement are some of the reasons ethnographers have argued that there is no duality in Hindu thoughts on the body. Van der Veer argues, for example, that "the transformation of the body through ritual action implies instead [of quasi-Cartesian dualism] a 'refinement' of mental qualities" (1989: 458). What van der Veer misses in this construction, and what Marriott failed to recognize before him, is that the soul and the body are in Hindu thought perpetually and irreconcilably split apart: the state of embodiment and the state of liberation are popularly and textually discussed as fundamentally opposed. The body is the vessel of human experience and religious experience, I heard repeatedly from my informants, but liberation is precisely not an embodied experience. Liberation, the final goal of the Hindu ascetic religious endeavor, relegates all previous experience to the social and material plane.

The two models in supposed conflict here—a monistic continuum on one hand and a soul-matter dualism on the other—are not irreconcilable in Hindu thought, but operate simultaneously in their own domains. Posing a continuum of purity and pollution, or a gradual line from gross to subtle matter, speaks to a method of functioning in the material world, but the metaphor of soul-body dualism at the core of the renouncer's religious project ultimately trumps materiality. The split between body and soul refers to a goal of final liberation, where the constraints of sociality and materiality no longer function. Hindu practitioners engage in physical disciplines to approach a disembodied state because their bodies are the only available tools.

In the face of large and convincing literatures that deconstruct structuralism, Cartesianism, and irreconcilable splits between the human mind and body, I hardly wish to reinstitute dualism as the only defining mode of thought and experience. Efforts to explain bodily experience in holistic ways—that deconstruct the difference between subject and object, for example, or that rely on sense or perception as valuable sources of knowledge—are certainly productive for anthropology. But I do want to suggest that dualism is a useful heuristic tool, and that our fears of structuralism and Cartesianism may have eclipsed or precluded the cross-cultural uses of dualism as a model. My two points, very simply, are first, that dualism is not exclusively a Western concept and second, that a split between body and soul is precisely the metaphor Hindu renouncers use to articulate their social separateness. At least in name, the institution of renunciation defies caste: using renouncers' worldviews on embodiment may help us review Indological models of caste-based bodily experience as well as challenge assumptions about the unity of soul and body in Indian systems of thought. As Dumont argued, dualism is a concept internal to Hindu religious life and is, in many regards, correct as a way of understanding renouncer worldviews.

NOTES

Introduction

1. For scholarly work on the textual tenets of renunciation, see especially Denton 2004; Olivelle 1992; Zaehner 1973; Heesterman 1964.

2. See Narayan (1993a) and Abu-Lughod (1991) on fieldwork methodologies by "halfies," or people who are personally connected to the places where they do research.

3. See Feldhaus (1995) for a thorough exploration of how rivers may stand in for each other in Hindu India, and Slusser (1982) for a comprehensive account of the myth and lore of temples and rivers in the Kathmandu Valley. See Rademacher (2005) for contemporary ethnographic work on the Bagmati.

4. The *Gītā,* an account of the meeting between the warrior Arjuna and the deity Kṛṣna, is one of the most popular religious texts in India, and one with which every renouncer I spoke with was basically familiar, if only in an oral version. The popular image of renouncers insists on their religious and philosophical authority, and most of my informants duly quoted from or cited the principles of the *Gītā* as a way to demonstrate a basic credential.

5. See Burghart's groundbreaking work on ascetic social orders (1983a, 1983b).

6. Early writings on globalization tended to claim that the predicament of displaced or dispersed communities—how culture is reproduced without a shared experience of place—was a recent phenomenon (Appadurai 1996; Kaplan 1996; Bhabha 1994; Clifford 1992, 1997). The example of the South Asian renouncer community shows us that the communal practices of wandering, travel, and movement across space far precede modernity. Creating cultural links across space is, in this instance, as much a "traditional" enterprise as it is a "modern" or a "postmodern" one.

7. As a discipline, anthropology has grown increasingly sensitive to multi-sited field methods (Clifford and Marcus 1986) so that ethnographers can work with immigrant communities, diasporas (Silliman 2001), pilgrimage groups (Gold 1988; Morinis 1992), and labor populations who move across international or interregional borders (Mills 1999; Ong 1999), for example.

8. In one sense, I followed Taussig's description of "pilgrimage as method," although I took it more literally than he may have intended (1997:197).

9. Varied cosmic maps suggest that mythical events occur in different degrees of specificity: the local, the regional, and the subcontinental. Sircar details many *śakti pīṭha* lists (1973), but popular legend also enumerates the *pīṭhas* differently (Dowman 1981). Certainly in Kathmandu, Guhyeśwarī is seen as the site of the goddess's vulva, or the center of creation; on larger, subcontinental lists, it is listed as a *pīṭha*, or power spot, of the goddess's anus, since the temple of Kamakhya in Assam represents the vulva.

10. My thanks to Kaja McGowan for this very helpful advice.

11. See Griaule 1965; Crapanzano 1980; Narayan 1989; Behar 1993 for ethnographies with similar approaches.

12. See especially Narayan (1989) on the image of renouncer as charlatan.

13. These are my estimates, based in part on discussions with photographer and researcher Dolf Hartsuiker. The numbers of renouncers in South Asia has fluctuated over time: different authors have debated whether the number is decreasing in contemporary India because of alternative social options (Gross 1992; Ghurye 1995[1953]). Population figures for the total renouncer community are very difficult to ascertain and monitor (see Sinha and Saraswati [1978] for good Banaras estimates in the 1970s). Certainly the number is relatively high in absolute terms, but represents only a minute fraction (less than 0.2%, if my estimates are close) of the total South Asian population.

14. See Khandelwal (1997, 2001, 2004) for work on the women renouncer community in Hardwar and Khandelwal, Hausner, and Gold (2006) for recent work on women renouncers in South Asia as a region.

15. A knowledgeable Western *sādhu* told me that a full 90% of women *sādhus* in his order were either Nepali or of Nepali origin, and this figure was largely borne out by my own research.

16. Caldwell (1999) touches on the sticky methodological quandary of how to learn a tradition that requires both initiation and a scholarly distance.

17. Denton (2004) cogently argues that the difference between Varanasi widows who live in ashrams and renouncers is precisely the ritual of initiation. The need for a ritual of initiation to be classified as a *sādhu* also points to the importance of having a *guru*, or someone qualified to perform the rite.

18. My informants' insistence that knowledge comes in part from practice resonates strongly with Bourdieu (1977) and Asad (1997), who argue that the experience of religion, culture, or language comes through embodied practice, which conveys knowledge of a different order and kind than does an academic exercise.

19. See Lamb (2000) on the powers of women who fall outside householder norms. Also see Lochtefeld (1992) for another account of Rādhā Giri's charisma.

20. See Bharati (1961) and Rampuri (2005) for autobiographical accounts of being a Western *sādhu*. Neill (1970) presents the only work I have seen that compares Western travelers to *sādhus*.

21. See Khandelwal (2006) on the historical development of service as a concept and practice affiliated with renunciation.

22. For two well-known photography books on sādhus, see Bedi (1991) and Hartsuiker (1993). Hartsuiker spent many years getting to know his subjects (personal communication, 2001).

The Body and Sādhu Society

1. See Desikachar (1995) for a translation of Patañjali's yoga sutras. For discussions of union from a different tradition, see McDaniel (1989) and Dimock (1966) on Bengali mysticism.

2. See Mohanty (1991) for a good example of the feminist discussion of fluid subjectivity, or how individual subjectivity may shift in its alliances and oppositions depending on political, historical, and social circumstances. See Mascia-Lees, Sharpe, and Cohen (1989) for an application of feminist thinking on fluid subjecthood to anthropology.

3. See especially Rudolph and Rudolph (1983[1967]) on Gandhi's use of the symbol of the renouncer.

4. See also Khandelwal (2001) for similar findings of youngest daughters of large families permitted by their parents, albeit reluctantly, to become *sannyāsinīs,* and for consideration of *sannyāsa* as a "site of undetermination" for women (2004).

5. See Guha (1987) for a historical case that suggests that women might have become *sādhvīs* as an alternative to abortion.

6. See Obeyesekere (1981) for a psychoanalytic discussion of hair among Sri Lankan women ascetics. Also see Hershman (1974) and Leach (1958) for discussions of hair as related to sexuality, and the magical properties of hair.

7. See also Daniel (1984) for an ethnographic account of pilgrimage where stripping away the five sheaths is the primary goal.

8. The "sharing of a body" turned out to be the seminal concept in Bengali kinship classification: Inden and Nicholas (1977) demonstrated that rather than classify extended family "by blood" and "by law" as American kinship is delineated (cf. Schneider 1968), Bengalis classify all family by the sharing of a common body. Members of a family are considered *eka-deha* and *eka-śarīra,* literally of "one body."

9. Substance exchange with the earth, for example, is explicit for Alter's informants (1992:158).

10. For a full discussion of *darśan,* or the possibility of attaining realization through sight of a *guru* or deity, see Eck (1998).

11. This view is shared by Gold's householder *yogī* informants, who suggest that death is the end of relationships, since the mortal body is the sustainer of social connectedness (1992).

12. See also Heesterman (1982) for a textual reading of renouncer-householder social interactions.

13. The "concept of spirit possession," Parry adds, "seems to suggest a quite radical duality between the flesh and the spirit," as do the legends about accomplished renouncers who borrow bodies to have experiences they otherwise could not (1992:512).

14. More examples include Staal (1983–1984), Kasulis (1993), and Irigaray (2002).

15. Also, see Azouvi (2002) on how French philosophers' relationship to Descartes shifts dramatically over time. Interpretations of Descartes, Azouvi argues, are more closely related to contemporary political trends than to Descartes' actual theses. As one reviewer nicely summarizes, Cartesian arguments have "always been distorted to fit contemporary prejudices" (*Times Literary Supplement*).

16. See Inden (1990) for an application of Said's classic arguments (1978) about Western projections of the so-called Orient to India in particular.

17. Parry (1985) also suggests that the relationship between body and spirit in Catholicism may be a more monist position than is usually cited, as well. For Christian monastic views on the split between body and soul, see Asad 1997; Bottomley 1979; Brown 1982; Bynum 1987, 1992.

The Social Structures of Sādhu Life

1. Olivelle (1992) explains in detail how this group of texts, written over more than a millennium, can be brought together to assess how the institution of renunciation, *sannyāsa,* has been theologically formulated. Some were probably written just around the beginning of the common era; many—including the *Upaniṣad* from which this quote was taken—were written much later, around the twelfth century CE.

2. See Olivelle (1993) for a textual history of the four *āśramas.* In earlier texts, each was seen as a "mode of religious life" that could be seen as a "lifelong undertaking"; much later, they were seen as sequential stages (Olivelle 1992:52). He argues that the earliest discussions of *sannyāsa* as a life choice date from the fifth century BCE.

3. Pinch argues that Udāsīn sects tend to align themselves religiously and politically with Śaiva *daśnāmī* orders (1996:41).

4. The four Śaṅkarācārya *maṭhs,* or monasteries, are located in Badrinath, Uttaranchal, in the north, Puri, Orissa, in the east, Srngeri, Tamil Nadu, in the south, and Dwarka, Gujarat, in the west. A great deal of money and power is inherent in these positions; after I completed fieldwork for this book, the Śaṅkarācārya *maṭh* based in Srngeri was involved in a murder scandal.

5. See Hiriyanna (1993) for a good overview of the history and basic principles of this school of thought.

6. Rāmānuja is the most prominent but not the only founder of *bhakti* orders. Others include Nimbārka (probably twelfth century), and Madhva (thirteenth century), who advocated *bhakti* despite his affiliation with Vedānta lineages (Ghurye 1995[1953]).

7. Śaṅkarācārya's schools are known as Śaiva despite an insistence on devotion without form or attribute. This is probably because the ascetics which Śaṅkara organized were exclusively worshippers of Śiva, or at least a prototypical deity who most closely resembles Paśupati, the Lord of the Animals, or Rudra, both later interpreted as manifestations of Śiva. (See Lorenzen 1972.)

8. While most renouncers invoke Śiva, the deity of *caras,* or hashish, I also heard *sādhus* dedicate their pipes (or, alternatively, ask for alms) by calling, "Alakh!" Ghurye translates "Alakh" as "vernacular for the Sanskrit word 'Alakṣya' meaning 'not perceptible' hence formless, i.e. the Absolute Brāhma" (1995[1953]:106). Ghurye suggests that Śaṅkara intended that his orders engage in *saguṇa* practices, despite his philosophical orientation: "It is characteristic of Hindu religious synthesis, that even Śaṅkarācārya, the great logician and metaphysician that he was, saw good reason to permit and even to prescribe anthropomorphic worship as a step towards final spiritual realization" (1995[1953]:87–88).

9. This is also reflected in the history of Vedānta texts and commentaries (cf. Radhakrishnan and Moore 1957).

10. For a historical account of Nāth practice and ideology, see White (2003, 1996). The older Kāpālika and Paśupata, as well as the *tantric* Aghori and Kaula sects, are generally understood to be subdivisions of Nāth lineages (Lorenzen 1972; Parry 1985). Also see A. Gold (1992) and D. Gold (1996) on a Rajasthani caste of householder Nāths who are not renouncers but are initiated into Nāth lineages.

11. See Gold (1987); Babb (1986, 1983) on *gurus*. For *gurus* who are *sādhus*, see Narayan (1989:82–87).

12. There is a technical term for a sādhu without a *guru: vaimukh,* meaning without a head or a chief. Despite this technical allowance, I never met a *sādhu* who did not have a *guru* or who believed that someone could be a legitimate *sādhu* without one.

13. Pāgāl Bābā had actually heard of Rādhā Giri, not because she was a Giri, but because he knew the place on the river where her *dhūnī* was located, and the couple who had lived there previously.

14. Certainly these structures are male-dominated, and most *gurus* act as a patriarch in renouncer families. But see Khandelwal (1997) and Ramanujan (1982) on the image of respected renouncers as maternal.

15. See Inden and Nicholas (1977) for a classic study of Indian kinship, and interpretations of father-son relations, which remain a model for *guru*–disciple relations.

16. Olivelle shows that Brāhmanical society concerns itself with renouncer ideology as much as the other way around: Brāhmanical literature extols "marriage and procreation, the central institutions of the old worlds" as a "total and uncompromising rejection of the celibate ideal" (1992:49).

17. See Alter, who studied wrestlers and wrestling *akhāṛās* for a description of the range of activities that take place in *akhāṛās* in contemporary Banaras (1992:8–9).

18. Of the ten lines, members of seven orders are usually initiated into *akhāṛās* (Gross 1992:147). The three lines that do not initiate warriors—which are not coincidentally limited to renouncers of high-caste background—are the Tīrtha, Āśrama, and Sarasvatī lineages (Hartsuiker 1993).

19. Hartsuiker (1993) argues that the seventh *akhāṛā,* the Agni Akhāṛā, was ratified as a full *akhāṛā* as late as 1971.

20. There is also some evidence that dispersed mercenary groups of ascetic warriors existed before the thirteenth century, but these may not have been ratified as full *akhāṛā* regiments (Tod 1920).

21. See Pinch (1996:27–29) for theories on the relationship between militarism and higher numbers of lower-caste renouncers.

22. See Pinch (1996:25) and Lorenzen (1978:72) on why the term rebellion may be a "political overstatement."

23. At the request of the governor of the East India Company, Warren Hastings, the ruler of Nepal, Prithvi Narayan Shah, helped block renouncers from crossing the border into Nepal (Stiller 1989:51).

24. See Dirks (1997:185) on British attempts to control arenas of Indian religious tradition, particularly in the context of public space.

25. The Nāth temple in Paśupatināth alone (the Akhāṛā's second largest headquarters, after Dang, in southwestern Nepal) owns forty or so cattle as well as land, a considerable holding. See Bouillier (1991, 1998) on the holdings of Nepali Nāth lineages and their relation to the Nepali monarchy.

26. See van der Veer on finances as one aspect of power of contemporary Rāmānandi *sādhu* orders (1989:467), and also for discussion on the extent to which these financial transactions interact with those of the Brāhmanical pilgrimage industry (1988).

27. One account cites 18,000 casualties (Wilson 1861), but this is likely exaggerated.

28. The *nāgās* have their own administrative structure, the Śambhu Pañc, which is encompassed by but separate from the *akhāṛā* structure. See Gross (1992:147ff).

29. I was told there are four stages within renouncer life: *brahmacārī, nāgā, daṇḍa svāmī,* and *parahaṃsa* Most senior and elderly renouncers who participate in *akhāṛā* life are still *nāgā bābās,* however. I met only one *daṇḍa svāmī* during my work, and Ghurye states that the designation of *parahaṃsa* has been absorbed into the administrative rank of *maṇḍaleśvara* (1995[1953]:109). Hartsuiker (1993) argues that *daṇḍadhārīs*—holders of the staff—must be born as Brāhmans.

30. See Inden and Nicholas (1977) for an analysis of Bengali householder *saṃskāra* rituals.

31. It may be worth considering whether the symbolic power of the celibate ideal in South Asian political life (Alter 2000; Cohen 1995) derives partly from the military strength projected by ascetic orders.

32. See Anderson (1990) on the equivalence of religious power to political power.

33. Thapar (1979) argues that historically both kinds of ascetics have existed, falling on a continuum from someone totally disengaged from social life (whom Thapar would call an ascetic) to someone formally initiated into a social order (whom Thapar would call a renouncer). I argue that in contemporary South Asia, renouncers are connected with each other through the social structures I have outlined, even if they live far apart or in isolation.

Hardwar

1. Until its independence, Uttaranchal, composed of the two territories Garhwal and Kumaon, was the northernmost region of Uttar Pradesh.

2. On the Hindu nationalist movement, see also Jaffrelot (1996), Hansen (1999), and Hansen and Jaffrelot (1998).

3. The idea of motion is included in the very symbol of the Ganges, whose name etymologically relates to the Sanskrit verb *gam-*, "to go."

4. See Ewing (1997) and Freitag (1985) on how wandering places renouncers outside social life politically as well as spatially.

5. Different texts have slightly differing lists. The *Paramahamsaparivrājaka Upaniṣad* specifies that a renouncer may spend "one night in a village, three nights at a sacred bathing place, five nights in a town, and seven nights in a holy place" (verse 284 in Olivelle 1992:262). Different classes of renouncers may also be instructed in different lists (cf. *Nāradaparivrājaka Upaniṣad* 201–202 in Olivelle 1992:215).

6. See especially Narayan (1989) on the public image of the *sādhu* as charlatan.

7. I would call them "crossing-points," so as to encompass both spatial and temporal dimensions.

8. This may be another reason wandering tends to happen earlier in a *sādhu*'s life.

9. See Ostor, Fruzzetti, and Barnett (1982); Khare (1976); Kolenda (1987); Jeffery, Jeffery, and Lyon (1989) on householder kinship structures, family dynamics, and attachment to children.

10. Bhardwaj corroborates this observation with census statistics on pilgrimage demographics (1973:218).

11. Because Kashmir is politically contested territory between India and Pakistan, troop presence is heavy and civilian movement restricted.

12. See my essay on staying in place and community involvement (Hausner 2005).

13. Bhardwaj asserts early in his well-known book on Indian pilgrimage that meditation is always considered the foremost practice for liberation. Pilgrimage is "an *additional* redemptive practice, an adjunct to other forms of worship" (1973:4–5; italics in original).

14. On two occasions, both festival gatherings, I did see very focused group *sādhanā* among members of a Vaiṣṇava order. In these cases, the groups were roped off and sect leaders paraded the area in order to make sure that members of the public and other orders were kept physically distant.

15. Most of the Jūnā Akhāṛā *sādhvīs* I met at the 1998 Kumbh Melā in Hardwar lived together in a Pithoragarh ashram, near the Nepali border, and had traveled together to the Kumbh, where they lived in their own camp and moved about the city in small groups. See Denton (2004) for detailed descriptions of women's ashrams in Varanasi.

16. The word *dhūnī* is probably derived from the Sanskrit root *dhūp-*, "smoking" or "subfumigating" (Mayrhofer 1992). Ghurye is probably incorrect when he attributes it to the root *dhun-*, "to waft" (1995[1953]:137).

17. See Malamoud (1996[1989]) on heat and body functioning, and also Beck (1969) on the symbolism of heat in South India.

18. *Dhūnīs* do sometimes come in other shapes, which represent other *yantras,* or sacred designs.

19. See Heesterman (1993) in particular for an excellent analysis of Vedic sacrifice and the symbol of fire. A *dhūnī* might be seen as analogous to a householder's hearth, although in textual rituals a *sannyāsī* rather takes into his body the three sacred household fires when he leaves householder life.

20. Olivelle suggests that the ritual of depositing the continuous fires into the body were required by "Vedic practices related to travel" (1992:89), which were not necessarily limited to ascetics. Depositing the fires in the body allowed a traveler to adhere to the textual requirement of keeping sacred household fires burning continuously.

21. The first spoken text of the *Mahābhārata* reflects this tradition: a visiting renouncer is asked "From where have you come . . . and where have you whiled away your days, lotus-eyed one?" (verse 1.1.7 in van Buitenen 1973). In a different register, see Clifford (1992) on the distinction of "Where are you from?" and "Where are you between?"

Allahabad

1. We know that the Kumbhs have been taking place since at least the eighth century (when the wandering Chinese pilgrim Hsuen Tsang wrote about his experience at the Melā) and probably much longer, as part of the Māgh Melā.

2. This version is compelling in part for its insistence on illusion—particularly the illusion of a beautiful woman who is actually a male deity—as that which clouds the vision of the demons and relegates them to the world of death. See Leach (1961a) for a discussion on how sex-reversal in myth relates to the vanquishing of time.

3. Each city also hosts an *ardh* Kumbh, half Kumbh, on the sixth year of its cycle, which corresponds to a full Kumbh somewhere else. Allahabad is home to the Māgh Melā every year, possibly the Kumbh's historical antecedent.

4. This is why popular literature sometimes refers to renouncers as "god-men" or "holy men" (see Bedi 1991).

5. See Gaborieau (1982) for discussion of festivals as a way to link mortals and gods.

6. This may account for Prayag's pre-eminence among the four Kumbh Melās. The Hardwar Kumbh, usually described as the second most important Melā, takes place nine and a half years later, when Jupiter enters the constellation of Aquarius. Each Kumbh has its own import, however: in Hardwar, renouncers emphasized how the constellation Aquarius is symbolized by the pitcher, or the Kumbh itself.

7. The formal Nirañjanī Akhāṛā notice of the Kumbh announced procession and bathing dates using standard Hindi months, broken into the dark fortnight (from full moon to new moon) and the bright fortnight (from new moon to full moon). Gregorian calendar dates were also noted.

8. In the Indian system, Capricorn is represented by a crocodile, *makar*. As in Western astrology, both the characteristics of Capricorn and the symbol of the crocodile affect the period of time in question, as does Capricorn's link to the element earth, and its ruling planet Saturn, whose slow orbit and dark, dense qualities are such that its forces can be negative. I was also told that because crocodiles survive on earth and in water, Capricorn is linked to the element water, too, which symbolically connects the sign to the moon as well. The list of symbolic consonances will of course never be complete.

9. The solar transition into Capricorn, also the winter solstice when the sun begins moving northward, occurs on December 22 or 23 in the Gregorian calendar. The reason for these discrepant dates is because so-called Western astrological calculations use a tropical calendar, which accounts for a slippage in the placement of the constellations in the earth's sky over time (about a degree every seventy years), due to the tilt of the earth's axis. Most Indic astrological calculations use a sidereal calendar, which holds the constellations as fixed.

10. This quote is from an interview Bābā had with the BBC's Mark Tully, Allahabad, January 20, 2001.

Kathmandu

1. See, for example, the praises of the sage Yājñavalkya (Desikachar 2000).

2. The Nepali state has historically encouraged *sādhus* to come to Kathmandu for the festival by providing firewood, feasts, and even hashish at the temple during Śiva Rātrī. In the past few years, with a changing monarchy, this kind of support for renouncers has been less steady, and its future is uncertain.

3. McEvilley (1981) argues that yogic traditions originally emphasized bodily practices over mental practices, but that subsequent religious and historical movements eclipsed this focus on the physical body.

4. See O'Flaherty (1981) for her famous discussion on how the figure of Śiva encompasses both asceticism and eroticism.

5. The yogic breathing technique *kumbhaka prāṇāyāma* refers to retaining breath in the chest (Desikachar 1995).

6. See Hawley and Wulff (1996) for collected articles on the vast and important role of the divine feminine force in Hindu worship, and Kinsley (1997) for how manifestations of the divine feminine correspond to various features of the universe. See also Caldwell (1999) and Kondos (1986) on fierce or wrathful female deities.

7. Recall the Gaumukh *sādhu* who said, "The Himalaya is our father, and the Gaṅgā is our mother." Other *sādhus* referred to "Bhagvān" as their collective "*mātā pitā*," or mother and father.

8. See Levy (1990) on syncretism and Gellner (2001) on Newār religion. For comparative Newār and Vajrayana Buddhist worship at Paśupati and Guhyeśwarī, see Dowman (1981).

9. See Gold (1988:114) for a Rajasthani *bhajan* (possibly based on a poem by Kabir) which also uses the imagery of leaves falling from a tree as a metaphor for death. Also see Vaudeville (1974) for a translation of Kabir's original poem, in which falling leaves cry at their separation from the tree.

10. See Parry (1994) on the relationship between death rituals and fertility symbolism.

11. Again, see Parry for his pithy critique—and his convincing inversion—of "the monism of South Asian thought and the dualism of the West" (1992:511).

12. See the *Human Development Report* (2001) for good regional indicators of health and human welfare.

13. See Raheja and Gold (1994) for an ethnography of how their informants explain being born as women, and the ways they accept their fates.

14. See Lutz and Abu-Lughod (1990) for a good overview of the anthropology of emotion.

15. Khandelwal similarly found discussions with renouncers about sex and sexuality to be translated through the lens of emotion (2001, and personal conversation with Meena Khandelwal, November 2001).

16. See Salomon (1991) on Baul *tantric* poetry which argues that the Absolute manifests in progressive stages, which includes form.

17. See Beck (1976), for example, for elaboration on the symbolic equivalence between a South Indian temple and the human body. See also Basavanna's poem 820 in Ramanujan (1973), which is narrated as a poor man offering his body as a temple to Śiva.

18. See Rigopoulos (1998) for a full account of the history and symbolism of the deity Dattātreya.

19. Yoga texts offer detailed measurements of different kinds of *prāṇa* (including five *vayus,* or winds, which correlate to different bodily areas and functions). For a good summary, see Desikachar (1995).

20. Some *yogīs* also correlate the *cakras* with specific numbers, colors, animals, and personality characteristics (see Johari 1987).

21. See Storm (1999) for images and symbols of self-sacrifice in Hindu myth.

22. See also Gold (1996) on a caste of householder *yogīs* who deliberately cut the cartilage of the ear in order to sever the flow of sensuous desire.

23. Also see Alter (1994, 2000) and Cohen (1995) on the nationalist use of the symbol of celibacy, as well as Rudolph and Rudolph (1983[1967]) on Gandhi's use of celibacy.

24. O'Flaherty argues that the direction of the flow of semen is the major difference between Śiva as an ascetic, who directs his flow upwards, and Śiva as an erotic figure, who squanders his flow outward (1973).

25. Yoga Sutra verse 2.32 does link *tapas* and *svādhyāya,* but as separate elements of *niyama,* the branch of yoga practices relating to "personal discipline" (see Desikachar 1995:176, 240). This *sādhvī,* like most renouncers I spoke with, used the larger concept of discipline to contain all bodily practices.

26. See Khandelwal (2004, 2006) for a more detailed discussion on the prohibitions of sleep for renouncers.

Conclusion

1. Gross identifies nakedness, matted hair, and the use of ashes among ascetics as three prominent bodily symbols which signify a rejection of householder values and represent physical liminality: "in symbolizing a disregard for the body and sensual pursuits, [they] convey a sense of rejection of all socially sanctioned conventions and rules of conformity" (1992:304). See also Das (1976) for a discussion of liminality and the body in the Indian context.

2. See Heesterman (1993) for a text-based analysis of an attempt by Brāhmanical culture to encompass the whole, despite the impossibility of totality.

3. Eliade suggests that the concept of the inner sacrificial fire allowed "even the most autonomous ascetics and mystics to remain with the fold of Brāhmanism and later of Hinduism" (1958[1954]:112). Olivelle (1992) has a slightly different take, arguing that the renouncer ritual of internalizing sacrificial fires was a method of appropriating householder ritual.

4. The *Bṛhat-Sannyāsa Upaniṣad* suggests further that the outer world is sacrificed to the renouncer's body: "Having deposited the sacred fires in himself, an ascetic who offers the entire phenomenal world in the fire of knowledge is a great ascetic and a true fire-sacrificer" (verse 272 in Olivelle 1992:69).

5. Asad also points out Mauss's own interest in Eastern religious and mystical experience specifically. Also see Bourdieu (1990, 1977).

6. In anthropology, the body has come to stand for a practical ground of knowledge, as opposed, for example, to a discursive ground. In Advaita theories of reality,

on the other hand, both form *and* language are manifestations of dualist experience, and both would be set in opposition to non-dualist reality. See Leder (1990) and Butler (1993) for a discussion of the discursive constitution of matter. See also Moore (1994) for a good overview of feminist and anthropological positions on embodiment, including practical versus discursive forms of knowledge.

7. See especially Casey (1996); Harvey (2000); Massey (1994); and Moore (1986).

8. For theoretical discussions of singularity and community, see especially Agamben (1993); Nancy (1991[1986]); and Deleuze and Guattari (1987). My thanks to Cesare Casarino for introducing me to this literature. This is not quite the same question as whether *sādhus* are individuals, a topic of enormous magnitude in the South Asian literature, as well as in Euro-American philosophy: see, in anthropology, Mines (1994); Dumont (1980[1966]).

Appendix

1. A thorough examination of whether or not renouncers act as "individuals" more or less than householders do is best saved for another setting. An argument could be made that renouncers think of themselves as *less* like individuals, in their attempt to strip away ego identification, a paradox that Dumont was well aware of. See Olivelle (1992) for a historical defense of the rise of individualism coinciding with the rise of renouncer movements.

2. See Burghart (1983) and Das (1982[1977]) for compelling arguments that Brāhmans assert continued control of the social hierarchy by mediating the interactions between householders and renouncers. Brāhmans embody the category of opposition for both householders and renouncers: from the perspective of lower householder castes, Brāhmans take on the role of renouncer, and from the perspective of the celibate renouncer, they take on the role of married householder.

3. See also Sinha and Saraswati (1978) for an older but thorough ethnography of the ascetic community of Benaras, and Parry (1985) and Gupta (1993) for ethnographic works with Benaras Aghori ascetics in particular.

4. See also Grosz (1994) for an excellent overview of phenomenological thought and interpretations of experience.

5. See especially McNay (1991) on Foucault's docile bodies (1979), and on how he ignores agency.

6. See especially Ewing (1997) on religious subjectivity in South Asian anthropology.

7. See Martin (1987) for a study on women resisting medical authority over their bodies. In part these moves in feminist theory reflected a popular women's movement to reclaim their bodies and knowledge about them from the realm of medical science.

8. But see Bynum (1992) for arguments on how the body is not necessarily anti-transcendent in historical religious endeavor, and how transcendence is not necessarily anti-woman. She argues that medieval Catholic nuns' bodiliness enhanced their capacity for transcendence.

BIBLIOGRAPHY

Abu-Lughod, Lila. 1986. *Veiled Sentiments: Honor and Poetry in a Bedouin Society.* Berkeley: University of California Press.

———. 1990. "Can There Be a Feminist Ethnography?" *Women & Performance: A Journal of Feminist Theory* 5, no. 1:7–27.

———. 1991. "Writing Against Culture." In *Recapturing Anthropology: Working in the Present,* Richard Fox, ed.,137–162. Santa Fe, N.Mex.: School of American Research Press.

Agamben, Giorgio. 1993. *The Coming Community.* Michael Hardt, trans. Minneapolis: University of Minnesota Press.

Alter, Joseph. 1992. *The Wrestler's Body: Identity and Ideology in North India.* Berkeley: University of California Press.

———. 1994. "Celibacy, Sexuality, and the Transformation of Gender into Nationalism in North India." *Journal of Asian Studies* 53, no. 1:45–66.

———. 2000. *Gandhi's Body: Sex, Diet, and the Politics of Nationalism.* Philadelphia: University of Pennsylvania Press.

Alter, Stephen. 2001. *Sacred Waters: A Pilgrimage up the Ganges River to the Source of Hindu Culture.* New York: Harcourt.

Amatya, Saphalya. 1991. *Art and Culture of Nepal: An Attempt Towards Preservation.* Nirala Series 12. Jaipur & New Delhi: Nirala Publications.

Anderson, Benedict R. O'G. 1990. "The Idea of Power in Javanese Culture." In *Language and Power: Exploring Political Cultures in Indonesia.* Ithaca: Cornell University Press.

Appadurai, Arjun. 1986. "Is Homo Hierarchicus?" *American Ethnologist* 13:745–761.

———. 1992. "Putting Hierarchy in Its Place." In *Rereading Anthropology,* George Marcus, ed., 34–47. Durham: Duke University Press.

———. 1996. *Modernity at Large: Cultural Dimensions of Globalization.* Minneapolis: University of Minnesota Press.

Apte, Vaman Shivram. 1965. *The Practical Sanskrit-English Dictionary.* Rev. and enl. ed. Delhi: Motilal Banarsidass.

Aran, Lydia. 1978. *The Art of Nepal: A Guide to the Masterpieces of Sculpture, Painting and Woodcarving.* Kathmandu: Sahayogi Prakashan.

Arthvale, Parvati. 1930. *My Story: The Autobiography of a Hindu Widow.* Justin E. Abbott, trans. New York: Putnam.

Asad, Talal. 1983. "Anthropological Conceptions of Religion: Reflections on Geertz." *Man*, n.s. 18, no. 2:237–259.

———. 1993. *Genealogies of Religion: Discipline and Reasons of Power in Christianity and Islam.* Baltimore, Md.: Johns Hopkins University Press.

———. 1997. "Remarks on the Anthropology of the Body." In *Religion and the Body*, Sarah Coakley, ed., 42–52. Cambridge: Cambridge University Press.

Auge, Marc. 1995 [1992]. *Non-Places: Introduction to an Anthropology of Supermodernity.* John Howe, trans. London: Verso.

Azouvi, François. 2002. *Descartes et la France.* Paris: Fayard.

Babb, Lawrence. 1975. *The Divine Hierarchy: Popular Hinduism in Central India.* New York: Columbia University Press.

———. 1983. "The Physiology of Redemption." *History of Religions* 22, no. 4: 293–312.

———. 1986. *Redemptive Encounters: Three Modern Styles in the Hindu Tradition.* Delhi: Oxford University Press.

Balslev, Anindita Niyogi. 1999. *A Study of Time in Indian Philosophy.* New Delhi: Munshiram Manoharlal.

Bayly, Christopher A. 1983. *Rulers, Townsmen and Bazaars: North Indian Society in the Age of British Expansion, 1770–1870.* Cambridge: Cambridge University Press.

———. 1988. *Indian Society and the Making of the British Empire.* Cambridge: Cambridge University Press.

Beck, Brenda. 1969. "Colour and Heat in South Indian Ritual." *Man*, n.s. 4, no. 4:553–572.

———. 1976. "The Symbolic Merger of Body, Space, and Cosmos in Hindu Tamil Nadu." *Contributions to Indian Sociology*, n.s. 10, no. 2:213–243.

Bedi, Rajesh. 1991. *Sadhus: The Holy Men of India.* New Delhi: Brijbasi Printers.

Behar, Ruth. 1993. *Translated Woman: Crossing the Border with Esperanza's Story.* Boston: Beacon Press.

Bennett, Lynn. 1983. *Dangerous Wives and Sacred Sisters: Social and Symbolic Roles of High-Caste Women in Nepal.* New York: Columbia University Press.

Berreman, Gerald. 1972 [1963]. *Hindus of the Himalayas: Ethnography and Change.* 2nd ed. Berkeley: University of California Press.

Bhabha, Homi. 1994. *The Location of Culture.* London: Routledge.

Bhagat, M. G. 1976. *Ancient Indian Asceticism.* Delhi: Munshiram Manoharlal.

Bharati, Agehananda. 1961. *The Ochre Robe.* London: George Allen & Unwin.

———. 1963a. "Pilgrimage in the Indian Tradition." *History of Religions* 3, no. 1:135–167.

———. 1963b. "Actual and Ideal Himalayas: Hindu Views of the Mountains." Paper presented at the 9th International Congress of Anthropological and Ethnological Sciences. Chicago.

Bhardwaj, Surinder M. 1973. *Hindu Places of Pilgrimage in India: A Study in Cultural Geography.* Berkeley: University of California Press.

Bharucha, Rustom. 1993. *The Question of Faith.* Tracts for the Times/3. New Delhi: Orient Longman.

Blacking, J., ed. 1977. *The Anthropology of the Body.* New York: Academic Press.

Bloch, Maurice, and Jonathan Parry, eds. 1982. *Death and the Regeneration of Life.* Cambridge: Cambridge University Press.

Bordo, Susan. 1993. *Unbearable Weight: Feminism, Western Culture, and the Body.* Berkeley: University of California Press.

Bottomley, F. 1979. *Attitudes to the Body in Western Christendom.* London: Lepus Books.

Bouillier, Véronique. 1979. *Naitre Renoncant: Une Caste de Sannyasi Villageois au Népal Central.* Nanterre: Laboratoire d'Ethnologie.

———. 1991. "Growth and Decay of a Kanphata Yogi Monastery in South-West Nepal." *Indian Economic and Social History Review* 28, no. 2:151–170.

———. 1998. "The Royal Gift to the Ascetics: The Case of the Caughera Yogi Monastery." *Studies in Nepali History and Society* 3, no. 2 (December): 213–238. Kathmandu: Mandala Book Point.

Bourdieu, Pierre. 1977. *Outline of a Theory of Practice.* Richard Nice, trans. Stanford: Stanford University Press.

———. 1990. *The Logic of Practice.* Richard Nice, trans. Stanford: Stanford University Press.

Briggs, G. W. 1973 [1938]. *Gorakhnath and the Kanphata Yogis.* Delhi: Motilal Banarsidass.

Brown, Peter. 1982. *Society and the Holy in Late Antiquity.* Berkeley: University of California Press.

———. 1988. *The Body and Society: Men, Women, and Sexual Renunciation in Early Christianity.* New York: Columbia University Press.

Brunton, Paul. 1935. *A Search in Secret India.* New York: E. P. Dutton.

Bubriski, Kevin, and Keith Dowman. 1995. *Power Places of Kathmandu: Hindu and Buddhist Holy Sites in the Sacred Valley of Nepal.* Rochester, Vt.: Inner Traditions International.

Burghart, Richard. 1983a. "Renunciation in the Religious Traditions of South Asia." *Man,* n.s. 18:635–653.

———. 1983b. "Wandering Ascetics of the Ramanandi Sect." *History of Religions* 22:361–380.

Burghart, Richard, and Audrey Cantlie, eds. 1985. *Indian Religion.* London: Curzon Press.

Butler, Judith. 1993. *Bodies that Matter: On the Discursive Limits of "Sex."* New York: Routledge.

———. 1992. "Contingent Foundations: Feminism and the Question of Postmodernism." In *Feminists Theorize the Political,* Judith Butler and Joan Scott, eds., 3–21. New York: Routledge.

Bynum, Caroline W. 1987. *Holy Feast and Holy Fast: The Religious Significance of Food to Medieval Women.* Berkeley: University of California Press.

———. 1992. *Fragmentation and Redemption: Essays on Gender and the Human Body in Medieval Religion.* New York: Zone Books.

Calasso, Roberto. 1999. *Ka.* Tim Parks, trans. London: Vintage.

Caldwell, Sarah. 1999. *Oh Terrifying Mother: Sexuality, Violence, and the Worship of the Goddess Kali.* New Delhi: Oxford University Press.

Carman, John B., and Frédérique Apffel Marglin, eds. 1985. *Purity and Auspiciousness in Indian Society.* Leiden: E. J. Brill.

Casey, Edward S. 1996. "How to Get from Space to Place in a Fairly Short Stretch of Time: Phenomenological Prolegomena." In *Senses of Place,* Steven Feld and Keith H. Basso, eds., 13–52. Santa Fe, N.Mex.: School of American Research Press.

——. 1997. *The Fate of Place: A Philosophical History.* Berkeley: University of California Press.

Chandra, A. N. 1977. *The Sannyasi Rebellion.* Calcutta: Ratna Prakashan.

Chatterjee, Partha. 1990. "Colonialism, Nationalism, and Colonialized Women: The Contest in India." *American Ethnologist* 16, no. 4: 622–633.

Cixous, Helene. 1981. "The Laugh of the Medusa." In *New French Feminisms,* Elaine Marks and Isabelle de Courtivron, eds., 245–264. London: Harvester Press.

Clifford, James. 1988. *The Predicament of Culture: Twentieth-Century Ethnography, Literature, and Art.* Cambridge: Harvard University Press.

——. 1992. "Traveling Cultures." In *Cultural Studies,* Lawrence Grossberg, Cary Nelson, and Paula Treichler, eds., 96–117. New York: Routledge.

——. 1997. "Prologue: In Medias Res." In *Routes: Travel and Translation in the Late Twentieth Century.* Cambridge: Harvard University Press.

Clifford, James, and George Marcus, eds. 1986. *Writing Culture: The Poetics and Politics of Ethnography.* Berkeley: University of California Press.

Coakley, Sarah, ed. 1997. *Religion and the Body.* Cambridge: Cambridge University Press.

Cohen, Lawrence. 1995. "Semen, Irony, and the Atom Bomb." *Medical Anthropology Quarterly* 11, no. 3:301–303.

——. 1998. *No Aging in India: Alzheimer's, the Bad Family, and Other Modern Things.* Berkeley: University of California Press.

Cohn, Bernard S. 1964. "The Role of the Gosains in the Economy of Eighteenth and Nineteenth-Century Upper India." *Indian Economic and Social History Review* 1, no. 4:175–182.

——. 1987. *An Anthropologist among the Historians and Other Essays.* Delhi: Oxford University Press.

Cohn, Bernard S., and McKim Marriott. 1958. "Networks and Centers in the Integration of Indian Civilization." *Journal of Social Research, Bihar University* 1, no. 1:1–9.

Crapanzano, Vincent. 1980. *Tuhami, Portrait of a Moroccan.* Chicago: University of Chicago Press.

Csordas, Thomas. 1990. "Embodiment as a Paradigm for Anthropology." *Ethos* 18, no. 1:5–47.

——. 1994. "Introduction: The body as representation and being-in-the-world." In *Embodiment and Experience: The Existential Ground of Culture and Self,* Thomas Csordas, ed., 1–26. Cambridge Studies in Medical Anthropology. Cambridge: Cambridge University Press.

Csordas, Thomas, ed. 1994. *Embodiment and Experience: The Existential Ground of Culture and Self.* Cambridge: Cambridge University Press.

Dangol, Sanu Bhai. 1993. *The Pashupatinath: A Multi-Dimensional Observation on Shaivism, Pashupat Cult and the Pashupatinath.* Kathmandu: Pilgrims Book House.

Daniel, E. Valentine. 1984. *Fluid Signs: Being a Person the Tamil Way.* Berkeley: University of California Press.

Daniélou, Alain. 1985. *The Myths and Gods of India: The Classic Work on Hindu Polytheism.* Reprint. Princeton Bollingen 73. Rochester, Vt.: Inner Traditions International.

Das, Veena. 1974. "On the Categorization of Space in Hindu Ritual." In *Text and Context: The Social Anthropology of Tradition,* Ravindra K. Jain, ed., 9–27. Philadelphia: Institute for the Study of Human Issues.

———. 1976. "The Uses of Liminality: Society and Cosmos in Hinduism." *Contributions to Indian Sociology,* n.s. 10, no. 2:245–263.

———. 1982 [1977]. *Structure and Cognition: Aspects of Hindu Caste and Ritual.* 2nd ed. Delhi: Oxford University Press.

———. 1985. "Paradigms of Body Symbolism: An Analysis of Selected Themes in Hindu Culture." In *Indian Religion,* Richard Burghart and Audrey Cantlie, eds., 180–207. London: Curzon Press.

———. 1997. "Language and Body: Transactions in the Construction of Pain." In *Social Suffering,* Arthur Kleinman, Veena Das, and Margaret Lock, eds., 67–91. Berkeley: University of California Press.

Deleuze, Gilles, and Félix Guattari. 1987. *A Thousand Plateaus: Schizophrenia.* Brian Massumi, trans. Minneapolis: University of Minnesota Press.

Denton, Lynn T. 1991. Varieties of Hindu Female Asceticism. In *Roles and Rituals for Hindu Women,* J. Leslie, ed., 211–231. Rutherford, N.J.: Fairleigh Dickinson University Press.

———. 2004. *Female Ascetics in Hinduism.* Albany: State University of New York Press.

Desikachar, T. K. V. 1995. *The Heart of Yoga: Developing a Personal Practice.* Rochester, Vt.: Inner Traditions International.

Desikachar, T. K. V., trans. 2000. *Yogayājñavalkya Samhitā: The Yoga Treatise of Yājñavalkya.* Krishnamacarya Granthamala Series 4. Adyar: Krishnamacarya Yoga Mandiram.

Desjarlais, Robert. 1992. *Body and Emotion: The Aesthetics of Illness and Healing in the Nepal Himalayas.* Philadelphia: University of Pennsylvania Press.

Dilwali, Ashok. 1993. *Garhwal and Kumaon.* Hong Kong: Guidebook Co.

Dimock, Edward C. 1966. *The Place of the Hidden Moon: Erotic Mysticism in the Vaiṣṇava-Sahajiyā Cult of Bengal.* Chicago: University of Chicago Press.

Dirks, Nicholas. 1997. "The Policing of Tradition: Colonialism and Anthropology in Southern India." *Comparative Studies in Society and History* 39, no. 1:182–212.

———. 2001. *Castes of Mind: Colonialism and the Making of Modern India.* Princeton: Princeton University Press.

Doniger, Wendy. 1997. "Medical and Mythical Constructions of the Body in Hindu Texts." In *Religion and the Body,* Sarah Coakley, ed., 167–184. Cambridge: Cambridge University Press.

Doniger, Wendy, with Brian K. Smith, trans. 1991. *The Laws of Manu.* New York: Penguin Books.

Douglas, Mary. 1966. *Purity and Danger: An Analysis of the Concepts of Pollution and Taboo.* London: Routledge.

———. 1970. *Natural Symbols: Explorations in Cosmology.* London: Barrie and Rockliff.

Dowman, Keith. 1981. "A Buddhist Guide to the Power Places of the Kathmandu Valley." *Kailash: A Journal of Himalayan Studies* 8, no. 3–4:201–291.

Dubey, D. P. 2001a. *Prayāga: The Site of Kumbh Melā (In Temporal and Traditional Space).* New Delhi: Aryan Books International.

Dubey, D. P., ed. 2001b. *Kumbh Melā: Pilgrimage to the Greatest Cosmic Fair.* Allahabad: Society of Pilgrimage Studies.

Dumont, Louis. 1980 [1966]. *Homo Hierarchicus: The Caste System and Its Implications.* Mark Sainsbury, Louis Dumont, and Basia Gulati, trans. Chicago: University of Chicago Press.

Dumont, Louis, and David Pocock. 1959. "Pure and Impure." *Contributions to Indian Sociology* 3:9–39.

Durkheim, Emile. 1995 [1912]. *The Elementary Forms of Religious Life.* Karen E. Fields, trans. New York: Free Press.

Eck, Diana L. 1981. "India's '*Tīrthas*': 'Crossings' in Sacred Geography." *History of Religions* 20, no. 4:323–344.

———. 1982. *Banaras: City of Light.* New York: Knopf.

———. 1985. "Banaras: Cosmos and Paradise in the Hindu Imagination." *Contributions to Indian Sociology,* n.s. 19, no. 1:41–55.

———. 1996. "Gaṅgā: The Goddess Ganges in Hindu Sacred Geography." In *Devī: Goddesses of India,* John Stratton Hawley and Donna Wulff, eds., 137–153. Berkeley: University of California Press.

———. 1998. *Darśan: Seeing the Divine Image in India.* 3rd ed. New York: Columbia University Press.

Edward, James. 1983. "Semen Anxiety in South Asian Cultures: Cultural and Transcultural Significance." *Medical Anthropology* 7, no. 3 (Summer): 51–67.

Egnor, Margaret T. 1983. "Death and Nurturance in Indian Systems of Healing." *Social Science and Medicine* 17, no. 14:935–945.

Eliade, Mircea. 1958 [1954]. *Yoga: Immortality and Freedom.* Princeton Bollingen 56. Princeton: Princeton University Press.

Ewing, Katherine Pratt. 1997. *Arguing Sainthood: Modernity, Psychoanalysis, and Islam.* Durham: Duke University Press.

Fabian, Johannes. 1989. *Time and the Other: How Anthropology Makes Its Object.* New York: Columbia University Press.

Farquhar, J. N. 1918. *Modern Religious Movements in India.* New York: Macmillan.

———. 1925. "The Fighting Ascetics of India." *The Bulletin of the John Rylands Library* 9:431–452.

Featherstone, Mike, Mike Hepworth, and Bryan S. Turner, eds. 1991. *The Body: Social Process and Cultural Theory.* Theory, Culture and Society Series. London: Sage Publications.

Feher, Michael, with Ramona Nadoff and Nadia Tazi, eds. 1989. *Fragments for a History of the Human Body.* Parts 1–3. New York: Zone Books.

Feldhaus, Anne. 1995. *Water and Womanhood: Religious Meanings of Rivers in Maharashtra.* New York: Oxford University Press.

Forbes, William P., with V. K. Chaube. 2000. *The Glory of Nepal: A Mythological Guidebook to Kathmandu Valley.* Varanasi: Pilgrims Book House.

Foucault, Michel. 1979. *Discipline and Punish: The Birth of the Prison.* Alan Sheridan, trans. New York: Vintage.

———. 1980 [1976]. *The History of Sexuality. Volume 1: An Introduction.* Robert Hurley, trans. New York: Vintage.

Fox, Richard, ed. 1991. *Recapturing Anthropology: Working in the Present.* Santa Fe, N.Mex.: School of American Research Press.

Freitag, Sandria B. 1985. "Collective Crime and Authority in North India." In *Crime and Criminality in British India,* A. A. Yang, ed., 140–156. Tucson: University of Arizona Press.

Gaborieau, Marc. 1982. "Les Fêtes, le Temps, l'Espace: Structure du Calendrier Hindou dans sa Version Indo-Népalaise." *Homme* 22, no. 3:11–29.

Gallop, Jane. 1988. *Thinking Through the Body.* New York: Columbia University Press.

Geertz, Clifford. 1973. *The Interpretation of Cultures.* New York: Basic Books.

Gellner, David N. 2001. *The Anthropology of Buddhism and Hinduism: Weberian Themes.* New Delhi: Oxford University Press.

Ghosh, Jaimini. 1930. *Sannyasi and Fakir Raiders in Bengal.* Calcutta: Bengal Sectarian Book Depot.

Ghurye, G. S. 1995 [1953]. *Indian Sadhus.* Bombay: Popular Prakashan.

Glissant, Edouard. 1997. *Poetics of Relation.* Ann Arbor: University of Michigan Press.

Gold, Ann Grodzins. 1988. *Fruitful Journeys: The Ways of Rajasthani Pilgrims.* Berkeley: University of California Press.

———. 1989. "The Once and Future Yogi: Sentiments and Signs in the Tale of a Renouncer-King." *Journal of Asian Studies* 48, no. 4:770–786.

———. 1991. "Gender and Illusion in a Rajasthani Yogic Tradition." In *Gender, Genre and Power in South Asian Expressive Traditions,* Arjun Appadurai, Frank J. Korom, and Margaret A. Mills, eds., 102–135. Philadelphia: University of Pennsylvania Press.

———. 1992. *A Carnival of Parting: The Tales of King Gopi Chand and King Bharthari as Sung and Told by Madhu Natisar Nath of Ghatiyali, Rajasthan, India.* Berkeley: University of California Press.

Gold, Daniel. 1987. *The Lord as Guru: Hindi Sants in the Northern Indian Tradition.* New York: Oxford University Press.

———. 1996. "Experiences of Ear-Cutting: The Significances of a Ritual of Bodily Alteration for Householder Yogis." *Journal of Ritual Studies* 10, no. 1:91–112.

Grapard, Allan G. 1982. "Flying Mountains and Walkers of Emptiness: Toward a Definition of Sacred Space in Japanese Religions." *History of Religions* 21, no. 3:195–221.

Griaule, Marcel. 1965. *Conversations with Ogotemmeli: An Introduction to Dogon Religious Ideas.* International African Institute. London: Oxford University Press.

Gross, Robert Lewis. 1992. *The Sādhus of India: A Study of Hindu Asceticism.* Jaipur, New Delhi: Rawat Publications.

Grosz, Elizabeth, ed. 1991. *Feminism and the Body.* Special issue, *Hypatia* 6, no. 3.

———. 1994. *Volatile Bodies: Toward a Corporeal Feminism.* Bloomington: Indiana University Press.

Guha, Ranajit. 1987. "Chandra's Death." In *Subaltern Studies V: Writings on South Asian History and Society.* Delhi: Oxford University Press.

Gupta, Akhil, and James Ferguson, eds. 1997. *Culture, Power, Place: Explorations in Critical Anthropology.* Durham: Duke University Press.

Gupta, Roxanne Poormon. 1993. "The Politics of Heterodoxy and the Kina Rami Ascetics of Banaras." Ph.D. diss., Department of Anthropology, Syracuse University.

Gutschow, Niels, and Axel Michaels, eds. 1987. *Heritage of the Kathmandu Valley: Proceedings of an International Conference in Lubeck, June 1985*. Nepalica 4. St. Augustin: VGH Wissenschaftsverlag.

Hada, Jun. 2001. *Kathmandu Metropolitan City.* City Diagnostic Report for the City Development Strategy. Kathmandu: KMC/World Bank.

Hansen, Thomas Blom. 1999. *The Saffron Wave: Democracy and Hindu Nationalism in Modern India.* Princeton: Princeton University Press.

Hansen, Thomas Blom, and Christophe Jaffrelot, eds. 1998. *The BJP and the Compulsions of Politics in India.* Delhi: Oxford University Press.

Haraway, Donna. 1988. "Situated Knowledges: The Science Question in Feminism and the Privilege of Partial Perspective." *Feminist Studies* 14, no. 3: 575–599.

Harlan, Lindsey, and Paul B. Courtright, eds. 1995. *From the Margins of Hindu Marriage: Essays on Gender, Religion, and Culture.* New York: Oxford University Press.

Hartsuiker, Dolf. 1993. *Sādhus: Holy Men of India.* London: Thames and Hudson.

Harvey, David. 1989. *The Condition of Postmodernity: An Enquiry into the Origins of Cultural Change.* Oxford: Basil Blackwell.

———. 1996. "From Space to Place and Back Again." In *Justice, Nature, and the Geography of Difference.* Cambridge: Blackwell.

———. 2000. *Spaces of Hope.* Berkeley: University of California Press.

Hausner, Sondra L. 2002. "Hindu Renouncers and the Question of Caste." Paper presented at the American Anthropology Association Annual Meeting. New Orleans.

———. 2005. "Staying in Place: The Social Actions of Hindu *Yoginīs.*" *European Bulletin of Himalayan Research* 28 (Spring): 54–66.

———. 2006. "The Erotic Aesthetics of Ecstatic Ascetics." In *Holy Madness: Portraits of Tantric Siddhas,* Rob Linrothe, ed., 154–177. New York: RMA & Serindia.

Hausner, Sondra L., and Meena Khandelwal. 2006. "Introduction: Women on Their Own." In *Women's Renunciation in South Asia: Nuns, Yoginis, Saints, and Singers,* Meena Khandelwal, Sondra L. Hausner, and Ann Grodzins Gold, eds., 1–36. New York: Palgrave Macmillan.

Hawley, John Stratton, and Donna Marie Wulff, eds. 1996. *Devī: Goddesses of India.* Berkeley: University of California Press.

Heesterman, J. C. 1964. "Brahman, Ritual, and Renouncer." *Wiener Zeitschrift fur die Kunde Sud- und Ostasiens* 8:1–31.

———. 1982. "Householder and Wanderer." In *Way of Life: King, Householder and Renouncer (Essays in Honour of Louis Dumont),* T. N. Madan, ed., 251–271. New Delhi: Vikas.

———. 1993. *The Broken World of Sacrifice.* Chicago: University of Chicago Press.

Hershman, P. 1974. "Hair, Sex, and Dirt." *Man,* n.s. 9, no. 2 (June): 274–298.

Hindustan Times (Delhi). 2001. "First Non-Naga Akhara Makes a Grand Entry." January 12.

Hiriyanna, M. 1993. *Outlines of Indian Philosophy.* Delhi: Motilal Banarsidass.

Holmberg, David H. 1989. *Order in Paradox: Myth, Ritual, and Exchange among Nepal's Tamang.* Ithaca: Cornell University Press.

Hubert, H., and Marcel Mauss. 1964 [1929]. *Sacrifice: Its Nature and Function.* London: Cohen and West.

Human Development Report Office. 2001. *Human Development Report.* New York: United Nations Development Programme.

Hutt, Michael. 1997. *Modern Literary Nepali: An Introductory Reader.* Delhi: Oxford University Press.

Inden, Ronald. 1990. *Imagining India.* Oxford: Basil Blackwell.

Inden, Ronald B., and Ralph Nicholas. 1977. *Kinship in Bengali Culture.* Chicago: University of Chicago Press.

Independent (London). 1998. "Hindu Holy Men on Warpath at Ganges Festival." April 1.

Irigaray, Luce. 1985. *This Sex Which Is Not One.* Ithaca: Cornell University Press.

———. 2002 [1999]. *Between East and West: From Singularity to Community.* Stephen Pluhacek, trans. New York: Columbia University Press.

Jaffrelot, Christophe. 1996. *The Hindu Nationalist Movement in India.* New York: Columbia University Press.

Jaggar, Alison M., and Susan R. Bordo, eds. 1989. *Gender/Body/Knowledge: Feminist Reconstructions of Being and Knowing.* New Brunswick: Rutgers University Press.

Jeffery, Patricia, Roger Jeffery, and Andrew Lyon. 1989. *Women and Childbearing in India.* London: Zed Books.

Jha, Makhan. 1995. *The Sacred Complex of Kathmandu, Nepal: Religion of the Himalayan Kingdom.* New Delhi: Gyan Publishing House.

Johari, Harish. 1987. *Chakras: Energy Centers of Transformation.* Rochester: Destiny Books.

Kakar, Sudhir. 1989. *Intimate Relations: Exploring Indian Sexuality.* New Delhi: Penguin Books.

———. 1990 [1982]. *Shamans, Mystics, and Doctors: A Psychological Inquiry into India and its Healing Traditions.* Delhi: Oxford University Press.

Kaplan, Caren. 1996. *Questions of Travel: Postmodern Discourses of Displacement.* Durham: Duke University Press.

Kasulis, Thomas P., with Roger T. Ames and Wimal Dissanayake, eds. 1993. *Self as Body in Asian Theory and Practice.* Albany: State University of New York Press.

Keller, Evelyn Fox. 1985. *Reflections on Gender and Science.* New Haven: Yale University Press.

Keyes, Charles F. 1975. "Buddhist Pilgrimage Centers and the Twelve-Year Cycle: Northern Thai Moral Orders in Space and Time." *History of Religions* 15, no. 1 (August): 71–89.

Keyes, Charles F., and E. Valentine Danel, eds. 1983. *Karma: An Anthropological Inquiry.* Berkeley: University of California Press.

Khandelwal, Meena. 1997. "Ungendered Atma, Masculine Virility and Feminine Compassion: Ambiguities in Renunciant Discourses on Gender." *Contributions to Indian Sociology* 31, no. 1:79–107.

———. 2001. "Sexual Fluids, Emotions, Morality: Notes on the Gendering of Brahmacarya." In *Celibacy, Culture, and Society: The Anthropology of Sexual Abstinence,* Elisa J. Sobo and Sandra Bell, eds., 157–179. Madison: University of Wisconsin Press.

———. 2004. *Women in Ochre Robes: Gendering Hindu Renunciation.* Albany: State University of New York Press.

———. 2006. "Do Saints Need Sleep? Baiji's Renunciation as Service." In *Women's Renunciation in South Asia: Nuns, Yoginis, Saints, and Singers,* Meena Khandelwal, Sondra L. Hausner, and Ann Grodzins Gold, eds., 39–68. New York: Palgrave Macmillan.

Khandelwal, Meena, Sondra L. Hausner, and Ann Grodzins Gold, eds. 2006. *Women's Renunciation in South Asia: Nuns, Yoginis, Saints, and Singers.* New York: Palgrave Macmillan.

Khare, R. S. 1976. *Hindu Hearth and Home.* Delhi: Vikas.

Kinsley, David. 1974. "Through the Looking Glass": Divine Madness in the Hindu Religious Tradition." *History of Religions* 13, no. 4:270–305.

———. 1997. *The Ten Mahavidyas: Tantric Visions of the Divine Feminine.* Berkeley: University of California Press.

Kirby, Vicky. 1991. "Corporeal Habits: Addressing Essentialism Differently." *Feminism and the Body.* Special issue, *Hypatia* 6, no. 3:4–24.

Kolenda, Pauline. 1987. *Regional Differences in Family Structure in India.* Jaipur: Rawat Publications.

Kondos, Vivienne. 1986. "Images of the Fierce Goddess and Portrayals of Hindu Women." *Contributions to Hindu Sociology,* n.s. 20, no. 2:173–197.

Kumar, Nita. 1988. *The Artisans of Banaras: Popular Culture and Identity, 1880–1986.* Princeton: Princeton University Press.

Lacqueur, Thomas. 1990. *Making Sex: Body and Gender from the Greeks to Freud.* Cambridge: Harvard University Press.

Lamb, Sarah. 2000. *White Saris and Sweet Mangoes: Aging, Gender, and Body in North India.* Berkeley: University of California Press.

Law, Jane Marie, ed. 1995. *Religious Reflections on the Human Body.* Bloomington: Indiana University Press.

Leach, Edmund R. 1958. "Magical Hair." *Journal of the Royal Anthropological Institute* 88:147–164.

———. 1961a. "Time and False Noses." In *Rethinking Anthropology.* London: London School of Economics.

———. 1961b. "Rethinking Anthropology." In *Rethinking Anthropology.* London: London School of Economics.

Lefebvre, Henri. 1991 [1974]. *The Production of Space.* Donald Nicholson Smith, trans. Oxford: Blackwell.

Levi-Strauss, Claude. 1969a [1949]. *The Elementary Structures of Kinship.* Boston: Beacon Press.

———. 1969b. "Overture." In *The Raw and the Cooked.* New York: Harper and Row.

Levy, Robert I. 1990. *Mesocosm: Hinduism and the Organization of a Traditional Newar City in Nepal.* Berkeley: University of California Press.

Lochtefeld, James G. 1992. "Haridwara, Haradwara, Gangadwara: The Construction of Identity and Meaning in a Hindu Pilgrimage Place." Ph.D. diss., Department of Religion, Columbia University.

Lock, Margaret. 1993. "Cultivating the Body: Anthropology and Epistemologies of Bodily Practice and Knowledge." *Annual Review of Anthropology* 22:133–155.

Lopez, Donald S., ed. 1995. *Religions of India in Practice.* Princeton Readings in Religion. Princeton: Princeton University Press.

Lorenzen, David N. 1972. *The Kāpālikas and Kālāmukhas: Two Lost Śaivite Sects.* Los Angeles: University of California Press.

———. 1978. "Warrior Ascetics in Indian History." *Journal of the American Oriental Society* 98:61–75.

Lutz, Catherine A., and Lila Abu-Lughod, eds. 1990. *Language and the Politics of Emotion.* Cambridge: Cambridge University Press.

Lynch, Owen M., ed. 1990. *Divine Passions: The Social Construction of Emotion in India.* Berkeley: University of California Press.

Madan, T. N., ed. 1982. *Way of Life: King, Householder and Renouncer (Essays in Honour of Louis Dumont).* New Delhi: Vikas.

———. 1987. *Non-Renunciation: Themes and Interpretations of Hindu Culture.* Delhi: Oxford University Press.

Majpuria, Trilok Chandra, and Indra Majpuria. 1981. *Pashupatinath: The Divine Glory of the Guardian Deity of Nepal.* Gwalior: M. Devi.

Malamoud, Charles. 1996 [1989]. *Cooking the World: Ritual and Thought in Ancient India.* David White, trans. Delhi: Oxford University Press.

Malhotra, S. S. L. 1983. *Gangotri and Gaumukh: A Trek to the Holy Source.* New Delhi: Allied Publishers.

Marglin, Frédérique Apffel. 1977. "Power, Purity, and Pollution: Aspects of the Caste System Reconsidered." *Contributions to Indian Sociology,* n.s. 11, no. 2:245–270.

Marriott, McKim. 1976. "Hindu Transactions: Diversity without Dualism." In *Transaction and Meaning,* Bruce Kapferer, ed., 109–142. Philadelphia: Institute for the Study of Human Issues.

———. 1980. "The Open Hindu Person and Interpersonal Fluidity." Paper presented at Association for Asian Studies Annual Meeting. Washington, D.C.

Marriott, McKim, ed. 1989. *India through Hindu Categories.* Contributions to Indian Sociology Occasional Studies. New Delhi and London: Sage.

Martin, Emily. 1987. *The Woman in the Body: A Cultural Analysis of Reproduction.* Boston: Beacon Press.

———. 1992. "The End of the Body?" *American Ethnologist* 19, no. 1:121–140.

Mascia-Lees, Frances, Patricia Sharpe, and Colleen Ballerino Cohen. 1989. "The Postmodernist Turn in Anthropology: Cautions from A Feminist Perspective." *Signs* 15, no. 1:7–33.

Massey, Doreen. 1994. *Space, Place, and Gender.* Minneapolis: University of Minnesota Press.

Mauss, Marcel. 1973 [1935]. "Techniques of the Body." *Economy and Society* 2, no. 1:70–88.

Mayrhofer, Manfred. 1992. *Etymologisches Wörterbuch des Altindoarïschen. Vol. I.* Heidelberg: Carl Winter Universtät Sverlag.

McDaniel, June. 1989. *Madness of the Saints: Ecstatic Religion in Bengal.* Chicago: University of Chicago Press.

McEvilley, Thomas. 1981. "An Archaeology of Yoga." *RES* 1, no. 1:44–77.

McGregor, R. S. 1993. *The Oxford Hindi-English Dictionary.* Oxford: Oxford University Press.

McHugh, Ernestine L. 1989. "Concepts of the Person among the Gurungs on Nepal." *American Ethnologist* 16, no. 1:75–86.

McKean, Lise. 1996. *Divine Enterprise: Gurus and the Hindu Nationalist Movement.* Chicago: University of Chicago Press.

McNay, Lois. 1991. "The Foucauldian Body and the Exclusion of Experience." *Feminism and the Body.* Special issue, *Hypatia* 6, no. 3:125–139.

Mellor, Philip A., and Chris Shilling, eds. 1997. *Re-forming the body: Religion, Community and Modernity.* Theory, Culture and Society Series. London: Sage Publications.

Menon, Kalyani Devaki. 2006. "Passionate Renouncers: Hindu Nationalist Renouncers and the Politics of Hindutva." In *Women's Renunciation in South Asia: Nuns, Yoginis, Saints, and Singers,* Meena Khandelwal, Sondra L. Hausner, and Ann Grodzins Gold, eds., 141–169. New York: Palgrave Macmillan.

Merleau-Ponty, Maurice. 1962. *Phenomenology of Perception.* Colin Smith, trans. New York: Humanities Press.

Michaels, Axel. 2004. *Hinduism: Past and Present.* Barbara Harshav, trans. Princeton: Princeton University Press.

Michaels, Axel, and Govinda Tandan. 1995. "Deopatan and the Temple of Pashupati." In *Nepal: A Guide to the Art and Architecture of the Kathmandu Valley,* Michael Hutt, David N. Gellner, Axel Micahels, and Greta Rana, eds. Boston: Shambhala.

Miller, David. 1977. "The Guru as the Centre of Sacredness." *Studies in Religion* 6, no. 5:527–533.

Mills, Mary Beth. 1999. *Thai Women in the Global Labor Force: Consuming Desires, Contested Selves.* New Brunswick: Rutgers University Press.

Mines, Mattison. 1994. *Public Faces, Private Voices: Community and Individuality in South India.* Berkeley: University of California Press.

Mishra, Pankaj. 2004. *An End to Suffering: The Buddha in the World.* London: Picador.

Mohanty, Chandra Talpade. 1991. "Under Western Eyes: Feminist Scholarship and Colonial Discourses." In *Third World Women and the Politics of Feminism,* Chandra Mohanty, Ann Russo, and Lourdes Torres, eds., 51–80. Bloomington: Indiana University Press.

Monier-Williams, Sir Monier. 1999 [1899]. *A Sanskrit-English Dictionary.* New ed. Delhi: Motilal Banarsidass.

Moore, Henrietta. 1986. *Space, Text, and Gender.* London: Cambridge University Press.

———. 1994. *A Passion for Difference: Essays in Anthropology and Gender.* Bloomington: Indiana University Press.

Morinis, Alan, ed. 1992. *Sacred Journeys: The Anthropology of Pilgrimage.* Westport, Conn.: Greenwood Press.

Nabokov, Isabelle. 2000. *Religion Against the Self: An Ethnography of Tamil Rituals.* Oxford: Oxford University Press.

Nancy, Jean-Luc. 1991 [1986]. *The Inoperative Community.* Theory and History of Literature 76. Peter Connor, Lisa Garbus, Michael Holland, and Simona Sawhney, trans. Minneapolis: University of Minnesota Press.

Narayan, Kirin. 1989. *Storytellers, Saints, and Scoundrels: Folk Narrative in Hindu Religious Teaching.* Philadelphia: University of Pennsylvania Press.

———. 1993a. "How Native Is a 'Native' Anthropologist?" *American Anthropologist* 95, no. 3:671–686.

———. 1993b. "Refractions of the Field at Home: American Representations of Hindu Holy Men in the Nineteenth and Twentieth Centuries." *Cultural Anthropology* 8, no. 4:476–509.

Neill, Roderick. 1970. "Sadhus and Hippies." *Quest* 65 (April–June): 20–27.

Obeysekere, Gannanath. 1981. *Medusa's Hair: An Essay on Personal Symbols and Religious Experience.* Chicago: University of Chicago Press.

O'Flaherty, Wendy Doniger. 1981. *Śiva: The Erotic Ascetic.* Oxford: Oxford University Press.

Ojha, Catherine. 1981. "Feminine Asceticism in Hinduism: Its Traditions and Present Condition." *Man in India* 61, no. 3:254–285.

———. 1985. "The Tradition of Female Gurus." *Manushi* 31:2–8.

———. 1988. "Outside the Norms: Women Ascetics in Hindu Society." *Economic and Political Weekly,* April 30: 34–36.

Olivelle, Patrick. 1992. *Saṃnyāsa Upaniṣads: Hindu Scriptures on Asceticism and Renunciation.* New York: Oxford University Press.

———. 1993. *The Āśrama System: The History and Hermeneutics of a Religious Institution.* New York: Oxford University Press.

———. 1995. "Ascetic Withdrawal or Social Engagement." In *Religions of India in Practice,* Donald S. Lopez, Jr., ed., 533–546. Princeton: Princeton University Press.

Oman, J. C. 1984 [1905]. *Mystics, Ascetics, and Saints of India.* Delhi: Cosmo Publications.

Ong, Aihwa. 1999. *Flexible Citizenship: The Cultural Logics of Transnationality.* Durham: Duke University Press.

Orr, W. G. 1944. "Armed Religious Ascetics in Northern India." *Bulletin of John Rylands Library* 24, no. 1:81–100.

Ortner, Sherry B. 1974. "Is Female to Male as Nature Is to Culture?" In *Woman, Culture, and Society,* Michelle Zimbalist Rosaldo and Louise Lamphere, eds., 67–87. Stanford: Stanford University Press.

———. 1978. *Sherpas Through Their Rituals.* Cambridge Studies in Cultural Systems. Cambridge: Cambridge University Press.

———. 1984. "Theory in Anthropology since the Sixties." *Comparative Studies in Society and History* 26, no. 1:126–166.

Ostor, Akos, Lina Fruzzetti, and Steve Barnett, eds. 1982. *Concepts of Person: Kinship, Caste, and Marriage in India.* Cambridge: Harvard University Press.

Owens, Bruce McCoy. 1995. "Human Agency and Divine Power: Transforming Images and Recreating Gods among the Newar." *History of Religions* 34, no. 3:201–240.

Pal, Pratapaditya. 1975. *Nepal: Where the Gods are Young.* New York: Asia Society

Parry, Jonathan. 1985. "The Aghori Ascetics of Benaras." In *Indian Religion,* Richard Burghart and Audrey Cantlie, eds., 51–78. London: Curzon Press.

———. 1992. "The End of the Body." In *Fragments for a History of the Human Body,* Part 2, Michael Feher, et. al., eds., 490–517. New York: Zone.

———. 1994. *Death in Banaras.* Cambridge: Cambridge University Press.

Phillimore, Peter. 2001. "Private Lives and Public Identities: An Example of Female Celibacy in Northwest India." In *Celibacy, Culture, and Society: The Anthropology of Sexual Abstinence,* Elisa J. Sobo and Sandra Bell, eds., 29–46. Madison: University of Wisconsin Press.

Pinch, William R. 1996. *Peasants and Monks in British India.* Berkeley: University of California Press.

Pocock, D. F. 1964. "The Anthropology of Time Reckoning." *Contributions to Indian Sociology* 7 (March): 18–29.

Preston, James J. 1980. "Sacred Centers and Symbolic Networks in South Asia." *Mankind Quarterly* 20, no. 3–4:259–293.
Rademacher, Anne. 2005. "Culturing Urban Ecology: Development, Statemaking, and River Restoration in Kathmandu." Ph.D. diss., Department of Anthropology, Yale University.
Radhakrishnan, Sarvepalli, and Charles A. Moore. 1957. *A Sourcebook in Indian Philosophy.* Princeton: Princeton University Press.
Raheja, Gloria Goodwin. 1988. *The Poison in the Gift: Ritual, Prestation, and the Dominant Caste in a North Indian Village.* Chicago: University of Chicago Press.
Raheja, Gloria Goodwin, and Ann Grodzins Gold. 1994. *Listen to the Heron's Words: Reimagining Gender and Kinship in North India.* Berkeley: University of California Press.
Rai, Subas. 1998 [1993]. *Kumbh Melā: History & Religion; Astronomy and Cosmobiology.* Varanasi: Ganga Kaveri Publishing House.
Ram, Kanshi. 2000. *Śrīgaṅgāgananagītam.* Delhi 110007: Hansraj College.
Ramanujan, A. K. 1982. "On Woman Saints." In *The Divine Consort: Radha and the Goddesses of India,* John Stratton Hawley and Donna Marie Wulff, eds., 316–324. Berkeley: Berkeley Religious Studies Series.
Ramanujan, A. K., trans. 1973. *Speaking of Siva.* New Delhi: Penguin Books.
Rampuri. 2005. *Baba: Autobiography of a Blue-Eyed Yogi.* New York: Random House.
Rawat, Ajay S. 1989. *History of Garhwal 1358–1947: An Erstwhile Kingdom in the Himalayas.* New Delhi: Indus Publishing Co.
Rigopoulos, Antonio. 1998. *Dattātreya: The Immortal Guru, Yogin, and Avatara: A Study of the Transformative and Inclusive Character of a Multi-Faceted Hindu Deity.* Albany: State University of New York Press.
Rubin, Gayle. 1975. "The Traffic in Women: Notes on the Political Economy of Sex." In *Toward an Anthropology of Women,* Rayna Reiter, ed., 157–210. New York: Monthly Review Press.
Rudolph, Susanne Hoeber, and Lloyd I. Rudolph. 1983 [1967]. *Gandhi: The Traditional Roots of Charisma.* Chicago: University of Chicago Press.
Said, Edward E. 1978. *Orientalism.* New York: Pantheon.
Saili, Ganesh. 1996. *Char Dham: Home of the Gods.* Indus Travel India Series. Indus: New Delhi.
Salomon, Carol. 1991. "The Cosmogonic Riddles of Lalan Fakir." In *Gender, Genre and Power in South Asian Expressive Traditions,* Arjun Appadurai, Frank J. Korom, and Margaret A. Mills, eds., 267–304. Philadelphia: University of Pennsylvania Press.
Sanderson, Alexis. 1988. "Śaivism and the Tantric Traditions." In *The World's Religions,* Stewart Sutherland, et. al., eds., 660–704. London: Routledge.
Sarkar, J. 1950. *A History of the Dasnami Naga Sannyasis.* Allahabad: P. A. Mahanirvani.
Sax, William S. 1991. *Mountain Goddess: Gender and Politics in a Himalayan Pilgrimage.* Oxford: Oxford University Press.
Scheper-Hughes, Nancy, and Margaret Lock. 1987. "The Mindful Body: A Prolegomenon to Future Work in Medical Anthropology." *Medical Anthropology Quarterly* 1, no. 1:6–41.
Schneider, David. 1968. *American Kinship: A Cultural Account.* Englewood Cliffs, N.J.: Prentice-Hall.

Shilling, Chris. 1993. *The Body and Social Theory.* London: Sage Publications.

Shimkhada, Deepak. 1984. "Museum Without Walls: Wayside Sculpture in the Kathmandu Valley." Special Nepalese issue, *Arts of Asia* 14, no. 4:97–100.

———. 1985. "Pratapmalla's Pilgrimage: An Historical Painting from Nepal." *Oriental Art*, n.s. 30, no. 4:368–370.

Shweder, Richard A., and Robert A. LeVine, eds. 1984. *Culture Theory: Essays on Mind, Self, and Emotion.* Cambridge: Cambridge: University Press.

Silliman, Jael. 2001. *Jewish Portraits, Indian Frames: Women's Narratives from a Diaspora of Hope.* Hanover: University Press of New England.

Singer, Milton. 1972. *When a Great Tradition Modernizes: An Anthropological Approach to Indian Civilization.* New York: Praeger Publishers.

Singer, Philip. 1961. "Hindu Holy Men: A Study in Charisma." Ph.D. diss., Department of Anthropology, Syracuse University.

Singh, A. n.d. *The Gateway to the Gods: Hardwar Rishikesh Kankhal.* Hardwar 249401: Karam Singh Amar Singh Bookseller.

Singh, Naveen Kumar. nd. *A Pilgrimage to the Garhwal Himalayas: An Introduction Uttra [sic] Khand.* Delhi: B. S. Praminder Prakashan.

Sinha, S., and B. Saraswati. 1978. *Ascetics of Kashi: An Anthropological Exploration.* Varanasi: NR Bose Memorial Foundation.

Sircar, D. C. 1973. *The Śākta Pīṭhas.* Delhi: Motilal Banarsidass.

Slusser, Mary Shepherd. 1982. *Nepal Mandala: A Cultural Study of the Kathmandu Valley.* In 2 vols. Vol. 1: Text. Vol. 2: Plates. Princeton: Princeton University Press.

———. 1985. "On a Sixteenth-Century Pictorial Pilgrim's Guide from Nepal." *Archives of Asian Art* 38:6–36.

Sobo, Elisa J., and Sandra Bell, eds. 2001. *Celibacy, Culture, and Society: The Anthropology of Sexual Abstinence.* Madison: University of Wisconsin Press.

Staal, Frits. 1983–84. "Indian Concepts of the Body." *Somatics* 4, no. 3 (Autumn/Winter): 31–41.

Stiller, S. J. 1989. *Prithvinarayan Shah in the Light of Dibya Upadesh.* Kathmandu: Himalayan Book Centre.

Stoller, Paul. 1989. *The Taste of Ethnographic Things: The Senses in Anthropology.* Philadelphia: University of Pennsylvania Press.

———. 1997. *Sensuous Scholarship.* Philadelphia: University of Pennsylvania Press.

Storm, Mary Nancy. 1999. "The Heroic Image: Self-Sacrificial Decapitation in the Art of India." Ph.D. diss., Department of Art History, University of California, Los Angeles.

Suleiman, Susan, ed. 1986. *The Female Body in Western Culture.* Cambridge: Harvard University Press.

Svoboda, Robert E. 1986. *Aghora: At the Left Hand of God.* New Delhi: Rupa and Co.

Taussig, Michael. 1997. *The Magic of the State.* New York: Routledge.

Thapar, Romila. 1979. "Renunciation: The Making of a Counter-Culture?" In *Ancient Indian Social History: Some Interpretations.* Delhi: Orient Longmans.

———. 1982. "The Householder and the Renouncer in the Brahmanical and Buddhist Traditions." In *Way of Life: King, Householder and Renouncer (Essays in Honour of Louis Dumont),* T. N. Madan, ed., 273–298. New Delhi: Vikas.

Thompson, Catherine. 1985. "The Power to Pollute and the Power to Preserve: Perceptions of Hindu Power in a Hindu Village." *Social Science and Medicine* 21, no. 6:701–711.

Times Literary Supplement. Review of *Descartes et la France.* May 3, 2002.

Times of India (Bombay). 2001a. "Devotees' Dream, Organisers' Nightmare . . . Mammoth Kumbh Mela Begins." January 9.

———. 2001b. "Mahakumbh Begins: Faith Moves Monks and Masses Together." January 10.

———. 2001c. "Ganga Shifting Course; Mela Officials Keep Fingers Crossed." January 11.

Tiyavanich, Kamala. 1997. *Forest Recollections: Wandering Monks in Twentieth-Century Thailand.* Honolulu: University of Hawai'i Press.

Tod, Col. James. 1920. *Annals and Antiquities of Rajasthan.* London: Milford.

Toffin, Gerard. 1990. "Mythical and Symbolic Origins of the City: The Case of the Kathmandu Valley." *Diogenes* 30, no. 152:101–123.

Trawick, Margaret. 1990. *Notes on Love in a Tamil Family.* Berkeley: University of California Press.

Tripathi, B. D. 1978. *Sadhus of India: The Sociological View.* Bombay: Popular Prakashan.

Tully, Mark. 2001 [1991]. *The Kumbh Mela.* Varanasi: Indica Books.

Turnbull, Colin. 1992. "Postscript: Anthropology as Pilgrimage, Anthropologist as Pilgrim." In *Sacred Journeys: The Anthropology of Pilgrimage,* Alan Morinis, ed., 257–274. Westport, Conn.: Greenwood Press.

Turner, Bryan. 1984. *The Body and Society: Explorations in Social Theory.* Oxford: Basil Blackwell.

———. 1997. "The Body in Western Society: Social Theory and Its Perspectives." In *Religion and the Body,* Sarah Coakley, ed., 15–41. Cambridge: Cambridge University Press.

Turner, Ralph Lilley. 1997 [1931]. *A Comparative and Etymological Dictionary of the Nepali Language.* New Delhi: Allied Publishers.

Turner, Terence. 1977. "Transformation, Hierarchy and Transcendence: A Reformulation of Van Gennep's Model of the Structure of the Rites de Passage." In *Secular Ritual,* Sally Falk Moore and Barbara Myerhoff, eds., 53–70. Amsterdam: Van Gorcum.

———. 1980. "The Social Skin." In *Not Work Alone,* J. Cherfas and R. Lewin, eds., 112–140. London: Temple Smith.

———. 1994. "Bodies and Anti-Bodies: Flesh and Fetish in Contemporary Social Theory." In *Embodiment and Experience: The Existential Ground of Culture and Self,* Thomas Csordas, ed., 24–47. Cambridge: Cambridge University Press.

———. 1995. "Social Body and Embodied Subject: Bodiliness, Subjectivity, and Sociality among the Kayapo." *Cultural Anthropology* 10, no. 2:143–170.

Turner, Victor. 1967. *The Forest of Symbols: Aspects of Ndembu Ritual.* Ithaca: Cornell University Press.

———. 1969. *The Ritual Process: Structure and Anti-Structure.* Chicago: Aldine de Gruyter.

United Nations Population Fund. 2002. *The State of World Population.* New York: UNFPA.

van Buitenen, J. A. B., ed. and trans. 1973. *The Mahābhārata. Vol. 1: The Book of the Beginning.* Chicago: University of Chicago Press.

van der Veer, Peter. 1988. *Gods on Earth: The Management of Religious Experience and Identity in a North Indian Pilgrimage Center.* London: Athlone Press.

———. 1989. "The Power of Detachment: Disciplines of Body and Mind in the Ramanandi Order." *American Ethnologist* 16, no. 3:458–470.

Varenne, Jean. 1976. *Yoga and the Hindu Tradition.* Chicago: University of Chicago Press.

Vaudeville, Charlotte. 1974. *Kabir.* Oxford: Oxford University Press.

Wadley, Susan. 1995. "No Longer a Wife: Widows in Rural North India." In *From the Margins of Hindu Marriage: Essays on Gender, Religion, and Culture,* Lindsey Harlan and Paul B. Courtright, eds., 92–118. New York: Oxford University Press.

Weber, Max. 1958 [1920]. *The Religion of India: The Sociology of Hinduism and Buddhism.* Hans H. Gerth and Don Martindale, eds. and trans. New York: Free Press.

———. 1976 [1930]. *The Protestant Ethic and the Spirit of Capitalism.* Talcott Parsons, trans. London: Allen and Unwin.

White, David Gordon. 1996. *The Alchemical Body: Siddha Traditions in Medieval India.* Chicago: University of Chicago Press.

———. 2003. *Kiss of the Yoginī: "Tantric Sex" in its South Asian Contexts.* Chicago: University of Chicago Press.

Whitney, William Dwight. 1994 [1963]. *The Roots, Verb-Forms, and Primary Derivatives of the Sanskrit Language.* Delhi: Motilal Banarsidass.

Wiesner, Ulrich. 1978. *Nepalese Temple Architecture: Its Characteristics and its Relations to Indian Development.* Leiden: E.J. Brill.

Wilson, H. H. 1861. *A Sketch of the Religious Sects of the Hindus.* London: Trubner and Co.

Woodroffe, Sir John. 1929. *Shakti and Shakta: Essays and Addresses on the Shakta Tantrashastras.* London: Luzac and Co.

Zaehner, R. C., trans. 1973. *Bhagavad Gītā.* London: Oxford University Press.

Zimmer, Heinrich. 1946. *Myths and Symbols in Indian Art and Civilization.* Princeton: Princeton University Press.

Zimmerman, Francis. 1979. "Remarks on the Body in Ayurvedic Medicine." *South Asian Digest of Regional Writing* 18:10–26.

Zita, Jacquelyn N. 1998. *Body Talk: Philosophical Reflections on Sex and Gender.* New York: Columbia University Press.

INDEX

CONTEMPORARY INDIAN STUDIES

Published in association with the American Institute of Indian Studies

The Edward Cameron Dimock, Jr. Prize in the Indian Humanities

Temple to Love: Architecture and Devotion in Seventeenth-Century Bengal PIKA GHOSH

Art of the Court of Bijapur DEBORAH HUTTON

The Joseph W. Elder Prize in the Indian Social Sciences

The Regional Roots of Developmental Politics in India: A Divided Leviathan ASEEMA SINHA

Wandering with Sadhus: Ascetics in the Hindu Himalayas SONDRA L. HAUSNER

SONDRA L. HAUSNER *is Lecturer in the Anthropology of Migration at the University of Oxford.*